THE WORLD ACCORDING TO BEAVER

IRWYN APPLEBAUM

WITH AN INTRODUCTION BY JERRY MATHERS AS "THE BEAVER"

BANTAM BOOKS
TORONTO · NEW YORK · LONDON · SYDNEY

THE WORLD ACCORDING TO BEAVER
A Bantam Book / May 1984

Library of Congress Cataloging in Publication Data

Applebaum, Irwyn.
  The world according to Beaver.

  1. Leave it to Beaver (Television Program)
I. Leave it to Beaver (Television Program) II. Title.
PN1992.77.L4A67   1984   791.45'72   83-46004
          ISBN 0-553-34095-6

Published simultaneously in the United States and Canada

Bantam Books are published by Bantam Books, Inc. Its trademark, consisting of
the words "Bantam Books" and the portrayal of a rooster, is Registered in the
United States Patent and Trademark Office and in other countries. Marca Registrada.
Bantam Books, Inc., 666 Fifth Avenue, New York, New York 10103.

To *my* Cleavers,
the Applebaums:
Mom, Dad, Stu and Ed,
from their little goof.

CONTENTS

Well, Beaver, this may be hard for you to believe, but life isn't exactly like television.
— WARD

INTRODUCTION

*by Jerry Mathers,
as "The Beaver"*

There I was, eight years old and waiting my turn for the latest round of auditions for a television role. Acting was something I had been doing periodically since I was two years old so this was nothing new to me. This particular afternoon, however, I had something far more important than performing on my mind. So, while waiting my turn, I was fidgeting around and clearly wanted to be someplace else. The producers finally asked me what was bothering me.

"I gotta go to my Cub Scout meeting," I blurted out.

My mother was embarrassed and not a little upset with me because we had been specially called back for this audition, but the producers looked at me and decided I should have my wish. Off I went, greatly relieved to be set free, and completely unaware that my speaking up like that was largely responsible for the best thing that ever happened to me in my life: getting to play "the Beaver." The creators of the program for which I was auditioning that day—which would eventually go on to become "Leave It to Beaver"—told me later that they were impressed with my eagerness to go to my scout meeting since that was the exact quality of *real* little-boyishness that they hoped to see played out in every episode of their television series. Of course, I'm proud to have been able to bring the character of Theodore "Beaver" Cleaver to life during the six years and 234 half-hour episodes of the long and happy TV life of "Leave It to Beaver."

Between us, I figure Wally and I got into more messes in a half hour than most kids goof up in a full week, thanks in large part to trouble-making friends like Larry Mondello, Gilbert, or some goony girl, and, of course, that creepy, wise-guy rat, Eddie Haskell. (I still cringe when I hear him call me a "little squirt" on the reruns.) Luckily, we had June and Ward, the best mom and dad in the whole world, close by to teach us a lesson. Not that we ever retained those lessons for too long, but then we would never have had six seasons worth of shows if we'd always behaved like angels.

Sometimes I feel a little funny going back and watching the "Beaver" shows because for me it's like seeing a piece of childhood flashing before my eyes (was I ever really that young?). But I'm constantly amazed at how well the show holds up. Beaver and Wally's problems still hit home—not only for me, remembering back to the scrapes my friends and I got into as kids, but also as a parent now having to deal with my *own* kids. "Beaver" is a show that viewers will appreciate as long as there are kids and kids who grow up to be parents, because it's a show that appreciates kids.

Most important of all, the "Beaver" shows are still very funny. The series was produced with a high degree of care, quality, and love in the writing, directing, and performance that was rare back in the late fifties and early sixties when we were making it, and sadly, I think, is even rarer today.

For me, doing the "Beaver" series was great fun especially when we started filming at Universal Studios in the third year. Being a kid on a Hollywood studio lot was like being set loose in the biggest candy store in the world. I could poke my head into all sorts of fun places like the sets for *Spartacus,* or I could go home with latex scars and other movie monster effects our makeup man helped me to apply to my face.

Working at the studio I absorbed a lot of professional knowledge about movies and television that people spend years trying to study formally. I also got to meet a lot of famous people, although I was a little young to fully appreciate some of them. The figure I most remember was Alfred Hitchcock. The great director had seen me on a Lux Television Theater production and remembered me for the part of a small boy for his film *The Trouble With Harry* in 1956, my first significant feature film part. Several years later, I remember running around the Universal lot in my usual fashion during a series rehearsal break and stopping to watch a big chauffeur-driven Rolls Royce pull up. Out stepped Alfred Hitchcock whose own program was filming on the lot.

The imposing Hitchcock looked down at me and said, "Aaah, good day, Mister Mathers."

I just stood there in open-mouthed euphoria. No, not because the great *Hitchcock* remembered me. I was thrilled that an *adult* had called me, little Beaver, *Mister*.

One of the other things "Beaver" did for me was to get me killed. Well, not quite, for like Mark Twain, the rumors of my death were premature. I was in the Air National Guard during the Vietnam War. The wire services were in the habit of scouring the casualty lists for names from different areas, and somebody saw my name, or a name similar to mine, and reported that I had been killed in action, which then got picked up in the news media. It seems a lot of people remembered seeing me a few months earlier in my uniform and service haircut when I presented an Academy Award with Angela Cartwright (Linda on "The Danny Thomas Show"). So, when Shelly Winters went on the "Tonight" show after the news story broke and happened to mention my "death," pretty soon people believed it.

Rest assured, though, that I am still very much alive and so is the Beaver. I'm a people-oriented person so I get a lot of pleasure going out and meeting people during my personal appearances and hearing of all the enjoyment they have gotten and still get from "Leave It to Beaver." Three generations have now been entertained by Beav. The parents who watched the show with their kids are now grandparents. There have been songs about Beaver, parodies of Beaver, fan clubs and almost a whole Beaver cult on today's college campuses.

People just can't seem to get enough of Beaver which is why I think you'll have a lot of fun with *The World According to Beaver*. It captures the spirit and flavor of the shows and is chock-full of memorable scenes, characters, and laughs. It's the next best thing to having "Leave It to Beaver" reruns at your fingertips.

I hope you enjoy the book. I'm going to put on my green baseball cap, and go downstairs to see if there's any milk and cookies in the 'fridge and then go and see what kind of trouble I can get into today.

FOREWORD

♦

We could typewrite anything and make believe it's something.
—THE BEAVER

♦

Why typewrite anything about a television show and pretend it's *something*? And of all shows, why a *book* about "Leave It to Beaver," a program that hasn't aired a new episode in more than twenty years and whose hero was a little kid named Beaver Cleaver who was virtually allergic to reading and writing?

Let me offer my "because," as Beaver might say, my excuse, why an adult from a respectable family with two Ivy League degrees and a responsible job found joy and happiness working on a book about the Beaver.

First, however, let me warn you that if you are expecting herewith a cold, objective, academic analysis of some silly television show, put this book down and take a nap. I am an unashamed child of the TV generation who has always been convinced that I was born two weeks before the first installment of Davy Crockett because my parents wanted me to be home in time to watch it. So there's no way I could be objective about a television show about which I have vivid memories of Saturday nights, sitting in my pajamas on the rug of my parents' living room in Flushing, New York, in front of the television console in the blond wood cabinet waiting for "Roaring Twenties" to come to an end so I could watch my favorite program, at a time when I was so young I pronounced it "Leeba Dabeeba." During the intervening years, my pronounciation has improved and my fondness for the Beav has deepened and, if such a thing is possible, matured.

Which led to writing this book. Quite simply, *The World According to Beaver* is a labor of love and laughter, which is entirely as it should be, because "Leave It to Beaver" was a television series dedicated to love and laughter. Each week for six years from 1957 to 1963 America loved to laugh at the latest exploits of Beaver, the cute little kid in his baseball cap, and of the Cleaver family—father Ward, mother June and brother Wally—who constantly had to get Beaver out of some very funny predicaments in the little middle-American town of Mayfield.

But Beaver's appeal went beyond humor, for there were many shows that offered more yocks per minute, just as there were many shows that featured more well-known actors and more glamorous production values. The show's great strength was its creative soul, the guiding spirit committed to making "Leave It to Beaver" what I like to think of as television's best 5-H Club series, a show created to be Humorous, Heartwarming, Homiletic, Human and Wholesome (who said spelling counted?).

"Leave It to Beaver" was a comedy about family life and the laughs very often started in the belly but crept up to the heart. Most of all, throughout the shows pulsed a strong current of human understanding. The Cleavers lavished a lot of love and respect upon one another. The shows were sentimental but were rarely sloppy. In coping with Life in the course of each episode someone was always learning a lesson or imparting some reassuring, easily digestible wisdom. No situation was too imposing for this family to handle by drawing upon the solid reserve of moral fiber and stout optimism that flowed through the Cleaver veins. The family stood united, ready to share any burden.

"Leave It to Beaver" presented an idealistic view of life, existing in the unrealistic universe of television situation comedy where problems are laid out and resolved in under thirty minutes, with dramatically timed breaks for commercials. Ward and June Cleaver were superparents, who always dressed neatly, had a meticulous home, rarely fought with each other and always had time to devote to raising their children without raising their voices. For their part, Beaver and Wally never strayed too far from the straight and narrow and managed to avoid being either rotten kids or crazy teenagers.

The Cleavers' warm-oatmeal home life was the "holy gruel" which many parents and kids watching the show would seek all their lives, and never come close to emulating in the privacy of their own homes. Things just never were that perfect in anybody's home. Many have since criticized the Cleaver view of life. Some think it sets up impossible expectations for children who will feel dangerously shortchanged when comparing their home life to Beaver's and Wally's. Other's laugh *at* the boys, howling with disbelieving glee that any two saps would *want* to be that close to their parents.

Most of us just enjoyed spending time each week with the Cleaver family because the series presented family entertainment with a difference—a special understanding of what it means to be a *kid*. For the "Beaver" view of life was just that—Beaver's. Unlike other family shows "Leave It to Beaver" had no adult star; no Donna Reed or Danny Thomas or even Florence Henderson to demand attention. It was the kids rather than the parents that made the Beaver's world go 'round. The writers had a rare ability to remember what it felt like to wiggle their toes in the mud of childhood and their scripts focused on the *kids'* perceptions of how crazy living

with *adults* could be, rather than the adults tsk-tsking over their crazy kids, which was the rule on other family shows.

The scripts were prepared from the white-bread staff of life, but carefully smeared with the chunky peanut butter of a kid's mind. "Beaver" never tried to be big-funny, but it was almost unerringly true-funny; true to the kinds of childish fears, peer pressure and doubts about coming of age that all of us go through. Beaver's troubles were never major catastrophes and they were situations that everybody watching the show has either experienced or could easily imagine.

In this respect, Beaver has a great deal in common with another cultural favorite, Charlie Brown. What Charles Schulz told a 1983 TV interviewer about his comic strip applies directly to Beaver: "It's about the struggle for survival when you're a little kid . . . There's a big struggle going on on the front sidewalk and in the school playground. That's what the whole so-called Peanuts thing is all about."

Beaver was a very ordinary kid. Perhaps his face was cuter than the average little boy's, but he was a fairly unremarkable lad. He was neither a genius, nor a dolt, not a great athlete, but not a spastic either; just a friendly, likeable, freckle-faced youngster, who liked to get dirty and mess around. He was a refreshing change from just about every other TV kid who was either coated in plastic or impossibly precocious. Beaver was just, well, the Beaver. He was *our* hero, an Every-goof, a kid trying to understand the adult world and just trying to get through till tomorrow, like the rest of us.

With its kid-consciousness, "Leave It to Beaver" has remained fresher than other family shows. Back in the fifties and early sixties the stars of the other shows drew more viewers and their canned Father-and-Mother-are-more-interesting-than-the-kids approach generally won higher ratings than "Beaver." While we watched Ozzie and Harriet and Ricky Nelson, laughed at Danny Thomas's eye-rolling, quick-tempered brand of fathering, wished that our moms were as sweet and pretty as Donna Reed, and while many girls longed to be Princess or Kitten on "Father Knows Best," most kids appreciated Beaver and Wally as "kids like us" and that's why they are the TV kids we keep coming back to in our minds. Because of its original approach, "Leave It to Beaver" remains funny and rings true today whereas most of the other family shows seem rather stale. Even those who think it's corny and silly to watch Beaver worry about hooking his good pants on a rusty nail, when today kids are hooked on drugs, can better relate to Beaver than any other TV kid. When most TV shows elicit the nod of sleep, Beaver still inspires the nod of recognition.

Now, more than a quarter of a century since the series began, the video exploits of Beaver and the Cleavers are still sparking waves of love and laughter from millions of viewers at all hours of the day in syndicated reruns on local television stations all around the country. In fact, since 1957, barely a single week has passed without people actively watching "Leave It to Beaver." Few television characters have had the staying power of Beaver Cleaver. He has developed into one of the most popular heroes in television history. Today's TV super-stars may have the flashpowder impact of six-figure deals, pin-up posters, talk show glitter and cover stories splashed across *People* and *The National Enquirer,* but Beaver Cleaver's star has burned brightly all these years in the most powerful medium of all: the collective memories of a nation of viewers.

The World According to Beaver attempts to explore and celebrate the special view of life that was the Beaver's. It's a concentrated dose of Beaver lore, Beaver facts and Beaver fun—all available for viewing any time of the day or night, without commercials. First, there's a behind-the-scenes look at the creative energy that went into building a first-class TV show. Then there will be a tour of Beaver's world: his family, friends, community and, most of all, how he reacted to impor-tant events in his life like going to school, getting into trouble and trying to understand girls. The best way to present the show's unique flavor, I felt, was to let it speak for itself, so you will find this book filled with hundreds of actual quotes specially selected from scripts and videotapes of the episodes. Then there's a synopsis of every one of the 234 episodes. Finally there's a look at what life has been like for the "Beaver" stars and for the show itself in the years since the last episode. Throughout, there are also dozens of photos taken directly from the shows as well as exclusive backstage shots.

All your favorite "Beaver" people—Eddie Haskell, Lumpy Rutherford, Larry Mondello, Miss Landers and many more—are here; all your favorite Beaver moments are here including falling in the soup bowl and riding the Big Dipper roller coaster, and I think you'll even find some surprises. Consider this book, then, the *Portable Beaver, Beaver's Famous Quotations,* the *Beaver Companion,* or just a way to spend a bunch of hours laughing and remembering the Beaver. If you have half as much fun reading this as I've had putting it together, I know you're in for a swell time.

◆

I will always be glad I tackled this project because it gave me an excuse to fairly wallow in the wonderful "Beaver" shows. In the process I became an even greater admirer of the extraordinarily gifted individuals who were able to take the situation comedy format, which was already becoming tiresome by 1957, and create a classic series that still surprises and entertains to this day. Most of all, one has to doff one's cap to Messrs. Joe Connelly and Bob Mosher, the founding fathers and guiding lights of "Beaver." The many writers and directors they worked with during the six years also raised—and rose to—the high standards of the series.

I am especially grateful to those actors involved in the show who generously opened their hearts and memories and let me share vicariously their close feelings and devotion for "Leave It to Beaver": Jerry Mathers, Tony Dow, Barbara Billingsley, Ken Osmond, Richard Correll, and Richard Deacon.

There are many terrific people who graciously lent their support and talents to me in doing this book and they all have my sincerest thanks. Special thanks to the folks at Bantam Books who believed a little extra in me and the Beav: Jack

Romanos, Linda Grey, Nina Hoffman, Sol Skolnick, Sally Williams, Sandra Su, Deborah Futter and Dave Stern; to Charles Bloch and Sue Terry, and most especially, my intrepid editor, Fred Klein.

Nancy Cushing-Jones, vice-president, MCA Publishing, was invaluable in her support and hard digging through the Beaver archives. Thanks, too, to the brave photographic efforts of Aspasia and Bruce Howard Newman. A very grateful bow to the hard-working and extremely talented Beaver fans at Jackson Typesetting. I should also publicly acknowledge the wide varieties of Entenmann's baked goods which got me through more long nights than I would care to recount.

No amount of thanks can properly express my appreciation and admiration of the design artistry of Barbara N. Cohen who made this book look like the S-H-A-R-P-est thing to hit May-field since Wally's new suit.

And there is one person without whom this book would never have come to be. For her encouragement, wisdom, experience, advice, energy, sense of humor, patience and willingness to throw herself into this whole mad adventure, I hereby hug my beloved Lucille.

THE WORLD BEFORE BEAVER

America in the mid-fifties was in a pretty good mood. The events of the world temporarily settled down to a dull roar. The Korean Armistice had been signed for several years and World War II seemed to have settled into the past. On the home front the wounds of McCarthyism were beginning to heal. The economy was good enough and the times were peaceful enough to give rise to a kind of "silly season" where much of the energy was devoted to the pursuit of pleasure.

In Eisenhower we had a "presidential pop" and it appeared to be an excellent time to raise a family which was just what much of the country was doing. Even Elizabeth Taylor was getting into the act with her firstborn, and another American actress, Grace Kelly, was bringing a fairy tale to life by wedding her Prince. Suburbs were growing and *McCalls* was promoting "family togetherness" as the key theme for the period. The postwar baby-boomers were beginning to reach puberty and as a result were becoming a powerful cultural force all their own.

By 1957, rock 'n' roll was firmly in place as the pacesetter for teenagers, providing not only the beat, but the inspiration for dress, language and heroes like Elvis Presley who, parlaying his success in records, had already begun a film career. By fall of that year teenagers had even invaded the bookshelves and the theater as the novel *Gidget* and the musical *West Side Story* debuted. Teenagers were proving to be big business as demonstrated by the popularity of transistor radios and records, movies like *The Blackboard Jungle* and *Rebel Without a Cause,* and the journal of ten-cent sophomoric wit and wisdom, *MAD Magazine.* (In the following year, the truly awesome buying power of the baby-boomers would become dramatically evident with the introduction of Wham-O's hula hoop.) Even the 1957 U.S. open chess champion, Bobby Fischer, was a 14-year-old.

But there was one part of the cultural life of the country that was unquestionably rising to an all-pervasive dominance—television. By 1957, the TV set was firmly entrenched in the home, so much so that in declaring September 8th–14th National Television Week, The National Association of Radio and Television Broadcasters chose as their theme, "Television—A Member of the Family."

The nationwide acceptance of television brought the world into the living room of America. Turning on their TV sets in the fall of 1957, Americans were confronted with the sights as well as the sounds of such disturbing events as the Arkansas National Guard barring black students from Little Rock's Central High School and the announcement that the Russians had successfully launched *Sputnik.* With reality brought to life before their eyes, perhaps it was no wonder that TV also became the nation's most turned-to diversion, enabling Americans to escape from the worries of their everyday life.

In the television universe, the young people certainly did not rule, but here, too, they were demanding a lot of attention. In 1957, a kiddie TV pioneer, "Howdy Doody," was already celebrating its tenth anniversary, and "The Mickey Mouse Club" and "Andy's Gang" (with Froggy and his magic twanger) were spellbinding junior viewers along with such daytime favorites as "The Little Rascals," "Superman," and "The Lone Ranger," which was marking its 25th broadcast year. Even on Art Linkletter's daily "House Party," one of the most popular segments was *Kids Say the Darndest Things*. Most influential of all was a local Philadelphia show, "Bandstand," that was celebrating its fifth anniversary by going national on ABC-TV with a ninety-minute weekday version entitled "American Bandstand" featuring host Dick Clark and the most poular teen heartthrobs of the day, like Sal Mineo, Pat Boone and Tab Hunter, along with the hottest records and newest dance steps.

For prime-time viewers *TV Guide* predicted that 1957–58 would be "a season to make your eyes pop," with fewer comedians, fewer hour-long dramas, fewer quiz shows, more musical programs and adult westerns and "more documentary programs that picture our world today." Viewers would miss the antics of "I Love Lucy," 1956's most popular series, since Lucy and Ricky decided they needed a rest. Jimmy Durante also said his last goodnight to Mrs. Calabash, wherever she was, just before the season began. Returning TV winners included "Gunsmoke" (which would take over the top spot through the end of the decade), "The Ed Sullivan Show," "The Jack Benny Show," "The Danny Thomas Show" (with a new TV wife), "The Adventures of Ozzie and Harriet," "Father Knows Best," "Alfred Hitchcock Presents" and "G. E. Theater," starring Ronald Reagan.

Making their first appearances on TV screens in the fall of 1957 were a slew of series which would become beloved video chestnuts: Raymond Burr as Perry Mason, Ward Bond and Robert Horton in "Wagon Train," James Garner in "Maverick," Richard Boone as Paladin in "Have Gun, Will Travel," Lee Marvin in "M Squad," John Forsythe in "Bachelor Father" and Walter Brennan and Richard Crenna in "The Real McCoys."

Slipped in there among the shows premiering with so much hoopla there was a simple little domestic comdey on CBS, the show with the odd name, "Leave It to Beaver."

. . . AND THEN, THERE WAS BEAVER

Just ten days before exisitentialist angst's greatest moment of triumph, when Albert Camus would be awarded the Nobel Prize for literature, masses of Americans were preoccupied by the struggles of a somewhat lesser order of seriousness. An individual was worried sick that a note his teacher sent home to his mother would result in his getting " 'spelled" from the second grade. The individual was one Beaver Cleaver. The date was October 4, 1957, and the situation occurred in *Beaver Gets 'Spelled,* the premiere episode of "Leave It to Beaver."

To trace the birth of the Beaver, one has to go back to what might appear to be an unlikely source, "Amos 'n' Andy." Their years of writing for the black characters of that long-running series honed the script-writing skills of the two former advertising copywriters who would go on to create the lily-white world of "Leave It to Beaver." Bob Mosher and Joe Connelly had been working together as a writing team since leaving J. Walter Thompson agency in New York around 1942. They contributed comedy material to the Edgar Bergen and Phil Harris radio shows, among others, and then won a regular spot writing scripts for "Amos 'n' Andy." Regular is an understatement: Mosher and Connelly wrote more than *fifteen hundred* scripts over the course of twelve years for the escapades of Amos, Andy, Sapphire, Kingfish and the other characters. They wrote for radio and television and continued to write radio scripts even after they had other projects.

They developed a Ray Milland anthology TV series which was a flop and then decided to try their hands at a movie screenplay when Connelly happened upon a quirky situation at his son's parochial school. The original script eventually was filmed as *The Private War of Major Benson,* starring Charlton Heston, and won the writing team an Academy Award nomination in 1957. That very year was to prove a banner one for the duo because during that same period they turned once again to draw upon the humor they saw in the natural conflicts between adults and children to create another television pilot.

Connelly and Mosher's goal was to try to come up with a concept for their family comedy which was different from the other shows already on television. They wanted to do an adult story about kids which would present life the way they remembered seeing it when they were kids. The more they sat and reminisced about their childhoods and exchanged stories about their own kids, the more they believed they had something relatively fresh and entertaining that TV audiences might enjoy. Both writers had difficult childhoods. Connelly's parents separated while he was rather young and Mosher was raised by an aunt because his father died when Mosher was a small child. They both were raising families of their own. In 1958 Connelly had six children and Mosher had two, so they were naturally kid-oriented.

They wanted to do a show that celebrated the best things about families but one which concentrated on the kids for a change. They didn't want another show about wiseacre kids who would have been sold into slavery by their parents in real life if they ever tried to do some of the silly things they were allowed to do on TV. The show should be "clean and honest."

They decided to work around a husband and wife raising two sons in a small suburb or middle-American town. In choosing the nickname Beaver for the youngest son they evoked the image of a friendly little creature with a toothy smile, not unlike Little Beaver from the old "Red Ryder" serial. Beaver was inspired by Connelly's eight-year-old son, Ricky. They called the older brother Wally and so, to focus the show around the kids, they titled their pilot script "Wally and Beaver," rather than some variation on the "Father," "Daddy," or "Star's Name" formula used by most TV shows.

The next step was to get a pilot script completed and to begin casting. They knew that the two boys would be crucial to the success of the show, especially the youngest. They inter-

viewed hundreds of child actors and kept calling back Jerry Mathers, a boy who had a great deal of acting experience even though he was only eight years old. Jerry became Beaver and the rest of the casting was completed. The response to the "Wally and Beaver" pilot was positive and it looked like Remington Rand would come aboard to be a major sponsor of a series commitment on the CBS network.

Some changes were necessary, however. Jerry Mathers was, if anything, even livelier and cuter than they had hoped. Barbara Billingsley, who had performed in many grade B films and TV dramas but in only one previous series, a short-lived number entitled "Professional Wife," proved a fine choice for the mother, June Cleaver. However, the actors selected for Wally and the father, Ward, needed replacing. More "cattle calls" were set up for 12-year-old boys and Tony Dow, son of former "Our Gang" actress, Muriel Montrose, got the part. Even though he had no acting aspirations and, in fact, lucked into his first role by tagging along to help a friend audition for a

TV pilot, "Johnny Wildlife," he was a good-looking, clean-cut, athletic boy with tremendous ability as a swimmer and diver. He had a natural appeal which played well with Jerry.

Joe Connelly and Bob Mosher

That left Ward. Jerry recalls being asked to read parts with several adult candidates for his TV father. One, Hugh Beaumont, was an actor with whom he had worked previously. Beaumont was a Methodist lay preacher who had made a lot of religious films. Jerry was hired for one of them and was having trouble with crying on cue before the camera. Beaumont, seeing his trouble, pulled the youngster aside and suggested that he bury his head in his hands and laugh, which would produce the same sound as crying. It worked and Jerry was so grateful that he remembers praying the night following Beaumont's audition that he would be the new Ward. Whatever the reason, he got the role and the Cleaver family was complete.

The last major change was the title. Remington Rand was growing leery of "Wally and Beaver," fearing that it sounded too much like a nature show. A new title was requested, one that would also indicate the light-hearted nature of the series. And thus came "Leave It to Beaver."

MAKING ''BEAVER''

As Connelly and Mosher created the first season's shows they established the ground rules and work atmosphere that would help carry the show through its entire run. First and foremost were the scripts. They personally wrote the majority of the "Beaver" episodes and closely supervised every teleplay before it was produced. Among the other writers who contributed "Beaver" scripts over the years were Bill Manhoff, Mel Diamond, Ben Gershman, Fran van Hartesvelt, George Tibbles, Katherine and Dale Eunson, Bob Ross, Alan Manings, and the team of Dick Conway and Roland MacLane who wrote many of the shows in the final two seasons.

Connelly and Mosher tried to avoid contrived, set-up jokes and worked hard to develop humorous characters who could be funny in simple situations. This was the same kind of attention to character depth they brought to "Amos 'n' Andy" where they helped to refine Kingfish to be not really evil but a conniver, and Amos to be gullible rather than stupid. They tried to mold Beaver and Wally and their friends into believable little people with real shortcomings. And they were determined to let the characters age as the actors changed and grew in their own lives. While Jerry Mathers was in his cutest years, the early shows revolved around Beaver. As he moved into his awkward pre-teen years and Tony Dow blossomed as a teenager the emphasis of the series shifted more toward Wally.

In planning "Beaver" Connelly told an interviewer, "If we hire a writer we tell him not to make up situations but to look into his own background. It's not a 'situation' comedy where you have to create a situation for a particular effect. Our emphasis is on a natural story line." When they were looking for material for their scripts Connelly and Mosher were not above adapting scenes directly from the lives of their own kids. An early show was *The Haircut*, in which Beaver loses his haircut money and does such a bad job of trying to cut his own hair that Wally agrees to help with the trimming, giving Beaver his own Mr. T-style hairdo. A similar incident occurred to Mosher's son Bobby who, like Beaver, had to wear a stocking cap to cover his ragged haircut when he had to play an angel in his school play. Connelly's oldest son, Jay, combed his hair meticulously, which soon became a trait of Wally's. Mosher's kids faked taking a bath by wetting and rumpling their towels and throwing dirt in the water to leave a ring when it drained. Beaver's way of chopping off syllables from words to ease their pronounciation was inspired by Ricky Connelly who said things like " 'got" for "forgot" and " 'spelled" for "expelled."

Of course, such reliance on family source material could have its drawbacks. Connelly told one reporter, during an argument his kids would sometimes blurt out, "Why don't you practice some of that jazz on the show around here?" Mosher noted that, "One evening my son was sent to his room as punishment for something he'd done. He went up quietly enough, but before he closed his door behind him, he yelled down: "I'll never give you another story for your show as long as I live!"

Richard Correll, who eventually joined "Beaver" as Beaver's friend Richard Rickover, was a close friend of the Connelly family because his father, Charles Correll, was Amos of "Amos 'n' Andy." He recalls that Connelly drew liberally from his kids and their friends to shape key "Beaver" characters. Wally was patterned after Connelly's oldest son, Jay; Eddie Haskell was inspired by a friend of Jay's and Larry Mondello was based on Terry Fotre, one of Ricky's friends, who was heavy, wore a baseball cap and was always eating. Correll also recalls, "Joe would get the kids together for an outing, like for a birthday, and take a bunch of us to Disneyland and he'd always have a pad of paper handy to copy down things we would say. I remember one time he took us out to dinner and I was complaining about having to take a bath since the restaurant was so dimly lit nobody would notice if I was dirty. That turned into a line Beaver says when the Cleavers go out for dinner."

In choosing the directors for the show Connelly and Mosher were as careful as they were with the writers, looking for people who had the patience and skill to work with child actors and to properly pace the gentle humor of the scripts. The two directors who handled the most shows were Norman Tokar, who worked on the first three seasons and Norman Abbott who helmed most of the final two seasons. Among other directors were Gene Reynolds (who went on to direct "M*A*S*H"), David Butler (who had done a number of Hope/Crosby "Road" pictures and Shirley Temple films), and Hugh Beaumont.

For the first two seasons, "Beaver" was filmed at Republic Studio and then moved over to Universal Studios. Unlike many TV series which ground out two episodes a week, "Beaver" produced one show per week, largely because the child actors were only allowed to work four hours a day. They also had to have three hours of schooling a day, often with private tutors.

(Despite all that activity the boys usually managed to work in an after-lunch basketball game.)

The script for each season's 39 shows was delivered to the performers late in the week prior to production. Monday the cast would have a reading of the script, with any awkward lines or scenes being pinpointed for rewrites. Tuesday afternoon the script would be rehearsed in a complete run-through for the camera and lighting crew. Individual scenes were then filmed over the next three days with a single camera. On most days, the scenes with the child actors were filmed first and the adult actors had to film their scenes after 5:00 P.M.

Most of the actors have very fond memories of making the series. Jerry Mathers and Tony Dow got along well on the set and Jerry particularly remembers looking up to Tony for his athletic abilities. It was a friendly set with almost a family spirit between cast and crew. Barbara Billingsley was especially motherly in her attention to the children, displaying a genuine interest in their hobbies and school work that was very much in character with her role as June. Most of the young actors remember Mosher as being calm, quiet and personable whereas Connelly was the more flamboyant, loud—and at times wild— fun-loving adult. (Correll recalls that in the terrible Bel Air fire in the early sixties, Connelly broke through police barricades, climbed atop his roof with a fire hose and watered down his house and grounds, fending off evacuation teams with a .45 from his gun collection. As a result, his was one of the few houses that survived the fire.

An unexpected problem arose with the first episode that was produced. It was a seemingly innocent premise: the boys send away for a genuine Everglades alligator advertised in the back of a comic book. The problem arises when the boys were shown hiding their 'gator in their toilet tank. It seems showing a toilet on a TV series was a network taboo, so the episode was postponed until dispensation could be negotiated. When *Captain Jack* did air in the second week, toilet scene intact, a small, liberating blow for TV realism was struck.

Jerry Mathers with Director Norman Tokar.

In lieu of *Captain Jack*, "Beaver" debuted with *Beaver Gets 'Spelled*, *The Black Eye* (Beaver gets belted by a *girl*) and *The Haircut* rounded out the first month of episodes. The series originally aired on Friday nights at 7:30 P.M. (EST) on CBS. On October 4, 1957 its network competition was "Saber of London," a short-lived suspense show on NBC, and "Rin Tin Tin" on ABC. Later that same night viewers could watch Charlton Heston guest star on Schlitz Playhouse and Edward R. Murrow interview June Havoc on "Person to Person." CBS did not mount a major promotional campaign for "Beaver," and never quite knew what to do with the series. Midway through the season the show was moved to Wednesday at 8:00 P.M.

The critical reception to "Beaver" was generally favorable although the *New York Times* asserted that "Leave It to Beaver" was "too broad and artificial to be persuasive." John Crosby in the *New York Herald Tribune* said the show was "charming and sincere" and featured the "wonderful candor and directness with which children disconcert and enchant you." The *New York Daily News* critic said, "Put it down as a pure delight." *Variety* compared the first show favorably with *Tom Sawyer,* and in reviewing the fourth season debut, noted the show had "never been a yock show in the sense of generating big and sustained laughs, but it has consistently poured forth warmth, wit and wisdom without condescension or pretense." *Look* commented that the series "eschews slapstick to concentrate on humorous realism." *TV Guide* pronounced it as the "sleeper of the 1957–58 season" and later on, "one of the most honest, most human and most satisfying situation comedies on TV."

"Beaver" switched in fall 1958 to ABC where it remained. There were four time changes during the ensuing years however: from October 1958 to June 1959 it appeared on Thursdays from 7:30–8:00 P.M.; during the summer of 1959 reruns were aired at 9:00 P.M. on Thursday; from October 1959 through September 1962 the show aired at 8:30 on Saturday; and during the 1962–63 season the show returned to Thursday night, now at 8:30.

Through the years the ratings were always solid, but never high enough for a top-twenty berth, even though other family comedies like "Make Room For Daddy," "Father Knows Best," "The Donna Reed Show" and even "Dennis the Menace" and

Valentines Day promotional picture with Angela Cartwright

"The Real McCoys" (which the network promoted for its "hill-belly laughs") were all able to shoot their way past the dominant TV westerns of the late fifties and early sixties into top-twenty ratings.

But during the six years it appeared on the networks, no matter what else was going on in the world or on television, viewers could turn to Mayfield for relief. While Lana Turner's daughter was arrested for killing her mother's lover in 1958, Beaver and Wally were merely breaking Ward's car window. On the eve of the July 1960 Democratic National Convention, America could sweat out Wally's choice of a blind date for the high school dance. If they didn't choose to watch the third TV production of *Peter Pan,* in December 1960, viewers could thrill to *Wally's Glamour Girl.* The week the press questioned President Kennedy in the first live presidential press conference telecast, Ward questioned Beaver about his "secret life" written up in his diary. While Newton Minnow, Chairman of the FCC may have called TV "a vast wasteland" in May 1961, Beaver was honorably serving his Mayfield community by collecting for the Community Chest. In 1962, the week

John Glenn climbed into his space suit for the first manned orbit of earth, Beaver traipsed down the street in a bunny costume.

During its next to last season, "Beaver" ran against some stiff competition such as "The Defenders," with its highly charged courtroom cases of controversial topics like abortion and the death penalty. Ward's meting out punishment for Beaver's faking a book report offered viewers a clear alternative. In the final season, the courtroom *and* the operating room plagued "Beaver" as it ran against "Perry Mason" and "Dr. Kildare." That last season, however, "Beaver" was part of a golden sitcom line-up for ABC with "The Adventures of Ozzie

and Harriet," "The Donna Reed Show," "Leave It to Beaver" and "My Three Sons."

"Beaver" was not renewed for the 1963–64 season. "My Three Sons" would move into its time slot. Connelly and Mosher would move on to "The Munsters," and the actors went on to high school, college or other roles. The country would move on as well. Two and half months following the last "Beaver" episode President Kennedy would be assassinated and soon Mayfield would seem a lot farther away for all of us. But thanks to the magic of reruns, it would never be totally beyond reach.

Promotional Pictures:
St. Patrick's Day (facing page),
Summer (left), Easter (right.)

THE CLEAVER FAMILY

The Most Interesting Character
I Have Ever Known
by Beaver Cleaver

The most interesting character I
have ever known is my father
Mr Ward Cleaver. He does not have
an interesting job he just works
hard and takes care of all of us.
He never shot things in Africa or
saved anybody that was drowning
but thats all right with me because
when I am sick he brings me
ice cream and when I tell him
things or ask him things he
always lissens to me. He used up
a whole Saturday to make things
in the garage. He may not be
intresting to you or someone else
because hes not your father
hes mine.

WARD CLEAVER

If there is ever a Super Bowl competition for television fathers, Ward Cleaver should be the coach.

He wasn't the smartest father, nor the best-looking, nor the wisest—certainly not the funniest—but he was the most *understanding* man who ever accepted the daunting mantle of video fatherhood. Ozzie Nelson, Jim Anderson of "Father Knows Best," Steve Douglas of "My Three Sons," Danny Thomas, or Dr. Alex Stone of the "Donna Reed Show" were all good family captains, but Ward Cleaver was better able to steer his sons through the rocky shoals of growing up because he remembered so precisely how easily the rowboat of boyhood could turn into the *Titanic.*

Ward was many people's ideal pater familias. He always had time for his kids. He cared about their problems and always had a ready solution. He taught them how to do things. He never lost his temper. He meted out punishment fairly. He was a good breadwinner, a loving husband and still gave the kids some slack to grown on—and he did it all without hardly ever loosening his tie.

Actually, as portrayed by Hugh Beaumont and written in the scripts, Ward was a less-than-perfect human; he had bad days at the office, he lost his patience, he gave bad advice, he could be pedantic and stiff in his moral lectures, he was known to shout, he ignored his children. He just never suffered such lapses into normal parental behavior for very long. By the episode's end Ward would reach into his reserve of love and empathy to resolve the problems at hand and shore up the family's foundation of communication, shared feelings and respect.

◆

JUNE: You know something, Ward? You're a very nice man.
WARD: Aw, I'm just a sentimental old farm boy.

◆

One of the reasons that Ward is such a dedicated father is that he had such a "real boy" childhood. Although there are a few references to growing up in Mayfield and Shaker Heights, Ward most frequently refers to his happy childhood on his family's farm. According to Ward, his father was a "very solid, sober citizen, with both feet on the ground." Ward was named after his father, but the only reference to this is his library card, which reads "Ward Cleaver, Jr." Ward's grandfather was a Civil War hero. He also had an older brother and sister and several uncles on his father's side.

When he wasn't doing his farm chores or walking to and from school, Ward lead a Tom Sawyer-like outdoors existence. He rode horses bareback, ice skated, played ball and made kites. He also went to horror movies and "Our Gang" comedies, and had his own subscription to *Wierd Tales*. He got into fights with his siblings and even hinted at getting into more than his fair share of scrapes as a playful youth. His father would listen to excuses but believed firmly in the old-fashioned toolshed psychology for training his children. Sparing the rod on his boys, Ward did not quite follow in his father's footsteps.

Ward worked his way through State University where he played on the basketball team and was elected president of his fraternity. In World War II he served as an engineer in the Seabees.

◆

WARD: My parents used to always drive out in the country on Sunday afternoons to visit friends. This one day I waited until the last minute to tell them they would have to go without me.

JUNE: That was pretty thoughtless.

WARD: Well, it wasn't thoughtless at all. I had something else to do, something more important.

JUNE: Important enough to disappoint your parents?

WARD: At the time I thought it was. It was my first date with you.

◆

The love that flows through the Cleaver household is not strictly between parents and children. There is a lot of love between Ward and June. It's not the kind of mushy stuff that would make Beaver turn away at the movies, but a steady glow of affection that suffuses the entire family, even during the darkest troubles.

When Ward comes home from the office the genuine smile on his face shows that he really is *happy* to be home and is looking forward to kissing his wife hello and spending the evening with her. Meanwhile, most of the husbands who were watching Ward on "Leave It to Beaver" every week probably gave bigger smiles to their television sets than to their wives when they came home. In some of the early episodes Ward and June were more demonstrative and showed some of the lovely spirit of a young couple with a cuddle, a nuzzle and a hug or two. As they got older they settled into a more formal fondness. By his own admission Ward is the type "who says it with seatcovers" rather than with flowers.

◆

BEAVER: A guy never thinks his father can do anything except go to work and come back.

◆

Since he took his role as breadwinner seriously, Ward plowed much of his energy into his workday. While he had enough sketching talent to become a commercial artist, he sought a more reliable income. He obviously secured his position from the TV Fathers Employment Agency which provided most male heads of the 50s and 60s television households with steady but undefined work.

Each morning Ward drives to a downtown Mayfield office building to work for a company that is engaged in some form of profitable enterprise. He's a white-collar, company man, often taking "reports" home with him from "the salt mines" to pore over.

Ward has a bit of the Babbitt middle-class businessman in him. He takes pride in his community, willingly serves on the mayor's committee for a new youth center and on parents' committees at his sons' schools. On Thursdays he goes to the Mayfield Businessman's Luncheon. He takes pride in the fact that he can now afford a bigger home, a better car and a country club membership. He likes to golf and hunt and two weeks of every year he takes his family up to a cabin by Shadow Lake for vacation. The Cleavers are not rich, but they are comfortable.

◆

BEAVER: Hey, Wally, you know when we were talking to Dad before, I thought he was going to tell us all that stuff about how he had to walk five miles to school.
WALLY: Yeah, through three feet of snow.
BEAVER: When he first started telling us, I think it was three miles and two feet of snow.
WALLY: Yeah, it seems like every year the distance gets farther and the snow gets deeper.

◆

Businessman is Ward's profession. His career is father, an avocation he never stops practicing. Even by the standards of the more family-oriented 50s and 60s Ward Cleaver is an unusually attentive and devoted father. By today's measure, he's a veritable freak of human nature. He carries some of his business modus operandi over to his family life by wearing his tie and jacket around the house. But he is not reserved about rolling up his sleeves and dealing with his family. He bemusedly refers to himself at one point as the "Great White Father and Peacemaker." If so, he is a benevolent ruler. Like any good ruler he has a throne room—his den—where he dispenses lectures, advice and comfort. However, he's fully capable of unloading a fount of wisdom or discipline in any room of the house.

He wants his sons to be better than he was: he wants them to learn the rules of mature behavior while they're still young and to be active, interested in their lessons and in the world around them. To build better boys his tools are lectures, aphorisms, common sense and parables which sometimes pass over the heads of his sons. His ability to listen, his willingness to mix discretion with discipline and a long memory back to the moments when he squirmed through his own childhood all help to make Ward a wondrously understanding and ever inspiring father.

He expects a lot of Wally and Beaver and knows enough to back off when his dreams have exceeded his sons' reach. At times Ward learns almost as much as he teaches. Even when he's too firm with the boys they soon realize he's only over-reacting for their own good and doing it with more compassion than any of their friends' fathers.

◆

BEAVER: Dad, you're almost like one of the fellas.
WARD: Well, Beaver, I think that's the nicest
               thing you ever said to me.

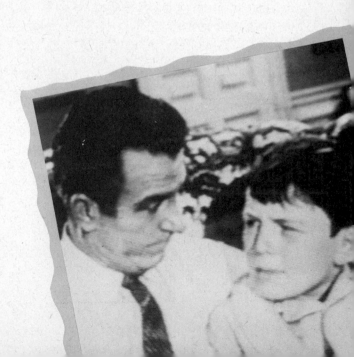

WARD AT THE
SALT MINES

What does Ward Cleaver do for a living?
A solve-it-yourself mystery.
The clues:

- He drives to his office in downtown Mayfield every weekday morning and some Saturdays. The building number is 9034. He usually works until four P.M.

- His firm has several offices in addition to the vital Mayfield branch, including one in Mexico City. The home office, where *the brass* keep a watchful eye, is in New York.

- Ward and his coworkers prepare a lot of reports. Ward has a secretary and is sometimes seen dictating into a recording machine.

- Fred Rutherford is the only fellow employee we meet. He is fiercely competitive with Ward, always snooping about his desk, trying to horn in on Ward's projects.

- Although it's never definitely stated that Ward is Fred's superior, Ward does have a corner office while Fred does not.

- Mentions are made of the following work-related documents: "the Miller audits," "the Thompson deal," and "next year's production schedule."

- On various occasions, Ward looks over some property for the office, attends a *sales meeting,* takes June to a company conference because "the company likes for the wives to meet," goes on a business trip to St. Louis, mentions the company's media department, and says they took "a new survey down at the office about women's marketing habits."

- Whatever he does, Ward sometimes has to stay late and at least once came home so tired he actually lay down on the sofa—*in his suit.*

JUNE'S RULES TO LIVE BY

Watch your manners.

Sit up straight.

Don't play too hard.

Be careful.

Don't get your feet wet.

Don't eat a lot of *junk* and spoil your dinner.

You need all the vegetables you can get.

If you're served something you don't like just eat it anyway.

Don't talk with your mouth full.

Don't eat with your elbows on the table.

You'll always be safe if you tell the truth.

There's no reason for anyone not to be dressed properly.

Be enthusiastic.

JUNE CLEAVER

WARD: What type of girl would you have Wally marry?

JUNE: Oh, some very sensible girl from a nice family . . . one with both feet on the ground, who's a good cook and can keep a nice house and see that he's happy.

WARD: Dear, I got the last one of those.

◆

It would come as no surprise if there were men walking around today with "June" tattooed on their arms instead of "Mom." For millions of viewers June Evelyn Bronson Cleaver has grown to become the quintessential American mother. If the Garden of Eden was starting anew as a suburb, June would be the ideal Eve—pretty, tireless wife, mother and homemaker.

◆

What's all this excitement out here? I'm breading cutlets.

◆

To be sure, June considers herself a fulfilled woman according to the most traditionally conservative American view of womanhood: a girl goes to school to find a good provider, gets married, sets up his home, bears his children and his problems at the sacrifice of any greater ambition of her own. She is the homebody extraordinaire, allowed to fly from the nest only long enough to do the family shopping, attend school and church meetings and visit relatives and friends. Even her hobbies are home oriented—like crocheting and making curtains.

June has taken the brunt of the criticism on behalf of that beaming ladies' auxiliary of TV moms who seem to have brains in their heads only large enough to concern themselves with planning a dinner menu and scheming to get the grumpy father to bend his stubborn will. Like Ward, June was even considered a little fantastic during the Eisenhower years and today seems like a dinosaur of doting motherhood. Now, perhaps viewers laugh as much at June as with her, at her unruffled WASP demeanor, her absolute concern for the prim and proper way to carry on, at her slavish attention to housework and cleanliness. With the enlightenment of the women's movement our view of a mother's role inside and outside the home has been expanded. No matter how much of an impossible cliché June Cleaver may seem at times, beneath her breast beats a warm and loving heart, and that will never go out of style. At some point all of us long for such comfort and it's nice to know that the image of June Cleaver still glows brightly, with a soothing hand, a hot dinner and a glass of milk to cure whatever ails us.

Like her husband, June's childhood days are only sketchily filled in by the scripts. She grew up in East St. Louis, attended boarding school and spent summers with her maiden Aunt

Martha. Thus she comes by her very eastern finishing school view of life honestly, striving to carry out proud—though undefined—Bronson family traditions. Her greatest honor came at summer camp where she won a blue bathing cap in a swimming meet. Her reading tended toward *Little Women* and *Dorothy Vernon of Haddon Hall.* By her teen years June had arrived in the Mayfield area where she met Ward Cleaver when he was sixteen. They both attended State. He was definitely the best student of the two. She had little work experience, although she types competently and she did volunteer at the USO during World War II.

Dinner will be ready soon. Go upstairs and wash up and put on a clean shirt.

If the position of wife were ever to be a licensed profession, June Cleaver would qualify—manicured hands down—because she takes her duties so seriously. There is the proper way to do everything: the neat and orderly and polite way, and that's the June Cleaver way.

That personal pride begins with her dress. Virtually every waking minute is spent in a sensible dress, high heels, make-up and choker necklace. Her standard "street clothes" are not complete until she has a hat on her head and gloves on her hands. You can count on the fingers of one hand the number of times June is caught wearing pants. Her face is always shining, there is rarely any trace of perspiration (and never, never any sweat), no hair is ever out of place, even when she's cleaning, and she never raises her voice above a gentle midwestern lilt.

I have milk and cookies for you.

The kitchen is the central core of June Cleaver's life. Although a spotless range and oven have replaced the hearth, June still prepares two elaborate hot meals each day, three on weekends, with tender loving care. Her coffeepot is ever ready for her husband and there's milk, cookies, fruit and often cake for her boys when they come home from school.

Better than the food, though, is the fact that *Mom* is waiting. How many other moms are there to reassure their kids that no matter how big a mess they may have made of their lives that day, the family hasn't left them behind and moved to another town? June is sitting there whipping up a chocolate cake for dessert, checking on the roast and eager to know why her sons are late. While today's mothers worry about the deadly substances their darlings are putting into their bodies, there is something quaint about watching June insist that Beaver eat his Brussels sprouts. She shrieks when one of her sons sticks his finger directly in a mayonnaise jar or drinks right out of a pitcher instead of using a glass. She's a woman who still believes in the healing power of a Jell-O mold. June believes that cleanliness is next to godliness and she is willing to move even closer to her maker by getting up on a step ladder to apply a vacuum cleaner to the molding above the den door. She even finds satisfaction in thumbtacking down new kitchen shelf paper.

♦

Ward, I'm very worried about the Beaver.

♦

There are times when even her husband and sons make light of June's obsessive concern for manners, comportment and grooming. She's one woman trying to tame two rowdy boys (and one occasional recidivist adult male husband) into presentable shape before a watchful world. She is usually the parent who is apprehensive about the way the boys will conduct themselves socially, yet she is also more prone to spoil them, protect them, and even baby them. She and Ward provide a nice parental balance supporting one another's weaknesses in particular situations. Ward handles the really difficult problems but June—especially in the early shows—proves to be the more flexible and inventive voice of parental reason that gets her lads out of more than a few messes. And while she'll never be one of the guys, like Ward on his good-father days, Ward himself pays her a great tribute by saying that "for an ex-girl" she's pretty understanding at times.

JUNE: Well, Beaver, I'm your mother. I don't always know what goes on in your head, but if you're hurt or unhappy, then I don't ever have to guess.

BEAVER: Why not?

JUNE: Because I'm hurt and unhappy, too.

BEAVER: Right away?

JUNE: Almost right away.

BEAVER: Without me even saying anything?

JUNE: Beaver, you don't have to say anything. When you were a baby you couldn't talk; you couldn't tell me you were cold or hungry or had a pain, but I always knew, and somehow—well—that never changes.

BEAVER: You know Mom, sometimes, when I get home from school and a teacher yelled at me, or I had a fight with some of the kids or something, you'll give me an extra sort of look when I come in the door. Is that what you mean?

JUNE: Yes, Beaver.

BEAVER: Can fathers do it?

JUNE: Yes.

BEAVER: I think mothers do it better than fathers do.

BEAVER CLEAVER

WALLY: Hi, Mom, what are you doing?

JUNE: Just sewing more name tags in Beaver's clothes.

WALLY: "Theodore Cleaver." Hey, you know, Mom, it's a good thing you didn't put "Beaver" in there. If he conked out on the trip or something they'd bury him in a pet cemetery. . . . Oh, I'm sorry, Mom. For a minute there I forgot he was your kid.

◆

A cheery, toothy grin bursting forth from a dimpled, freckled, bright-eyed face beneath a green baseball cap—that's Theodore "Beaver" Cleaver. Look up "All-American Little Boy" in the dictionary and they should have Beaver's picture, or maybe just his dirty fingerprints.

The obvious question is how fine, upstanding parents like Ward and June Cleaver ever named their son "Beaver." As Beaver explains it, it's his given name, "my brother given it to me." "Theodore" proved too big a mouthful for young Wally to pronounce and when it came out "Tweeter" Ward and June thought "Beaver" sounded a little better. Thus was a legendary name bestowed. Just to add a touch of distinction he's frequently referred to as *the* Beaver.

The youngest Cleaver boy makes himself as busy as his animal namesake, but instead of building dams this Beaver spends his time messing things up. Beaver is fresh, naughty, bright, and cute as a button. It's probably the latter trait which is his most outstanding. With his squeaky voice, dirty hands and wide-eyed, friendly curiosity Beaver is the kind of kid people like just for doing nothing.

Of course, to his family he's a bit of a handful. There are always scrapes his parents have to get him out of and trouble that he drags his brother into. He can be a crybaby or an irritating pest but he's always cute.

◆

WALLY: You know what you are, Beaver? You're an optimist.
BEAVER: What's that?
WALLY: Well, that's the kinda guy, if he fell off a cliff, all the way down he'd be saying, "Everything's gonna be okay."

◆

Each morning Beaver awakens knowing that somehow he's going to get tripped and skin his knees on the sidewalk of life. He just wants to be a happy kid but trouble keeps roughing him up. He remains a black-eyed optimist in his constant struggle to become smarter and better able to cope with slowly approaching adulthood.

Beaver's actually a very ordinary boy. He's a fair student, with above average intelligence but only average drive and ambition. He'd much rather be liked by his peers than be considered a "big shot." Like the other Cleaver men he's too decent and trusting for his rotten friends who usually take advantage of him or goad him into trouble. He tries hard to absorb the protective moral jelly his parents keep dispensing but he usually applies it either too late or too weakly to protect himself from the fires of temptation. His greatest pleasures in life are getting dirty, collecting junk and, as he gets older, baseball. His greatest dislikes are school and girls.

He is secure in the tightly wrapped coccoon of his parents' home but feels more and more constricted as he grows up and realizes he's supposed to break free. Still, he stands lovingly and loyally behind his brother, even when Wally goes flaky over girls, and by his parents, even when he begins to realize they can never fulfill all of his expectations. He's a kid who, when he learns his father wasn't a hero in the war but only dug dirt, still swells up his little chest with pride because his dad served "in the same war as the president" and had to be "the best dirt leveler in the whole Seabees."

As he slouches toward his teen years Beaver becomes even more awkward and perhaps more cowering than cute, but he never gives up for too long his capacity to wish things better and to muddle through. Naive, apprehensive, sometimes downright stupid—Beaver can be all of these and more. He's a lightning rod for trouble since he's a little more unlucky and a lot more trusting than the rest of us. We love watching Beaver because we all have days when life pastes a "kick me" sign on our behind as it so often does to Beaver, and no matter how old or cynical we may get there are still times when we would like to think that Ward and June are out there somewhere worrying about *us* and the messes we're getting into.

◆

He's got that little kid expression on his face all
the time, but he's not really as goofy as he looks.

—WALLY

JUNE: Beaver, I just hope you realize that wherever you
go or whatever you do there's always somebody
watching you.

BEAVER: Sure, Mom. You watch me, Dad watches me, when
I'm at school the teacher watches me and when I
go to the movies the ushers watch me.

JUNE: No, Beaver, I mean somebody else.

BEAVER: Gee, Mom, do you mean like, God?

JUNE: Mmm-hmmm, and if you do something bad you're
going to hurt Him.

BEAVER: I wouldn't want to do anything to hurt God. He's
got enough trouble with the Russians and all.

JUNE: Well, Beaver, I just hope you never will.

BEAVER: Oh, sure, Mom.

WALLY CLEAVER

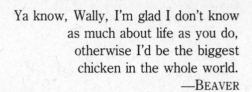

Ya know, Wally, I'm glad I don't know
as much about life as you do,
otherwise I'd be the biggest
chicken in the whole world.
—BEAVER

There are two things you count on an older brother for: to
wise you up to things and to beat up on guys who are bullying
you. As the family's oldest son, he is also expected to accept
increasing burdens of responsibility around the house and to
learn to be a man. All in all, Wallace "Wally" Cleaver is a pretty
neat older brother.

Ward and June's eldest is an unpretentious, good-looking,
athletic youth with a good head on his shoulders, strong muscles
in his arms, good hands and an almost sweetly shy personality.
Wally has never gotten his fair amount of appreciation over the
years for his key role in the series. In addition to his sheer
likability, Wally has a pretty good pug nose for getting into
trouble; one that could match Beaver's at times. A good many
of the episodes actually focus on Wally's dilemmas rather than
Beaver's, especially in the later seasons.

Although he sometimes cracks under the strain of having
such a little goof for a brother, who he always has to protect,
Wally stands beside the Beaver most of the time. He is the
ideal middle man, helping to explain the intricacies of the adult
world to Beaver while at the same time interpreting the muddle-
headed confusions of Beaver's mind to his parents.

Wally is a very concerned brother and even when he carelessly
leads Beaver into murky waters—sometimes literally—he drags

them both back to safety, not much the worse for their adventures. He's Beaver's first real friend, and remains the one friend his brother can rely on when his other buddies doublecross him. In return, Beaver listens to Wally's problems with a willing, if not always comprehending, ear.

As the boys grow older Wally naturally gets embarrassed having his little brother hanging around. There is more friction between the boys and the sparks occasionally explode, but through measles, toads and girlfriends, Wally ends up being a good brother. He blazes the trail to dating, high school, working, and cars, and takes the pioneer's hard knocks while leading the way. Through it all he remains a good, obedient son.

His classmates like Wally because he's so "natural." He's friendly, a good student, a prime athlete, yet doesn't let any of his accomplishments go to his head. June would add that he's well-mannered, polite and conscientious. One of his many girlfriends in the senior year of high school even whispers that he looks like Lloyd Bridges. Even his most obnoxious friend finds good things to say about Wally:

◆

I'm not sayin' you're in my class, but you're not a clod or anything.

—EDDIE HASKELL

◆

PETE: Hey, you guys ever lie around here just thinking about stuff?
BEAVER: Thinking about what?
PETE: Oh, I don't know, like what's up in the sky, clouds and God and stuff?
BEAVER: Me and Wally don't do much thinking.
WALLY: Sometimes I think about stuff like that but it's mostly at night.

SECRETS OF THE CLEAVER HOME

I'm glad we don't have a girl. Our staircase isn't
wide enough for her to throw her bridal bouquet
from.

—JUNE

There are actually two Cleaver homes. For the first two
seasons the family lived at 485 Maple Drive. The distinguishing
characteristics of this house were its picket fence, the bunk
beds in the boys' bedroom (Beaver on top), the pretty neighbor lady, Mrs. Donaldson, and the fact that it didn't have a
den, although there was a space in the living room for Ward's
desk, and the tire swing in the back yard.

What most of us remember as the Cleaver home, though,
was the house the family moved to between the second
and third season. Here is an inside look at 211 Pine Street:

- There is no front fence, but there are camelia bushes and a
  nice plot of lawn for the boys to mow.

- The front door is often left unlocked but there's a key in the
  mailbox.

- One of the first sights upon entering the house is a framed
  reproduction of Gainsborough's *Blue Boy*.

- An ongoing wish of June's is for a downstairs bathroom.

- The kitchen tablecloth pattern matches the plaid of the kitchen
  chairs. The kitchen also has a cookie drawer in addition to a
  cookie jar.

- Ward and June have separate twin beds in their bedroom.
  They do have a portable television in their room, however.

INSIDE THE BOYS'
BEDROOM

Nobody can hurt you when you're sleepin' in bed.
—BEAVER

- Things come in pairs in the Cleaver brothers' bedroom. There are two oars standing in the corners, two small clown drawings on the wall, two pennants over their beds (one marked "W," the other marked "F," and two sinks in the bathroom.

- As you face the beds from the doorway, Beaver sleeps on the right and Wally on the left bed. The bedspreads are a windowpane pattern. (June likes checks and plaids.) Pillows are a little soft and lumpy from excess pillow fighting.

- The dresser has an ample supply of hair tonic and after-shave.

- Wally's favorite place to hide from his parents is under his bed, Beaver's safe spot is the closet floor.

- The boys share a homework desk, a comfortable chair and a floor lamp with a whaling ship motif.

- Any spot is fair game for throwing dirty socks, although they reach their rankest state underneath the mattress.

- Great unanswered bedroom questions: What do the "W" and "F" banners stand for? Why do the boys share a bedroom since the house has a spare guest room?

A VISITOR'S GUIDE TO MAYFIELD

MAN ON BUS: The next stop we make is Mayfield.
BEAVER: Gee, it's not where I'm supposed to be goin', but at least it's someplace I've been.

◆

We all feel that the pleasant little burg of Mayfield is someplace we've been. It is one of the most remembered TV towns, perhaps second only to Metropolis. This is rather ironic, considering that the creators of the show went out of their way to disguise the location of Mayfield so that they didn't get tied to any one geographical area. They went so far, Jerry Mathers recalls, as to alter the mileage signs on the bus station set when Beaver goes on a trip so that viewers wouldn't be able to get out an atlas and try to pinpoint the town.

Careful viewers will note all kinds of discrepancies and inconsistencies about locales throughout the episodes. From the balmy weather and infrequent rains Mayfield looks like a southern California suburb but characters mention traveling to California. Ohio sites like Shaker Heights and Cincinnati are mentioned, but Mayfield is also described at various points as being only twenty miles from the Ocean. Places in and around Mayfield also shift location from episode to episode.

Maybe Connelly and Mosher had the right idea. Leave Mayfield right where it is, in the golden heart of imaginary middle America, a nice place to raise your family, a small center for commerce and comfortable prosperity.

If you're lucky enough to find yourself in Mayfield, here are the key sites and services you won't want to miss:

◆

PUBLIC BUILDINGS AND LANDMARKS

485 Maple Drive—The Cleavers's first home. Wave hello to Mr. Benner, the new owner.

211 Pine Street—The current Cleaver home. Stop by the kitchen door to see if the first batch of cookies is done.

Grant Avenue Grammar School—Where Beaver and Wally spent kindergarten through eighth grade.

Mayfield High—Wally's high school, where Beaver is headed. Fed by four grammar schools. School freaks can also see Union High and City High, among others.

Haydn Memorial Library—All the Haydns are dead, but Mr. Davenport, the head librarian, is available for consultation.

Old MacMahon House—Mayfield's haunted house.

MAYFIELD FUN SPOTS

Metzger's Field—*The* park for ballplaying or for fighting.

Miller's Pond—Just right for boating, polliwog hunting or falling in with all your clothes on.

Captain Jack's Alligator Farm—Home of Captain Jack, the noted alligator authority and Captain Jack, the notorious Clever 'gator.

Mayfield Zoo—Say hi to Stanley the monkey.

State Street Bridge—Best bridge in town for spittin'.

Piedmont Street Bridge—Neatest place to have your feet jiggled by oncoming traffic.

Hank's Bar & Grill—Mayfield's premier beer joint. If the music or beer gets flat head for The Red Top, The Bird Cage, The Green Door, The Blue Moon Tavern or Monihan's.

SHOPS AND SERVICES

Uncle Artie's Magic Shop—Stock up on rubber cheese slices and soap candy.

Margaret Manning Adoption Society—Be wary. Awfully tricky about reuniting runaway boys with their real parents.

Miss Spencer's School of Dance—Try to arrange your trip around her darling Saturday afternoon dances for young ladies and young gentlemen.

Fats Flannaghan's Junkyard—First-rate source for all kinds of good junk. You might also get lucky at the dump on the other side of Euclid Avenue.

The Book Nook—The best in new and used reading material. Ask for the latest "Red River Sam" yarn or *The World According to Beaver*.

Nelson's Bakery—Good eating bargain: their day-old eclairs.

GETAWAYS

Bellport—A nearby town that pretends to be a little ritzier than Mayfield; features a swingin' amusement park with the Big Dipper.

Friend's Lake—Some 50–60 miles from Mayfield, lovely spot for a picnic or vacation. There's also Shadow Lake and, for a longer trip, you might wish to journey 90 miles to Crystal Falls.

THE GUYS

"Good evening, Mrs. Cleaver, Mr. Cleaver."

EDDIE HASKELL

A kid like Eddie Haskell only comes along about
once in a couple hundred years.

—WALLY CLEAVER

◆

Without question, Edward Clark Haskell is one of television's
best-loved, most often quoted wise guys. He probably ranks right
beside Phil Silvers's Sgt. Bilko for blue ribbon obnoxiousness.

Eddie and Wally have been best friends since the second
grade, which should qualify Wally for a purple heart, and
definitely proves that even a rat can have a best friend. For,
as they said about Errol Flynn, you could always count on
Eddie—to let you down.

Eddie's two trademarks are his unctious politeness to adults
and his weasly, sharp-tongued meanness to everybody else.
He is a model white-collar delinquent, a creep who goads
people into trouble rather than perpetrating the crime himself.
He was a born shirker, not worker, and a strain on any parent,
especially his own long-suffering mother and father, Agnes and
George. Mary Ellen Rogers's father refers to him as an "over-
stimulated adolescent"; but really, when it comes to Eddie,
when you've said "creep," you've said it all.

EDDIE: Relax, Sam; how many times have I let you down?
BEAVER: A couple of hundred times.
EDDIE: You stay out of this, boy creep.

◆

EDDIE HASKELL
MY PAL

BEAVER: Hey, Wally—how come Eddie's such a creep?
WALLY: 'Cause he works at it.

♦

EDDIE: Maybe I can help. Look, I've been in every kind of trouble there is.

♦

JUNE: Eddie seems to know a lot about the law.
WALLY: Yeah, he told his father, in three years he's goin' over the wall.

♦

JUNE: Beaver, if you can't say something nice about a person, it's better not to say anything.
BEAVER: Okay— (A beat) I guess we better talk about something besides Eddie.

♦

BEAVER: Wally, there wasn't anything funny about Dad yelling at ya; why was Eddie laughing?
WALLY: Well, you know Eddie; he's always laughing at stuff that isn't funny.

♦

BEAVER: That Eddie Haskell even whistles like a wise guy.

♦

EDDIE: Hi, Beaver.
BEAVER: Okay, Eddie, what do you want from me?
EDDIE: What are you talking about?
BEAVER: This is the first time in my whole life you called
            me "Beaver" instead of "shrimp" or "squirt" or
            something.

◆

WALLY: Boy, I don't know about takin' advice from Eddie.
BEAVER: I wouldn't take advice from him on good stuff, but
            when you want to know how to be a real rat, you
            couldn't go to a better guy.

◆

WALLY: Cut it out, Eddie—you always do what your father
            tells you.
EDDIE: Yeah, but I'm just playin' it cool till I'm eighteen.

◆

WALLY: Ya know something, Eddie? If they gave a prize for
            running off at the mouth, you'd be valedictorian.

◆

BEAVER: Does everybody have a conscience?
WALLY: Of course they do.
BEAVER: I'll betcha Eddie Haskell doesn't have one.

◆

EDDIE'S ADVICE ON HOW TO GET WHAT YOU WANT OUT OF LIFE

If you ask them, they always say no; just tell your pop, and then if he says no, you can start whining around.

◆

This is vacation. Your parents aren't allowed to make you work all the time. It's a state law.

◆

Nothing's a dirty trick if it's funny enough.

◆

Look, why should I do my parents a favor and call 'em? If you start treating them too good, the next thing you know, they'll start pushing you around.

◆

If we don't stick together, we're gonna lose the cold war with the adults.

◆

My pop made me stay around the house one Saturday. You know what I did? I went out in the yard and started bouncin' a ball off the roof. Pretty soon my old man came out and tole me to get lost.

◆

EDDIE,
THE OBNOXIOUS

EDDIE: It was *awfully* nice seeing you again, Mrs. Cleaver.

◆

JUNE: I wonder why we're always so suspicious of Eddie?
WARD: Any teenager who is that polite and well-mannered will bear watching.

◆

EDDIE: Mrs. Cleaver, you've done something new to your hair.
JUNE: Not a thing.
EDDIE: Oh, it looks very nice.

◆

EDDIE: We're going to see *Spartacus*. I'm quite a student of history, and I'd like to see if it contains any inaccuracies.
WARD: Don't you let Kirk Douglas get away with anything, Eddie.

◆

EDDIE: I was thinking of writing a book on my experiences with the fishing fleet. Entering college with a book on the best-seller list will certainly give me an edge with my English prof. Don't you think, Mr. Cleaver?

◆

EDDIE: I probably wouldn't have done it if Clarence hadn't
         been there to urge me on.

◆

JUNE: Eddie, are you having a good time?
EDDIE: Oh, yes, Mrs. Cleaver. I think a *small* house like
         this makes a party so intimate.

◆

EDDIE: Good morning, Mrs. Cleaver. That's a very pretty
         dress.

◆

EDDIE: Gee, your kitchen always looks so clean.
JUNE: Why, thank you, Eddie.
EDDIE: My mother says it looks as though you never do
         any work in here.

◆

EDDIE: Put your thumb back in your mouth, sonny. I'm
         talking.
WARD: (Entering) Oh, excuse me, fellas; phone call, Beaver.
EDDIE: Hurry back, Beaver. I was really enjoying our
         conversation.

◆

EDDIE: Mrs. Cleaver, I don't like to carry tales, but I just
         saw little Theodore going down the street. I believe
         he had some of Mr. Cleaver's gardening tools hidden
         in his wagon.
JUNE: Yes, we know, Eddie. He and Gilbert have a job
         cutting lawns.

EDDIE: Oh, I'm glad to hear it's a worthwhile project, Mrs. Cleaver. I know you would appreciate me letting you know if Theodore was engaged in some sort of mischief.

◆

EDDIE: Thank you for having me to lunch, Mrs. Cleaver. I hope it's no trouble.

JUNE: No, Eddie—we're just having chopped egg sandwiches.

EDDIE: That will be delicious. (After he walks out with Wally) Boy, Wally—chopped egg sandwiches. Can't you talk your mother into somethin' with meat in it?

◆

EDDIE: (With a big smile) Good morning, Theodore.

BEAVER: Eddie, how come you're only polite to me when my mother's here?

◆

EDDIE: I'm getting a job after school and on weekends. I convinced my father it's the best thing to do if I'm going to look forward to a business career.

JUNE: Yes, well, Wally might like to get a job, but of course he has his track practice every afternoon.

EDDIE: Well, perhaps I'm making the right decision, Mrs. Cleaver. After all, I've heard of very few men who've become millionaires running the two-twenty.

◆

EDDIE: I make it a point not to lie around in bed Saturday mornings. It spoils my work habits for the school week.

◆

WALLY: Eddie, we can't go without my brother.

EDDIE: Who needs him? He already paid his dough for the ticket. . . . Oh, good morning, Mrs. Cleaver. We're worried about Theodore, Mrs. Cleaver. Poor little fellow—I wouldn't want him to miss this outing for anything.

JUNE: Really, Eddie?

EDDIE: Oh, yes—I've always felt that older boys should devote more time to the little ones.

EDDIE, THE PARENT'S NIGHTMARE

JUNE: Wally's invited away for the weekend.

WARD: Don't tell me the Haskells invited him over to be a good influence for Eddie again.

◆

JUNE: Maybe we need Eddie Haskell.

WARD: What?

JUNE: Well, if it weren't for Eddie, who could we blame Wally's faults on?

◆

EDDIE: When I walk in the kitchen, your mother's always givin' me that look. You know—like I'm a roach or somethin'.

◆

EDDIE: Your father doesn't like me.

WALLY: Why would you say that?

EDDIE: On account of the way he looks at me when he opens the door; sometimes I think he'd be happier to see Khrushchev standing there.

◆

EDDIE: Thank you, Mr. Cleaver. You know, if I had done something like this to my father, he would have clobbered me.

WARD: Don't think I didn't consider it, Eddie.

◆

EDDIE: Hi ya, Beaver—you gnaw down any trees today? Heh, heh, heh.

◆

WALLY: Hey, Eddie—how come you're always givin' Beaver the business?

EDDIE: I'm not givin' him the business. I'm just tryin' to wise him up. I don't want him goin' out in the world and gettin' slaughtered.

◆

EDDIE: Is the warden going to let you have wheels?

BEAVER: Huh?

EDDIE: Is your father going to let Wally buy the car? If you need a translation, why don't you go to the UN?

◆

LUMPY: Dad wouldn't want me to hurt his standing in the community.

EDDIE: He's got you for a son, and he doesn't want to hurt his standing in the community!

◆

EDDIE: Well, well, well, squirt, what are you and Gilbert going to do, form an ignorant club?

◆

EDDIE: Yeah, Wally, what do you want to help out those kids for; what are you doing, bucking for eagle scout or something?

◆

EDDIE: Where you been, Larry—out frightenin' babies? Heh, heh, heh.

◆

EDDIE: Ah, you're talking to an expert. I owe my success to the fine art of the insult. Hit them with both barrels, and they'll back right off.

BEAVER: Hey, maybe it'll work.

EDDIE: Sure it will; there's a million good girl-insults. Get a load of this. "Hey, you, I've seen better-looking faces on iodine bottles." That's only the beginning. Here's one that will really slow 'em down. You get a bunch of guys together, and then you point at this one girl and then say, "Hey, now I remember you; you're the cover girl for *Mad Magazine*."

◆

EDDIE: Hey, I hear they got you in solitary confinement. What'd you do, spill jam on your bib again?

BEAVER: No, I stayed out late, so I'm not allowed out on school nights.

EDDIE: Hey, that's rough. If that ever happened to me, eight or nine girls would kill themselves.

◆

EDDIE: Beaver, where do you get this "*we*" stuff? What do you think we're running here, group therapy?

THE SERIOUS EDDIE

EDDIE: I really fixed myself up good, the old Haskell touch.

◆

EDDIE: It's not that I was afraid; it's just that I feel kind of weird when I got to be anyplace by myself.
BEAVER: Gee, Eddie, I didn't know you ever felt weird about anything.
EDDIE: Yeah, Beaver, when I'm around other people, I can act like a big shot and get away with it.
BEAVER: Yeah, you're real good at that.
EDDIE: Yeah, but it's not good in life for a guy to act like a big shot to himself.
BEAVER: Yeah, I guess even a creep's gotta have friends.

◆

WALLY: Gee, Eddie, then how come you're always jumpin'
         on other guys and makin' fun of them?
EDDIE: Look, Sam, if you can make the other guy feel like
         a goon first, *you* don't feel like so much of a goon.
WALLY: Gee, I don't figure that out.
EDDIE: Of course you don't, Wally. That's 'cause you never
         went to kindergarten with a home permanent.

◆

EDDIE: You got a lot of stuff goin' for you at school. But
         how'd you like to be like me? I gotta make a noise
         like a brass band, or nobody would even notice me.
WALLY: Ah, you're not that bad, Eddie.
EDDIE: Oh, yes, I am. Half the time my blood relatives
         can't stand me.

◆

EDDIE: (Shaking his head) Boy, everybody around here's
         wise to me. I might have to move to a new town
         and start over.

◆

BEAVER: Hey, Mom, you know how you were saying there
         might be another Eddie? Well, I think I might have
         seen him . . . This morning when we were doing
         the dishes, the other Eddie wasn't there for long,
         but he was there, all right.
JUNE: Well, maybe Eddie really is going to change.
BEAVER: No, I don't think so, Mom. Well, about a half hour
         later, I offered him a piece of my candy, and he
         rubbed it in my hair. I guess the old Eddie is going
         to be with us a while longer.

◆

LUMPY RUTHERFORD

Oh, you needn't worry about Clarence. When it comes to brains, he's got a head on him like the Rock of Gibraltar.

—Mr. Rutherford

♦

"All your life you've been kind of a pleasant slob," Eddie says to Clarence "Lumpy" Rutherford. He is both bigger and dumber than his friends, older and less mature. Beaver refers to Eddie and Lumpy (a mind-boggling combo by anyone's estimation) as "Creeps, Incorporated." In his own words, Lumpy admits, "I'm a mess."

Fred says Lumpy is built like Burt Lancaster, but a brick outhouse would be a more apt description. Gilbert observes that "from the back, Lumpy looks like a man, but from the front he just looks like a stupid kid." Aside from his gut, Lumpy's most distinguishing characteristic is that his head is somewhat "lopsided," which Fred attributes to his having slept too much on one side of his head when he was a baby.

He is older than Wally, and in the early episodes, he is the first bully that the Cleaver boys must deal with. Pretty soon his true cowardly, lumbering self shows through, and they see him for a kind of harmless buffoon. As he continues to "swell up," everybody gets a good laugh at Lumpy's expense, but as long as he's getting his three squares and a few snacks in between and his father is not yelling at him too much, he's a happy enough boob, sporting a silly sort of dodo's grin. When things are going poorly, which is most of the time, he still whines for his "Daddy."

Lumpy's two prized possessions are his comic-book collection and his jalopy. His favorite preoccupation is getting fed, and he can move through eats like a thresher through wheat. His schoolwork is so poor that he is left back in high school, prompting Mr. Hyatt, his homeroom teacher, to remark that Lumpy is "making sophomore class his permanent home." Fred handicaps his college chances by trying to determine which instrument the state band is in short supply of, which is how Lumpy switches from clarinet to tuba, but what saves his enormous hide is his football guard-playing ability, which earns him a scholarship (which he almost loses because of his flunking grades). The scholarship gives his social standing a much-needed boost, since most of the guys and none of the girls will talk to him.

LUMPY: What are you staring at me for, Gilbert?
GILBERT: Well, my mother keeps telling me not to grow up
          like you, and I just wanted to see what she meant.

◆

LUMPY: Daddy, there's nothing good on television, and I
          can't find my comic books.
FRED: Well, then, go read a book.
LUMPY: Gee, Daddy, you don't have to be mean to me just
          'cause Violet got gypped.

◆

BEAVER: When I went over there, I figured I could make an
          impression on Lumpy's brain, but when he looked
          in the glass and called himself "a doll," I figured it
          was kind of hopeless.

◆

MR. GANNON: Having trouble with the test questions, Ruther-
               ford?
LUMPY: Oh, no, sir. This is the same test you gave
               me last year.
MR. GANNON: That's right. We fought through World War I
               before, didn't we, Clarence?

◆

EDDIE: Listen, every night before supper he goes down to
          the malt shop for a sundae. He's not supporting
          that blubber on skim milk, you know.

◆

LUMPY: Look, squirt, if you're putting us on, I'll break you
          in two and hang you out to dry.
BEAVER: Boy, I bet you think you're as strong as King
          Kong.
LUMPY: Maybe I am.
BEAVER: Well, maybe you are, because you sure look like
          him.

◆

EDDIE: I'll swing by and get Lumpy. He's not gonna attract
          any chicks, but at least he's ballast.

◆

LUMPY: Hey, Wally, we're watchin' the kids, but who's
          watchin' us, huh? Heh, heh, heh.
GIRL: The way you dance, everyone in the place.

◆

LARRY MONDELLO

Get another loaf of bread—Larry's
going to be here for lunch!

—JUNE

Larry Mondello, red-haired, freckle-faced, whiny-voiced, potbellied perpetual loser, is also Beaver's *best* best friend. Called "Frankie" early on, Larry never, ever looks really *happy*, but he comes closest when he's got something working in his jaws. He's most often remembered as the kid who is always digging something out of his pocket to eat, usually an apple. In fact, he probably eats more apples on camera than Mr. Ed.

For a young fellow only half a year older than Beaver, Larry cuts a somewhat awesome figure. He wears a baseball cap like Beaver, but the similarity stops there. Larry's a BIG BOY; in the fifth grade, he weighs 114 pounds to Beaver's 74 (soaking wet). When his mother bakes a cake for the school bake sale, Larry eats it before he delivers it. Larry can be a rather sweet blob of a boy; however, he manages to get Beaver dunked in hot water almost as often as Eddie Haskell burns Wally. The main difference is that Larry is more stupidly plodding about his troublemaking than Eddie or even Gilbert. Larry is always more interested in being close to a Wise potato chip than in being a wise guy.

We get to know a little bit more about the Mondellos' home life than about any of the families of the Cleaver boys' other friends, and what we see is not a very pretty picture. Wally says that at the Mondellos "somebody is always eating, and if they're not eating, they're hollerin'."

Larry's father is always "away on business," often in Cincinnati, for some unexplained reason, and it is left to Mrs.

Mondello to raise Larry and his older sister. This task proves far too great a strain for his mother, and as a result, she is a very nervous, worried woman who can't wait for her husband to get home to "get to the bottom of things." To hear Larry tell it, his father's way of getting to the bottom of things is via direct pressure to Larry's bottom.

Larry has an older married brother who used to enjoy hitting him on the arm before he moved away, and his sister writes in her diary, "My little brother is horrible and eats like a pig." She, in turn, gives her mother nervous headaches because she is not married yet, though one wonders why Mrs. Mondello is so eager to get her daughter railroaded into the kind of marital nightmare she appears to be living out.

JUNE: Larry's home sick today.
WALLY: No wonder, the way he ate last night.

◆

JUNE: I think you better tell the boys to come out.

WARD: That won't be necessary. I think the smell of hot dogs will bring Larry out in the open.

◆

BEAVER: Larry, how come you eat your cake first?

LARRY: If I eat the sandwiches first, I might not have room for the cake.

◆

JUNE: Well, there's one thing I'll say for Larry; a punch in the stomach didn't affect his appetite any.

WARD: Oh, the way that boy ate! It was like watching a mongoose. I don't think I've seen anyone eat ketchup on corn before.

◆

MRS. MONDELLO: The people from the drugstore called; last week somebody in this house spent $3.25 on sodas, candy bars, milk shakes, and bubble gum.

LARRY: Maybe Dad did it, Mom.

◆

LARRY: It's pretty neat, Beaver, your father siding with you. In my house, they're always siding with my older sister.

BEAVER: How come?

LARRY: On account of if they don't, she gets headaches.

BEAVER: Couldn't you get headaches?

LARRY: Uh-uh. She thought of it first.

GILBERT BATES

Okay, I may be a dirty rat, but I'm not a dumb rat.

◆

The sheer brazen obnoxiousness of Eddie Haskell is burned into most of our memories, but as a junior wise guy, Gilbert Grover Bates has never quite gotten his due. Gilbert is Beaver's "Eddie," which is really too bad for Beaver, because Gilbert is generally a quieter, sneakier, and meaner kind of rat than the cockier Eddie, so that Beaver is usually less prepared for the trouble that inevitably comes when he follows Gilbert's goading.

Right from the start, when Gilbert moves in across the street in "Beaver and Gilbert" during the second season, Beaver's in for it. When he first meets Beaver, Gilbert (whose family name is Gates initially) fills his head with wild stories about his training for the 1968 Olympics and his father's being an FBI man with "a bullet hole and everything." When Gilbert quickly manages to turn Beaver's friends against him, Beaver starts fighting him. This leads to Ward's discovering that Gilbert merely made up the stories because he had to move so often due to his father's job as a musician and that he was merely trying to make a flashy entrance into the neighborhood.

Gilbert truly comes into his full fresh-mouthed glory during the fourth season when Larry Mondello leaves Mayfield. Even Wally has some trouble beating back Gilbert's snappy answers for everything. Of course, Eddie Haskell, who is not about to cede any of his territory to a mere upstart, capitalizes on Gilbert's distinguishing physical characteristic, his big ears, and puts him in his place by calling him "hydrant head."

"Beaver's Birthday" provides just one example of Gilbert's unique brand of insinuating awfulness: Beaver is wrestling with his conscience (a match he always loses in the end) over

whether to use some of his birthday money to buy a new model car. Gilbert just happens to take him walking past the toy-store window with the car in it, talks him into buying it, puts the blame on Beaver, and then insists that they take the car to *his* house to play with it, but only after they stop for sodas, which—you guessed it—he gets Beaver to pay for. And of course, Gilbert's feet move even faster than his mouth just before the inevitable boom is lowered.

◆

BEAVER: You mean you gave my trains away to a girl just because she was pretty?

WALLY: Well, no I didn't give them to her just because she was pretty.

GILBERT: What'd she do, Wally, knock you down and *take* them away from you?

WALLY: Now look, Gilbert, you shut up.

GILBERT: You can't tell me to shut up! I'm not in your *family.*

◆

GILBERT: My mom told me to come home from school and clean up my room; then she didn't like the way I was doing it. Then I got a *real* break: My dad came home and told me to get out of the house because he couldn't stand to hear my mother yelling at me.

◆

GILBERT: Mr. Cleaver, could you call up my father and tell him you already gave us a lecture so I won't have to have another one?

◆

WARD: And when you make a mistake, admit it. If you don't, you only make matters worse.

GILBERT: If we knew we were going to make matters worse, we would have admitted it right away, sir.

◆

BEAVER: The guy I caddied for *cheated*. Oh, he didn't cheat a whole lot, just enough to win.

GILBERT: That's all you got to cheat, just enough to win.

◆

WARD: I think you should tell Gilbert that his idea didn't work.

BEAVER: I'm going to tell him all right, Dad. And I'm going to tell him when I'm sitting on him.

◆

THE OTHER GUYS

WHITEY WHITNEY

WHITEY: Hello, Mrs. Cleaver. This is Hubert Whitney.
JUNE: Who?
WHITEY: You know, Whitey. Mrs. Cleaver, if you're not yelling at Beaver, can I please talk to him?
JUNE: Well, Beaver isn't here now, and why would we be yelling at him?
WHITEY: I don't know; they're always yelling at me around here.

◆

Whitey can be very Hubertlike; Ward describes him as "always talking like he's been frightened by something." He's a diminutive slip of a boy with a high nasal voice and hair that just might have turned blond-white from nervousness.

Sometimes, particularly in the first few years, Whitey is almost as cute and as naive as Beaver. Quietly and without any fuss being made by the guys, Whitey gets the best grades of any boy in his class. This doesn't stop him from breaking out in hives for the whole month of August. In his own subtle way, Whitey can be a pretty crafty conniver, and he will always be remembered as the wise guy who got Beaver to climb up onto the soup billboard.

RICHARD RICKOVER

WALLY: Boy, Beaver, I don't know how you can stand that Richard. He's the creepiest kid I know.

BEAVER: He's not so creepy when *I'm* with him. He just acts that way around people.

◆

When Gilbert isn't around, it is up to Richard to get Beaver in trouble, although sometimes the two terrors team up for a double whammy. Richard is the youngest sibling in his family, and so, like Gilbert, he has become "wised up" out of necessity, always trying to get some advantage by figuring out an "angle." (Beaver is alone among his friends, who are the youngest in their families, in his willingness to smarten up at a more studied pace.)

A favorite Richardism is to remind Beaver that he's Beaver's best friend when he can't think of a better way to get his good buddy to do what he wants. Ward observes that Richard is "the only friend of Beaver's who doesn't sound afraid of adults," and Richard is also a boy who got a "D" in citizenship for hitting a girl on school property. He is the one who gives Beaver's name to the police when he's caught for window breaking and in his first appearance spills oil on Wally's good suit and then gets Beaver to use bleach on the stain, which wrecks the suit so badly that Eddie Haskell has to help Beaver out. Not every friend can get Beaver into a mess that's so terrible that Eddie has to bail him out. That, along with his mastery of the stacked cookie sandwich, are accomplishments not to be treated lightly.

◆

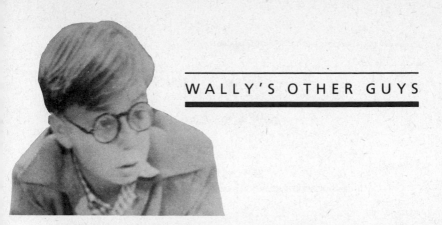

WALLY'S OTHER GUYS

TOOEY BROWN—is most noticeable because of his Coke-bottle-thick eyeglasses. He's been playing the clarinet since the fifth grade and looks it, but he's managed to find a broken-down motor scooter that he and Wally putter over.

CHESTER ANDERSON—is another grammar school pal of Wally's, a good-looking, levelheaded boy who is very similar to Wally in appearance and demeanor and is one of the few boys who will stand up to Lumpy. Like Wally, a natural captain of any sandlot baseball team.

BEAVER'S OTHER GUYS

HARRY HENDERSON—Filled Larry's enormous role as a fat foil for Beaver in a few episodes. A whiny, bespectacled boy who is probably best recalled for posing as the poster boy for Beaver's painting of Paul Revere.

BENJIE BELLAMY—The neighbor kid who talks to ants. While he frequently seems lost in his own little world, he touches down once or twice to get Beaver in trouble, as when he pours a paint bucket over himself or gets locked in the Cleaver bathroom.

THE GUYS WHO
WERE GIRLS

MARY ELLEN ROGERS

EDDIE: That Mary Ellen Rogers was asking for you. She said, "Give my love to Wally," and then she made a face like she was gonna get sick.

WALLY: I wonder what she did that for?

EDDIE: Aw, cut it out, Rock. Who do you think you're kidding?

As one of the most popular young men in Mayfield High, Wally hung around with a lot of guys, some of whom happened to be girls. There were many girls that he dated, but the young lady who stood out above the crowd of high school cuties was pert Mary Ellen Rogers. Her family lived around the corner from the Cleavers and since the eighth grade she was one of the first girls to come stalking Wally, using Beaver, ginger ale and donuts to get her man to take her to a school dance. Although she never seemed to make it to the big dates like the prom, Wally gives her his letterman's sweater—at least for a while—and if he's going out on a Friday or Saturday night there was a good chance Mary Ellen was the lucky girl.

◆

PENNY WOODS

If her face was on television parents wouldn't let little kids watch it.

—BEAVER

◆

As Beaver worked his way through Grant Avenue School, blond Penny Woods entered the classroom scene to more-or-less take over Judy's role as the girl most likely to make life miserable. With her blond hair and stuck-up face, Penny could be even more of a little female terror than Miss Hensler. But she could also be a little nicer, and as Beaver matured, the two natural adversaries actually lowered their verbal sparring gloves once in a while and became friendly—but just for a while.

◆

JUDY HENSLER

Miss Landers, do you want the list of people who were talking while you were out of the room?

◆

Judy Hensler is the Grant Avenue Grammar School Goody Two Shoes, the know-it-all squealer who always has one squinty eye peeled for offenders to report to the teacher. If Miss Landers forgets about the spelling test, you can count on Judy to raise her hand to remind her; if Beaver forgets to do his assignment, Judy will make sure the whole class knows about his lapse.

Fortified by hair braids so stiff they look like they're tied with iron and a perpetually sour expression, Judy is fond of throwing her good grades back in the face of her classmates and of warning them with self-appointed authority that they are going to get in trouble "for sure." Even the normally unflappably sweet Miss Landers occasionally snaps at Judy when she goes overboard. No one would argue with Larry's assessment that "Judy's the meanest girl in the whole school."

◆

THE MOST INTERESTING
CHARACTERS BEAVER
EVER MET

FRED RUTHERFORD

*See you down at the salt mines,
Ward, old man.*

◆

Perhaps the ultimate chrome-domed cornball,
Fred Rutherford has as much couth as hair. It
would be hard to gauge whether he is more
lovably annoying as Ward's best friend and
coworker or as Lumpy's father. His
conversation is strictly of the pompous,
callow, blowhard variety, sprinkled with such
charming phrases as, referring to the office as
the "salt mines" or the "sweat shop," and
referring to June as "the little bride."

When not toadying up to the cream of Mayfield's social
register or chasing after Ward's job by trying to curry favor
with the "big brass from New York," Fred corners anyone who
will pretend to pay attention so that he can brag about his "big
fella," Lumpy, saying things like, "Clarence has developed into
quite a young man around town, and very responsible for a lad
his age." And when no one but Clarence is around, he merci-
lessly berates the boy as a "knucklehead," a "big boob," and a
"stupid oaf."

Gwendolyn Rutherford (called Geraldine early on when there
is also reference to Fred's having *two* sons) is actually a
seemingly pleasant woman who takes the men of her household
with a large grain of salt, one that possibly emerged from the
"salt mines."

JUNE: Ward, Wally's best friend is Eddie Haskell, and yours
       is Fred Rutherford. What's wrong with this family?
WARD: Well, dear, can I help it if Wally and I are humanitarians?

◆

JUNE: Hello, Fred. Come on in here.
FRED: Oh, thank you, June, but my business is with the lord
       of the manor.

◆

FRED: Ward, this party that Gwen and I are throwing for
       Clarence has grown to tremendous proportions. We
       had to prune away the guest list quite a bit, but we
       want you and June to know that your Wally is still
       included.

◆

FRED: Have to keep a firm hand on boys nowadays, Ward.
       My Clarence answered me back the other day. I
       smacked him right in the mouth. None of this
       psychology for me.

◆

GUS, THE FIREMAN

◆

*When you get to be my age, you know a little
something about just about everything.*

◆

Gus is the one adult who is almost always available for
emergency consultation when Beaver needs it. His "office" is
the auxiliary firehouse where Lieutenant Gus keeps a somewhat

sleepy watch over "ol' number 7," the fire engine into which Beaver has put more elbow grease by polishing it than he ever applied to his own body.

Gus offers Beaver a ready ear and generally simple, sound advice, and the lure of the fire station is enough to bring Beaver around often. A skilled fix-it man, Gus can even come up with a cure when Beaver is left with an ailing carnival horse in the garage. After all, one thing Gus has plenty of is good, old-fashioned horse sense.

MISS LANDERS

BEAVER: Hey, Mom, would you get Miss Landers sumpin' kinda nice for a present 'cause she's not only a good teacher, she's a pretty good guy, too.

WALLY: You know something, Mom—I think he's stuck on his teacher.

BEAVER: No I'm not. I was stuck on her the first year I had her, but now I like her like I like Mom.

◆

Everybody ought to have a favorite teacher somewhere in their school career; somebody who encourages them and manages to make them feel good about having to go to school every day. For Beaver that special teacher is his grammar school instructor, lovely Miss Landers.

◆

BEAVER: She's a neat teacher, and she's fair, and she's pretty and she smells good, and she's always doing nice things.

◆

Beaver goes through all the stages with Miss Landers from teacher's pet trauma to crush to friend to having her invited home for dinner to suffering through the announcement of her engagement. Even though good old Miss Landers let him down by getting herself engaged—and presumably married—the kids were still able to call her Miss Landers. Perhaps it's appropriate that we never learn her new last name since we never learned her first name.

Miss Landers was the essence of sweetness, patience and the kind of spirit that could even get a class revved up about a silly civics project. And she imparted a lot of useful lessons beyond "booklearnin' " into the heads of her young scholars.

Some of you seem to think there's something shameful about a little boy and a little girl liking each other. Now let's think about it for a minute. Is it really so shameful? All of us here in this room are rather like one big family and I think our family could be a lot happier if we were considerate and friendly toward one another. And as far as little boys and little girls liking each other, well, you don't have to be silly about it, but I do think you should have mutual respect and learn to get along together. You know, if you do that, you'll be taking a big step toward becoming the kind of men and women we want you to be.

—MISS LANDERS

AUNT MARTHA

JUNE: Now, what's the matter with my Aunt Martha?
WARD: Well, nothing that you can put your finger on. It's just
        that whenever I'm in the room with her, I feel like I
        should be apologizing for something.

◆

June's maiden aunt is very dear to her because she was instrumental in raising June in the fine and proper Bronson family tradition, but to the Cleaver men, she's an unwelcome presence on her rare visits. She's a wonderful woman, Ward will admit, quickly adding, "But not for kids," a fair judgment about any woman who serves milk toast for breakfast and eggplant for dinner and makes Beaver wear a short-pants suit to school.

BEAVER: Is Aunt Martha the one who sends the soap every Christmas?

WARD: No, Aunt Martha understands boys better than that. She sends umbrellas.

WALLY: Oh, yeah. She's our *umbrella* aunt.

BEAVER: I remember her; she has birds on her hat.

◆

UNCLE BILLY

JUNE: Dear, aren't you afraid Uncle Billy is a little flamboyant for the boys?

◆

Ward's Uncle Billy is a swell windbag of a tall-tale teller, a kind of senior delinquent who is the natural hero of a young boy until he breaks his heart by not buying him a promised silken-wrapped bamboo fishing pole, as was the case with Beaver, or doesn't take him fishing, as was the case with Ward when he was growing up. Billy is good for ten whole dollars come birthday time, and when he takes care of the boys for a weekend, they have a ball, getting spending money and washing the dishes with the lawn hose. Still, Uncle Billy was always one of Ward's favorites, because he was the exact opposite of the other Cleaver boys, including Ward's father, who were *very* solid, sober citizens. Even with his wild stories and seemingly carefree, hearty disposition, Billy manages to teach Beaver a lesson or two, since it seems to be impossible for an adult Cleaver not to impart such knowledge.

◆

MOST INTERESTING
CHARACTERS
WE NEVER MEET

Larry Mondello's father.

Larry Mondello's sister.

Angela Valentine, the six-toed girl in Beaver's class who is suffering through some crisis whenever her name is mentioned—throwing up in the cloakroom or losing her mouth retainer in the school yard.

LIFE ACCORDING TO BEAVER

BEAVER: What makes rust, Dad?

WARD: Oxidation, it eats into the metal.

BEAVER: Why don't they make cans out of wood?

WARD: Wood rots.

BEAVER: Gee, there's something wrong with just about everything, isn't there, Dad?

WARD: Just about, I guess, Beav.

KID STUFF

JUNE: Did you notice the Beaver at lunch? I think there's
something wrong with him. He hardly ate anything.

WARD: Well, dear, he was probably lost in a dream world of his
own where there's no place for tuna fish sandwiches.

No matter how empathetic they might try to be, adults
can never fully step back into the half-tied shoes of the children
they once were. Being a kid means looking up at the world
through wide open eyes, eyes unclouded by the chill mists of
experience that eventually spirit us through the one-way door
to adulthood.

As a kid, each day's activities involve either enjoying life to
its innocent hilt or trying to figure out what your parents or
teachers want you to do instead, since one of the first laws of
childhood is that fun stuff is stuff no adult would be caught dead
doing. Probably the second kid law is that just about everything
you do can get you into trouble; the corollary of this is that

kids have no rights. As a kid grows older he yearns more and
more to blast out of the insular orbit of childhood and enter the
forbidding atmosphere of adulthood. This is not because adult
life looks so appealing but because it's what one is supposed to
become. Youth enjoys a decidedly short-term view of life,
taking each day's joys and troubles as they happen, for as
Beaver notes, "I'm just worried about getting by tomorrow."

◆

WARD: You fellas can't take the things Tom Sawyer did
         and try to do them today.
WALLY: Heck no, Dad. You try to do any of that stuff and
         they'd say you were some sort of delinquent.
WARD: Actually, those things were just part of growing up
         in Tom's day. There was nothing malicious or
         deliberate in anything he did, but times have
         changed; it's a more complicated world. If a fella
         tried to do those things today he'd be judged in a
         different light. . . .
BEAVER: Yeah, Dad. It was a lot easier being a kid in those
         days.
WARD: Well, Beaver, let's just say it's a lot harder being a
         kid these days.

◆

Being a kid was never easy for either a child or his parents,
but growing up in Space Age America creates more pressure
than any other period in history. Kids are expected to achieve
more at an earlier age, with fiercely competitive Little League
baseball, child psychology, crowded colleges, the threat of
communist dominance and even the need to get one's teeth
straightened. Still, as unusually sensitive parents, Ward and
June know that there are certain immutable laws and rhythms
of kid stuff that no amount of new-fangled modern problems
and concerns can alter.

YOU KNOW YOU'RE STILL
A KID WHEN . . .

- Your greatest fears are getting yelled at; getting punished; bullies; getting kissed by a girl; losing your teddy bear; haunted houses; getting a note home from your teacher.

- You express your anger by sulking in your room; giving "the silent treatment"; locking yourself in the bathroom; threatening to run away to join the Navy; pulling a girl's pigtail.

- You believe unwaveringly that your father can do *anything;* your mother's pretty neat too; your brother's okay when he's not punching you or going out with girls; you can *un*do things as easily as you can *do* them; that good cowboys wear white hats and bad knights get the most arrows shot into them.

- Your idea of fun is watching your brother get yelled at; reading a $1.98 "Red River Sam" western; watching killer and monster movies; joining a secret club; camping out even if it's only in your backyard and you're barely as tall as the tent.

- A big event is growing a new tooth; trading for a horse tooth; entering a raffle; being accepted as one of the "big guys"; getting a jacket or a bicycle that's brand new and not a hand-me-down; having a friend sleep overnight; staying up late on a school night.

- You have to tell your parents where you're going and you have to be home for lunch and dinner—or else.

- Your pockets, at any given time, contain marbles, rocks, chalk, bottle caps, baseball cards, pennies, dried worms.

- You want to be an atomic scientist this week even more than you wanted to be a garbage collector last week.

Monday

Went to school. Came home.
Had lunch. Ate it.

Tuesday

Went to school. Had lunch.
Came back home.

Wednesday

Went to school. Had lunch.
Came back home.

Thursday

Went to school. Had lunch.
Saw dead cat. Came back home.

Friday

Went to school. Had fight with
BIG KID. Beat him up!
He cried. Came back home.

BEAVER RUNS AWAY

♦

WARD: So, you're leaving home, huh?

BEAVER: Yes sir, and I'm not never coming back.

WARD: Well, don't you want to talk it over?

BEAVER: No sir. (Opens front door) Well, goodbye.

WARD: Goodbye.

BEAVER: Well, I'm really goin'.

WARD: So you said. I don't suppose you'd want to have your supper first?

BEAVER: No, I'm goin' right now.

WARD: (Extending his right hand) Goodbye. I'll tell your mother you've gone.

BEAVER: Thank you. (Pause) Well, goodbye.

WARD: Bye.

MESSIN' AROUND

Beav, you sure get a lot of fun out of
doin' nothin'.

—WALLY

◆

WALLY: I might mess around with Eddie and Lumpy.
JUNE: Doing what?
WALLY: Gee, Mom, if I knew what we were going to do, it
wouldn't be any fun to do it.

◆

To a boy growing up in Mayfield, "messin' around" is what
he does when he's not doing something he has to do like going
to school or church or eating lunch. Messin' around is as
natural as breathing and sometimes not much more active. It's
not big stuff like going to the dentist or taking a car trip or
having a job. It's passing-the-time stuff, having-fun stuff, just-
trying-to-stay-out-of-trouble stuff; not earth shaking events but
the kind of activities that make life worth living.

Messin' around is what a boy does when no adults are
intruding on his time. Saturday is the best day of the week for
a kid beause it's the one day when neither school nor church
attendance loom on the horizon to cast their forbidding shadows
of proper behavior, responsibility and work. On Saturday he's
free to let his imagination run wild and any activity is fair
pursuit unless it might involve learning anything, like wandering
into a museum. Saturday night, if he's lucky, he gets to stay up
late and watch good killin' and monster movies on TV.

The most important element of good messin' around is that
it can entertain a kid for the least expenditure of money, a
commodity that's always in short supply. Everything must be

accomplished within the generally tight constraints of his allowance—if he's getting one that week. The major expenditure for the week is movie money: seventy-five cents, enough to buy a seat in the kiddie section and a soda after the show. No matter how beautiful the day outside, some of the choicest messin' around can occur slumped down inside the dank, dark confines of a movie theater during a matinee.

GOOD MESSIN' AROUND JUNK

- crush stuff in your father's vice
- look for night crawlers after dark
- spitting off a bridge
- watching a lady in a store window jiggle in an exercise belt
- going to Metzger's Field to play baseball or touch football

- going for ice cream sodas at the drug store
- chewing gum
- looking for four-leaf clovers
- hanging out at the dump or the junkyard
- looking for arrowheads
- by yourself fun: gunfights in the mirror; playing catch with yourself; playing quarterback *and* receiver with yourself; reading comic books
- pretending stuff: playing Korea in a war helmet; pretending to be on a desert island and watching for cannibals; death-rayin' guys from Mars
- trading marbles
- watching workmen change tires on a bus, put "skin" on the skeleton of a house or wreck a building
- getting your feet half-soled with tar by walking through the newly paved road
- going to the supermarket to see if they're giving out free samples
- playing with your army men or setting up your model fort for an Indian raid
- sitting through any combination of the following fine films: *Rope Justice; Hot-Rod Cuties; Vampires of the Amazon* and *The Man Beast from Mars*
- watching men paint the shells of turtles in the variety store
- filling bottles with gutter water
- catching polliwogs at Miller's Pond
- playing tic-tac-toe in the dirt with a stick
- trying to sharpen a licorice stick in your pencil sharpener

GROWN-UP STUFF

BEAVER: Boy, little kids are sure stupid. I wonder how they ever get brains enough to grow up with.

GILBERT: You don't need any brains to grow up. It just happens to ya.

BEAVER: Well I guess so.

YOU KNOW YOU'RE GROWING UP WHEN . . .

- You start getting fussy about yourself, taking a bath without strict orders from your parents or a warning notification from the health department.

- You buy yourself sensible clothes.

- You no longer find it acceptable to have your little brother's smelly old socks thrown into your clean shirt drawer.

- You don't like goofin' off as much as you used to.

- You actually look forward to going to dancing school.

- You start *thinkin'* about stuff when you're not doing anything.

- You enjoy pushing little kids around.

- You start shaving.

- You pass the test for a driver's license.

- You know exactly how many years it will be before you're eligible to vote.

- You stop blaming the other guys for getting you in trouble.

WARD: You know, Wally, shaving is just one of the outward signs of being a man, it's more important to try to be a man inside first.

WALLY: Yeah sure Dad.

◆

JUNE: Beaver, why in the world would you and Larry want to smoke?

BEAVER: Well, gee Mom, everybody's always saying how bad it is, telling kids not to do it, and I figured if grown-ups said it was so *bad,* there must be something real *good* about it.

◆

BEAVER: Wally, the rules are a lot easier on grown-ups than they are for little boys.

WALLY: Well sure they are Beaver, the grown-ups are the ones that make the rules.

◆

WARD: I guess you want to be one of the big guys pretty bad, huh, Beav.

BEAVER: I sure do.

WARD: Well, I can understand that. I went through the same thing myself. But I'll tell you something Beaver, if you want to be a big guy, you've got to be a real honest-to-goodness big guy. You see if you *lie,* you end up being just a make-believe big guy, and I'm sure that's not what you want.

◆

BEAVER: Boy, as a guy gets older having fun sure gets complicated.

WARD: It sure does, son.

◆

BEAVER: You know. Wally, you're starting to talk just like a grown-up.

WALLY: Well, it's just that a guy begins to realize that being grown up is a big responsibility.

BEAVER: Maybe that's why Dad worries about us so much. He knows all the stuff that can go wrong on a guy.

WALLY: Yeah, I guess I never knew I had it so good when I was a kid.

◆

WARD: You see, Beaver, in life, things change. You take all those things you were planning to do like swinging in the tire and playing war. Those things couldn't possibly be as much fun as they used to be now that you're older.

BEAVER: Gee, Dad, you mean I'll never have any fun hollering into a drainpipe or looking for polliwogs anymore?

WARD: Well, I'm afraid it will never be as much fun as it once was, Beaver.

BEAVER: Gee, Dad, I always thought growing up was the neatest thing that could happen to a guy.

WARD: Oh, well, growing up is a pretty neat thing, if you really grow up and it's all right to look back on the good times you had. The only thing is, when you try to relive them somehow they're never quite as good the second time around.

BEAVER: I guess it's like parking your gum on the windowsill overnight and then trying to chew it some more the next morning.

◆

BEAVER: Thanks for helping me, Mom. It's almost as good as having Wally help me.

JUNE: Thank you Beaver.

BEAVER: And besides, you won't run off and play baseball on me.

JUNE: Don't forget, one of these days both of you will run off on me.

BEAVER: Oh, I wouldn't do that Mom.

JUNE: Well, you think you won't now, but I'm sure you will.

BEAVER: Well, if you say so I guess I will. But I sure won't like it.

◆

BEAVER: Wouldn't it be neat if a guy could stay a kid all his life?

WALLY: Aw, you'd never get away with that. But you know when you get real old you have what they call a second childhood.

BEAVER: No foolin'? Boy, at least I got something to look forward to.

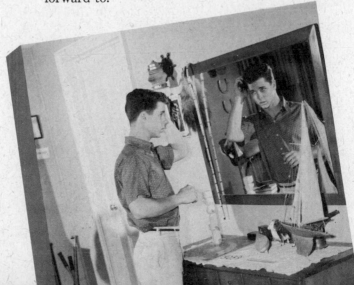

BEAVER: We can't just say we're going to be friends. We gotta have an agreement or something.

LARRY: Okay. (They shake hands solemnly)

BEAVER: I, Beaver Cleaver, swear to die for Larry Mondello and always stick up for him and never snitch on him and be his friend forever.

You might say that with the crew of friends Beaver and Wally have, who needs enemies? The Cleaver boys are loyal to their buddies—too loyal for their own good, since it's their friends who are usually the ones who are goading them into trouble. As a result, by being betrayed or let down by their pals, Beaver and Wally most frequently get a cold, hard initiation to the rotten ways of the world outside the warm bosom of the family.

Even when you're having a ball messin' around with the guys, you've got to be ever wary of "the business" rearing its ugly head. "The business" is peer pressure of the rankest variety; in fact, it often manifests itself in the brand of mean-spirited ribbing sometimes known as the "rank out." The milder form is mere teasing; the more severe varieties, when the whole pack of guys is ganging up on you, can really make you feel miserable. None of it is too lasting, though, and you still have the option of telling your pals to "dry up" or of clobberin' them if the going gets too rough.

◆

WALLY: Hey, you gonna make up with Larry?
BEAVER: Gee, Larry and I don't need to do that. Tomorrow I'll just say, "Hi, Larry," and he'll say, "Hi, Beaver," and then we'll go do somethin' and forget all about hatin' each other.

◆

WALLY: Boy, Beaver, wait'll the guys find out you were hanging around with a girl. They'll really give you the business.
BEAVER: But, gee, Wally, you hang around with girls and the guys don't give you the business.
WALLY: Well, that's beause I'm in high school. You can do a lot of stuff in high school without getting the business.

◆

BEAVER: I'd rather have the guys beat me up eight or nine times a day rather than call me a baby.

◆

BROTHERS

You know something, Wally, I'd rather do nothin'
with you than somethin' with anybody else.

—BEAVER

When a stranger on a bus asks Beaver if he and his friend
would like to sit together, Beaver replies, "Oh, he's not my
friend, mister; he's my brother," capturing in a nutshell the
special state of brotherhood.

As the Cleaver boys demonstrate over the years, a brother
can be the person you're closer to than anyone else in the
world, and at the same time, he can be the creep you hate
more than anyone on earth. He can be the person with whom
you share your most intimate thoughts or the person who
squeals those intimacies to your parents; he can be the person

with whom you band together against the burdens of growing up, or he can be your biggest stumbling block in life as you struggle to catch up to his footsteps.

No matter how bad things get, at least your brother isn't a girl, and he doesn't pinch. He can be your protector or your worst baiter, your hero or a source of family embarrassment. An older brother like Wally is not quite an adult, but he's wiser to the ways of the world, although he can still mess up almost as good as you can. A younger brother like Beaver can be a good little pal, someone you can order around, someone to cover for you, and he can also be an insufferable pest who's always hanging around.

He's the guy who helped you eat the heads off the Indians on your cowboys and Indians birthday cake and tore up his old underwear to make a tail for his new kite, which you flew all over town, the one you share a bed with on family vacations, the one who'll take you fishing for bullheads, the one you know how to annoy quicker than anyone, and the one you'll defend to the death. He's the big brother who will sock big guys for you, or he's the little brother who will get you into more trouble than you can easily get out of.

And he's even the person who, when he discovers girls, will start to go goofy and look at himself in the mirror and take baths when he doesn't have to, but even then, more often than not, he'll still come through for you, proving that, at least while you're growing up, blood is thicker than *goosh*.

◆

WALLY: Boy, Beaver, there's nothin' worse in the world than havin' a little dumb brother.

BEAVER: Yes there is—it's havin' a *big* dumb brother like you.

◆

JUNE: How can you sit there calmly with two brothers fighting upstairs?

WARD: All brothers fight . . . I remember my brother and I used to fight like cats and dogs. Once he bounced a rock right off the top of my head. I had to take five stitches in it.

JUNE: Your brother did that? I can hardly believe it.

WARD: Come to think of it, you're right. It was my sister.

◆

WALLY: Look, Mom, I've lived in the same room with Beaver for almost thirteen years now. You know, like in those prison pictures, the guy always knows more about his cell mate than the warden.

◆

BEAVER: Gee, Dad, what's the use of having a big brother if he can't sock guys for you?

◆

WALLY: Beaver? Oh, he was fine. He acted so good, I almost forgot he was my kid brother.

◆

BEAVER: Boy, I sure wish there was somebody in the family for me to yell at.

WALLY: That's your tough luck.

◆

BEAVER: Do you really like me, Wally?
WALLY: I guess so.
BEAVER: Do you like me a whole lot?
WALLY: Look, don't get sloppy on me. I might slug you one.

◆

It takes a certain kind of guy to catch polliwogs with . . . First you've got to find a guy who likes to lie on his stomach . . . You know something, Wally? The fun of catching polliwogs isn't really catching polliwogs. It's lying there with the other guy and talkin'. Like the time we were at the lake, and we were pretending the lake was an ocean, and the polliwogs were whales, and we was on a whaling ship. Remember, Wally? Well, we didn't catch one polliwog that day, but that was the best day I ever spent at the lake.

—BEAVER

TROUBLE

Wow, Beaver, a thing
like this makes Eddie
Haskell look like
Tinkerbelle.

— WALLY

As Beaver is so fond of noting, just about everything a kid
does gets him in trouble, so it comes as no surprise that his
days are trouble-filled.

Just a simple activity like going to the movies can get him in
all kinds of hot water: he can get hollered at for being cooped
up inside instead of being out in the fresh air, for going to see a
violent movie he's not supposed to, for practicing some of the
voodoo or hypnosis he learns from the film or he can get
caught trying to sneak his friend in the side door. And, of
course, he can get in trouble trying to raise the money to *go* to
the movies, since—like adults—most of his troubles have to do
with money and the lack of it.

Beaver's anxiety concerning punishment ranges from merely
being scared of getting yelled at, to fear of getting "clobbered,"
to "this is the worst mess I've ever gotten into," to "this is the
worst mess I will ever get into in my whole life," to "I wish I
was dead."

Naturally, the Cleaver boys are too well-bred—and too
chicken—to get into any severe trouble and thus they never

receive any severe punishment. As Ward metes out the sentences, he frequently makes the offenders suffer through an anxious period of anticipatory soul-searching in the den or in their bedroom. He is a firm but fair judge. For instance, for making an unauthorized long-distance phone call Beaver and his friends are required to put in an hour of yard work for a week after school. Other misdemeanors cause the loss of television and movie privileges. Even at his angriest, Ward is far more benevolent than the parents of the boys' friends, some of whom are "hittin' fathers" and almost all of whom throw their children out of the house when they get on their nerves.

I SHOULDA KNOWN BETTER
(Famous last words)

LARRY: How could you get in trouble drilling a little old hole?

◆

LARRY: You know something; you shouldn't have come over here in your good suit.

◆

LARRY: If there's no one here to catch us, then it's all right to do it.

◆

WARD: Well, there's a first time for everything. Maybe it's time for Beaver to do his first baby-sitting.

◆

MRS. WILSON: Oh, from what Ward has told Herb about your two boys, I figured Pudding would be as safe with them as she would be with J. Edgar Hoover.

◆

BEAVER: I am not chicken!

◆

BEAVER: Wally, I don't think this is gonna work.

◆

BEAVER: I am not *a'scared*!

◆

LARRY: What's the matter? Don't you like to do stuff you're not supposed to?

◆

WALLY: Boy, Beaver, you're really asking for it.

◆

BEAVER: I never thunk this would happen.

◆

EXCUSES, APOLOGIES AND TRYING TO BEAT THE RAP

BEAVER: Well, Dad, first of all I want to start off by telling you, you got a rat for a son.

◆

BEAVER: I think I fell down at recess today.
JUNE: Beaver, today is Saturday.

◆

BEAVER: Please don't cry, Mom. I'll do anything you want. I'll even kill myself if you don't cry.

◆

BEAVER: You gotta stay.
RICHARD: How come?
BEAVER: Because when I have a guest, I don't get punished so bad.

◆

WALLY: You look kinda funny. You're not thinking of crying, are ya?
BEAVER: No, not unless we get caught. Then I think we're going to be in so much trouble I'd better.

◆

BEAVER: You can get to sleep if you want to, but I'm going to spend the rest of the night thinking up snappy answers for Dad.

◆

WALLY: Wow, Beaver, you really told some big ones this time.

◆

BEAVER: Sometimes when a grown-up is mad at you, you can get in trouble just by saying hello.

◆

EDDIE: Look at the expression on these faces. You kids should be sent up the river on these expressions alone.

◆

WARD: Beaver, do you really think that's a good excuse?
BEAVER: No, sir, but it's the only one I got.

◆

WARD: Does that sound like the right thing to do, Wally?
WALLY: It doesn't now, but it sure did on Saturday.

◆

BEAVER: Wally, are there any Indians in Mayfield?
WALLY: Why, do you want one of them to scalp you before Dad gets home?

◆

BEAVER: Mom, do you like me *real* good?
JUNE: Of course I do.
BEAVER: Would you still like me *real* good if I was *real* bad?

◆

WARD: Beaver, you know what Larry was doing was wrong.
          You could have stopped him.
BEAVER: Gee, Dad, I have enough trouble keeping myself
          good without keeping all the other kids good.

◆

BEAVER: But that'd be lyin'.
RICHARD: Maybe, but tonight, when we say our prayers, we
          could ask for forgiveness.
BEAVER: I don't think you're allowed to do that.

◆

WARD: Beaver, it was a brand-new bike. To let it be
          stolen was a stupid thing to do. What in the world
          did you think when you found it gone?
BEAVER: I wished I was dead.
JUNE: You wished you were dead?
BEAVER: I wished it for about fifteen minutes, but nothin'
          happened, so I came home.

◆

WALLY: What are you gonna do?
BEAVER: I don't know. I guess the best thing is to run away
          to Mexico for the rest of my life.
WALLY: Yeah, but you better go to school first—you don't
          want to get yourself in trouble.

◆

"WAIT FOR ME IN THE DEN"
("What Do You Think Dad's Gonna Do?")

WALLY: You want us to wait up in our room?

WARD: I think that would be an excellent idea.

◆

BEAVER: Hey, Wally, we've been sitting up here almost a half hour. How come Dad hasn't come up yet?

WALLY: Gee, Beav, we did something real bad, and when you do somethin' real bad, it takes longer for Dad to figure out what he's going to do to us.

BEAVER: Well, whatever he's going to do to us, I wish he'd hurry up and do it so we could go outside and play.

WALLY: Beaver, what are you talking about? When he gets through with us, we'll be lucky if we get out to play for a whole year.

BEAVER: You think they'll send us to reform school?
WALLY: They might send me there, but you're too young for reform school.
BEAVER: Maybe they have a kindergarten reform school.

◆

BEAVER: What do you think they'll do to us, Gilbert?
GILBERT: They can't hit you or anything. That's against the law until you're twenty-one.
BEAVER: Yeah, but I think they're allowed to shake us.

◆

WALLY: Mom and Dad are in the next room discussing it.
BEAVER: Uh, oh, when they don't discuss stuff in front of ya, that's bad.

◆

BEAVER: But gee, Dad's never been a hittin' father.
WALLY: Well, if he's ever going to start bein' one, this oughta do it.

◆

WARD: Well, we want to be fair about it. What do you think a fair punishment would be?
BEAVER: No stewed figs for dessert.
WARD: Well, Beaver, you know you don't like stewed figs.

◆

WARD: You know what happens to boys who tell lies?
BEAVER: They don't get to watch television for the rest of their lives?

''THEY'LL BE SORRY!''

BEAVER: I'm not goin'. I don't care what you do to me; I'm not goin'. I don't care if you kill me or give me away to some poor people; I'm not goin'.

◆

WALLY: Well, where you going to run away to?
BEAVER: I don't know. I might run away and join some pirates and come back with a wooden leg. Mom and Dad wouldn't even recognize me.
WALLY: Aw, cut it out, Beaver. They don't have pirates anymore.
BEAVER: Then I might run away . . . and be a tramp! All by myself and eat all my food out of tin cans. (Takes bag of marbles from underneath his pillow)
WALLY: What are you taking these for?
BEAVER: In case I meet up with some other tramps. We might play marbles.

◆

LARRY: I'm sneakin' away tonight and shanghaiin' myself on a boat, and when my mother and father find out, they're gonna cry.

◆

BEAVER: Miss Landers, if you put that picture on the bulletin board, I'm going to run away to where nobody knows me and never come back to Mayfield again for the rest of my whole life till I die.

◆

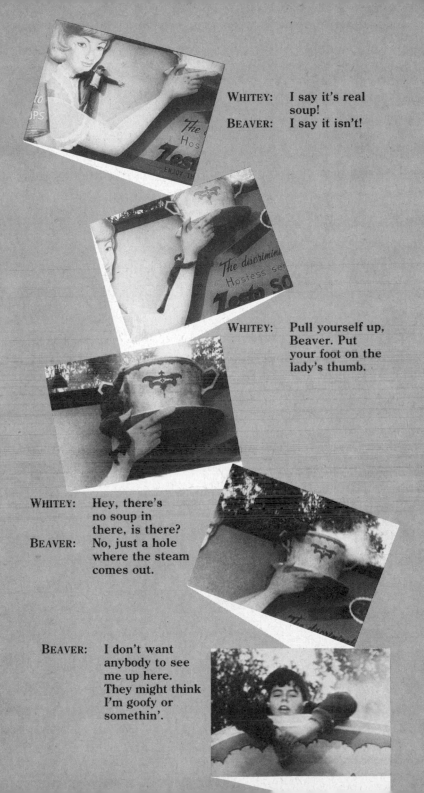

WHITEY: I say it's real soup!

BEAVER: I say it isn't!

WHITEY: Pull yourself up, Beaver. Put your foot on the lady's thumb.

WHITEY: Hey, there's no soup in there, is there?

BEAVER: No, just a hole where the steam comes out.

BEAVER: I don't want anybody to see me up here. They might think I'm goofy or somethin'.

LEARNING THE LESSON

LARRY: Gee, if you did everything your father tells you, you'd never have any fun.

BEAVER: But it's no fun havin' fun when you get in trouble.

◆

WARD: Beaver, was it worth all this?

BEAVER: Nothing's worth having your dad think you're a little sneak.

◆

WALLY: They said I should have told them yesterday.

BEAVER: Boy, it's not enough that you tell the truth anymore. It looks like you got to tell it at the right time, or else you still get clobbered.

◆

BEAVER: I think I really learned my lesson this time. I didn't even try to blame Gilbert for talking me into writing my book report from the movie.

WARD: Well, that is a big advance, to know enough to just blame yourself when you make a mistake.

◆

BEAVER: You know when I should have known things were going haywire? When Eddie Haskell was on *my* side.

◆

BEAVER: Yeah, that conscience stuff is really somethin' . . .
          Did your conscience ever bother you, Larry?
LARRY: Sure. Once, when I called my sister a big ugly
          toad, I felt funny right in my stomach.
BEAVER: Is that where your conscience is?
LARRY: That's where mine is . . .

◆

WALLY: Hey, Beav, you were crying. Did Dad hit you?
BEAVER: No.
WALLY: Did he yell at you?
BEAVER: No, he didn't yell at me.
WALLY: Well, golly, then what are you crying for?
BEAVER: Sometimes things get so messed up there's noth-
          ing else you can do.

◆

JUNE: Beaver, your father and I both want you to know if
          you ever have a problem, we want you to come
          and talk it over with us.
WARD: If anything's ever bothering you, don't keep it to
          yourself. You come to us with it, and be assured
          that we'll understand.
BEAVER: Gee, Dad, it sounds so neat I wish I was in trouble
          right now.

◆

And of course, the most important lesson of all is RESPON-
SIBILITY, and all that Beaver learns about it leads him to
conclude:

That responsibility stuff sure cuts down on a lot of fun.

GIRLS

Go see a girl? I'd rather smell a skunk!
—BEAVER

In Mayfield, any healthy, red-blooded little boy is supposed to hate girls and the Cleaver boys are no exception. Little girls may be full of sugar and spice and everything nice to some people but to the boys they're just full of trouble. Girls don't like dirt or blood or dead fish and you can't wrestle with them or do anything neat. Once in a while you'll find one who will make a muscle, but that's usually just a come-on to get you to take them to a dance or something.

And as it happens to most other little boys of Mayfield, as they grow older the girls seem less goony and more bewitchingly appealing. As they break through "the girl barrier" and progress from carrying school books home, to playing records at a girl's house, to soda dates, to movie marathons, to country club dances, they seek out wisdom from Doris Day and Gidget movies, from their peers and even, in desperation, from their parents, but usually they just grit their teeth and muddle through the sweet mysteries of dating on their own.

THE SEVEN WARNING SIGNS OF GOING FLAKY OVER A GIRL

1. You take a bath without getting official notice from your parents or the health department.

2. You put on a clean shirt two days in a row.

3. You attack your fingernails with a nail file instead of digging out the really crusty dirt with a paper clip.

4. You start splashing hair tonic, lilac water or Arabian Nights cologne on yourself—with a heavy hand.

5. You write the girl's name on your schoolbook covers and notebook margins or mention her name so often your parents start asking questions about her.

6. You begin to look forward to going to dancing school.

7. You memorize her class schedule so you can wait in the hall and watch her pass by.

BEAVER AND GIRLS

BEAVER: If I had my choice between a three-pound bass and a girl, I'd take the three-pound bass.

BEAVER: Boy, you know, Dad, Wally really gets a goofy look on his face when he talks to girls. His face gets all red and sweaty like he was catching a fever or something.

WARD: Well, you know, Beaver, it is a kind of a fever and

one that you'll be catching one of these days probably.

BEAVER: Well, I just hope when I get to Wally's age, there are shots for it or something.

◆

GILBERT: Boy, Beaver, she sure likes you.
BEAVER: She's really a kook.
GILBERT: She does act kind of goofy.
BEAVER: I wish she stayed in Bellport instead of moving down here. We got enough creepy girls running around here without importing any.

◆

WALLY: Julie's not a creepy girl or anything.
JUNE: We know she's a very nice girl, or you wouldn't be holding hands with her.

WALLY: I wasn't exactly holding hands with her . . . well, my hand was just hanging there, and she took it.

BEAVER: Boy, if a girl ever took my hand, I'd slug her with the other one.

◆

BEAVER: If I get married, I'm not gonna take my wife anywhere . . . not even to Disneyland.

JUNE: Beaver, why would you say a thing like that?

BEAVER: Well, just 'cause you're married, that doesn't mean you gotta like girls.

◆

BEAVER: Heck, Wally—girls are rats. They're even rats in Sunday school.

WALLY: What do you mean, they're rats in Sunday school?

BEAVER: Well, like this girl in the Bible. She took this neat guy and cut off his hair, and then she turned him over to some bad guys who dragged him away and stuck his eyes out, and they were mean to him, too.

WALLY: That was Samson and Delilah.

BEAVER: Sure, Wally. And if girls are even rats in the Bible, how do you expect 'em to be in person?

◆

WARD: Look, dear—he's going to be fine. He managed to survive measles, chicken pox, and poison ivy. I think we can see him safely through girls.

◆

BEAVER: Dad, cowboys and Indians—there's good guys and bad guys, isn't there? Is it the same with women?

WARD: Yeah, Beaver, I guess you could say there's good ones and bad ones.

◆

BEAVER: I've been thinking about it. Now that I'm never going to see Penny again after the party on Friday, I feel kind of funny. It's sort of like when my warts went away. I didn't think I was going to miss them, but I did.

◆

WALLY: I've seen her around. Look, Beaver, she's too much for you to handle.

BEAVER: What do you mean by that?

WALLY: You're still in the Pony League, she's batting in the World Series.

◆

WALLY: You don't give an expensive hunk of stuff to everybody you like.

BEAVER: Well, this is a different kind of liking—it's not Sunday school liking or Ten Commandments kind of liking—it's the kind of liking that—well, you know what I mean?

WALLY: Sure, but you're too young for that kind of liking.

BEAVER: If I'm too young for that kind of liking, how come I got that kind of liking?

WALLY: Search me. Maybe you've been seeing too many movies or something. But Beaver, feeling this way about a girl your age can get you nothing but trouble.

◆

BEAVER: There's something funny about this girl.

WARD: Funny?

BEAVER: Well, not funny, but it's kind of hard to explain. Sometimes when I'd look at her, I'd feel real good, and other times I'd feel like I was gonna get sick right to my stomach. But I guess you wouldn't understand.

WARD: I think I do, Beaver.

BEAVER: (A momentary pause) About girls, Dad—

WARD: Yes?

BEAVER: Does it ever get better?

WARD: I wish I could say so, son, but it gets an awful lot worse before it gets better.

◆

WARD: (Smelling after-shave) I think love has come to Beaver Cleaver.

◆

THE BIRDS AND THE BEES
(And the Peanuts and the Eggs)

BEAVER: (Looking at nest) I bet there's real birds in there; you know, inside the egg.

LINDA: Yeah, I wonder how they got in there.

BEAVER: I guess it's like peanuts. They're in there and that's that.

LINDA: Yes, but when peanuts get out they can't fly.

BEAVER: Yeah, but it's pretty neat the way it works, though.

WALLY AND GIRLS

JUNE: You think Wally's doing all this just for a girl?
WARD: Well, I don't think he's getting all dressed up just
         to impress the gym coach.

♦

EDDIE: Okay, Wally, I got my chariot over here. First
         we'll go by Mary Ellen Rogers's, then we'll go by
         Julie Foster's, then we'll hop over to Kathy
         Parker's. That way we give three different groups
         the benefit of our charm.

WALLY: Gee, Eddie, I still think we ought to phone first.

EDDIE: If it was just me, I'd phone first, but with you along, all doors are open. Even their fathers'll talk to us.

◆

BEAVER: Wally, I don't like Linda. Why should I feel bad because she's sitting in a tree with Larry?

WALLY: I don't know. I don't like Mary Ellen Rogers, either, but I feel kind of bad when I see her talking to some of the other guys in school. I guess that bad feeling is what makes people get married.

BEAVER: Search me, Wally.

◆

WALLY: I'm sorry about Herbie.

BEAVER: Oh, that's okay. I can always get another toad.

WALLY: Sure you can, Beav. I guess I can always get another girl.

◆

BEAVER: Hey, Wally, when you take Julie out, what are you going to talk to her about?

WALLY: I don't know. The same as we always talk about: school, sports, the other guys, I don't know.

EDDIE: And just what restaurant is going to be the scene of this fascinating conversation?

◆

EDDIE'S DATING TIPS

Well, come on, brother wolf, we don't want to keep Little Red Riding Hood and her friends waiting.

Look, Mr. Peepers, all you have to do is go up to her and say, "Hi, how about a date?"

It's better if we go by ourselves. That way you get to dance with all the other guys' girls, and then you don't get stuck with them and have to buy them stuff on the way home.

Watch the mush talk, lover boy. Her pop might be on the extension.

◆

Give her the bit about your old man being loaded with loot.

◆

I got my mother to call her mother, and her mother made her go out with me.

◆

EDDIE: What's the matter with you, jun-
           ior? You get drummed out of the
           Mouseketeers?
BEAVER: I got girl trouble.
EDDIE: Girl trouble? You? Now I've heard
           everything.
BEAVER: Cut it out, Eddie. It's not funny.
EDDIE: I'm sorry, I'm sorry. I wouldn't want
           to hurt your little feelings. Come on,
           loosen up. Why don't you tell Big
           Daddy your problems?
BEAVER: Well, I invited one girl to a dance,
           and now I've got a better offer.
EDDIE: Well, is that all? Simple. You just play
           a little game we operators call "Ditchin'
           the Dodo."
BEAVER: Ditchin' the Dodo?
EDDIE: Sure. You unload the crow and latch
           on to the dove.
BEAVER: I just couldn't go up and break my
           date with Peggy. And besides, my
           parents won't let me.
EDDIE: You don't break the date. You get
           her to break it.
BEAVER: But she wants to go with me.
EDDIE: So you do something that makes her
           not want to go with you. You do some-
           thing annoying. Make yourself obnox-
           ious. And believe me, Sam, with your
           personality it won't be too hard.

◆

EDDIE: Now you're operating; get in there
           and pitch, lover boy.

SCHOOL

I guess there's two things that'll always be in the
world—dirt and homework.

—WALLY CLEAVER

They say it's supposed to prepare you for life so maybe
that's why Beaver has such rotten times in school. School is
Beaver and Wally's week. It's where they spend the most time
and get into the most trouble. School is so central an institution
that it has an almost all-powerful hold over their lives. They
know there's no chance of having any fun on a *school night,* and
heck, there's special *school clothes* and even *school paper.*

Between the two of them, Beaver and Wally suffer through all of the sweaty school situations to which anyone who made it past kindergarten will be able to give a nod—or a cringe—of recognition: the dread of report cards; the anxiety of intelligence tests; being forced to look beyond the comics and sports pages of the newspaper for a "current events article"; struggling to understand Spanish when you have enough problems with English; trying hard not to get called upon to recite; the inescapable curse of homework; and worse, book reports and math quizzes; and getting graded in neatness, citizenship, comportment and even tenacity.

School is the world where squares carry briefcases and teachers carry the authority to send you to *the office*—to face the principal. Although Mrs. Rayburn, Grant Avenue Grammar School's fearless leader, is certainly no dragon lady, the threat of *the office* is sufficient to put all those future white-collar workers in a doomed state of mind when they grow up to head for their jobs. Then there's the mystery of what teachers actually do (and the shock of learning that some of them even watch television!), the fear of the janitor being allowed to twist your arm off if you horse around too much, or of the class laughing at you if you goof up and worst of all, getting a "dumb letter" sent home.

And school is even the place where they manage to learn a few things, scholastic and social, and where Beaver can hone his optimism to such a degree that he can say, with more brightness than he exhibited on the exam in question, "I got the highest of the ones who failed."

WHAT DID YOU LEARN IN SCHOOL TODAY?

BEAVER: Dad, in business, how often do you have to invert fractions?

WARD: Well, almost never, Beaver, but that's not the

question. Solving problems like these teaches you how to think and prepares you for your future life.

BEAVER: Gee, I didn't know school prepared you for anything. I thought it was just something you had to sit through.

♦

BEAVER: You know, Dad, reading's not so bad when you get used to it.

WARD: That's right, Beaver, and as you go through life, you'll find you can learn just about everything from reading: history, science, all the great thoughts anyone ever had.

BEAVER: Yeah, that's right, Dad. And you know something? If you couldn't read, you couldn't look up what was on television, either.

The Duck
by Theodore Cleaver
3rd grade

Once I wished I was a duck
Cause mostly ducks have lotsa luck
They swim around all day in a pool
And mostly never have to go to skool

Then I saw a duck
Hanging in a Butcher store
And I didn't wanna be
A duck no more.

BEAVER: I hope it's one of those neat colleges like I see in
            the movies where everyone is always singin' an'
            havin' fun all the time.

WARD: Beaver, let me tell you one of the hard facts of life.
            There just aren't any colleges like that in the whole
            world.

BEAVER: Yeah, I kinda figured that. I didn't really think any
            teacher would get up and sing lessons to his class,
            even if he was Bing Crosby.

◆

Wally, Beaver, Lumpy, Eddie (*singing in the car*)

> We're the fighting sons of Mayfield,
> Onward Mayfield High.
> We will always honor Mayfield,
> Mayfield do or die.

"TEACHERS ARE NOT THE NATURAL ENEMIES OF LITTLE BOYS"

BEAVER: If I don't bring an answer to Miss Canfield,
            she's going to send for Mom. Miss Canfield
            might even hit me!

WALLY: Only the coach can hit you.

◆

MISS CANFIELD: I'm afraid I made a mistake.
BEAVER: Do teachers make mistakes?
MISS CANFIELD: Oh, indeed they do. I think it must have
                   seemed to the other children as though I

was showing favoritism. We can't have that, can we, Beaver.

BEAVER: No, Miss Canfield. Does this mean I can't like you anymore?

MISS CANFIELD: Well, of course not.

BEAVER: I'm glad of that.

MISS CANFIELD: Well, Beaver, it couldn't be that important.

BEAVER: But it is. I asked my mom this morning when I could marry you.

MISS CANFIELD: Oh . . . well, Beaver, I'm quite a bit older than you are.

BEAVER: My mom says I'm grown up.

MISS CANFIELD: Well, of course you are, and before long, I'm sure you'll like some nice little girl your own age.

BEAVER: I don't think so, Miss Canfield. Little girls don't smell as nice as you do.

◆

MISS LANDERS: To deliberately miss a day of school means that you don't respect your school or the value of an education.

BEAVER: I respect the school. I never write on the walls or anything.

MISS LANDERS: Beaver, you might have learned something here today, no matter how small, that might have stood you in good stead the rest of your life. Why, it's just as though you took a day out of your life and threw it away. Do you understand that?

BEAVER: I think so. I guess if I'm going to throw any days away, I should do it with a Saturday.

MISS LANDERS: Well, Beaver, I don't think it's wise to throw any days away, but especially school days. There's so much to learn, Theodore, and so little time to learn it.

BEAVER: Well, I'm sorry, Miss Landers . . . and to make up for what I didn't learn today, I'll learn twice as much tomorrow as I'm supposed to.

◆

DING DONG SCHOOL— TROUBLE IN THE CLASSROOM

LUMPY: *F* Mr. Foster?

MR. FOSTER: Yes Rutherford, that's the lowest grade they allow me to give.

◆

WARD: Why don't you boys ever want to tell me anything? I'm really interested in what goes on at school.

WALLY: Nothing ever goes on at school, Dad.

WARD: Oh, now, Wally, I can hardly believe that.

WALLY: You go in the morning, and if you've done your homework, it's all right. If you haven't, they holler at ya. That's all there is to school.

◆

WALLY: Look, I been going to school all my life. You can't get in trouble by keeping your mouth shut.

◆

BEAVER: I didn't *write* it dumb—it came *out* dumb.

EDDIE: Hey, on problem number five in math, what did you get for an answer?
WALLY: What did you get?
EDDIE: I got three or four good answers.
WALLY: Let's see, mine came out to 61.873.
EDDIE: Very good.
WALLY: Is that what you got?
EDDIE: I got it now.
WALLY: Come on, Eddie. What are you trying to pull? Besides, the teacher is going to want to see how you arrived at the answer.

EDDIE: No, he won't. I got a gimmick. The solution
         I write out real crummy; the answer I write
         out real neat. By the time old man Brownley
         tries to figure out the solution, he's so shook
         he's happy to settle for the answer.

◆

Dear Miss Canfield,

    I have received your note dated two days

ago, the one sent home with Theodore. I

have whipped him, his father has whipped

him. He is sorry, we are very sorry.

                        Your friend,

                        Mrs. Ward Cleaver
                        (the Beavers mother)
                        Theodore's

Dear Miss Landers;

  We are all shocked by what Beaver said.

Especially my wife, who is a lady. I have

washed his mouth out with soap and beat him up

three times. I hope, because I have done this

so good, I won't have to come down to school . .

                   Yours truly,
                   Ward Cleaver, Theodore's father.

EDDIE:　Heck, I never thought any guy could get a ninety-two without cheatin'.

◆

BEAVER:　Hey, Richard, look at all the books.
RICHARD:　What do you want to look at books for?
BEAVER:　Our teacher, Mr. Blair, says that books are our friends and they speak to us.
RICHARD:　Tell me one book that ever said "hello" to you.
BEAVER:　It's just a teacher expression, like "Let's put on our thinking caps." If you wore a hat in the classroom, he'd send you right to the principal.

◆

BEAVER:　The *principal* sent for Dad? Oh, boy! Wally must have done it this time.
JUNE:　What do you mean?
BEAVER:　Well, when you're a little bad, you get sent down to the principal. And if you do somethin' badder, he gives you a note for your father, but when they ask you to bring your father into school, you know you've had it. (Happy thought) Hey, maybe Wally will even be expelled!

◆

HARRY:　I don't like takin' a test from a principal. What happens if you flunk it tomorrow?
PENNY:　They send you to dumb school, that's what they do. They got a whole big building full of dumb kids. They give you chocolate milk at recess and don't let you go to college.

◆

WHITEY: I didn't get my math homework dirty. My dog walked on it while I was doin' it.

◆

WALLY: Yeah, Dad. I did a thousand-word composition for Mr. Hanes, and he gave it back to me 'cause it was short.

WARD: Oh, so, you're writing it over, huh?

WALLY: No, I'm jamming in eighty more words.

◆

WARD: When did Miss Landers first ask you to do this?

BEAVER: Ummm . . . just about three weeks ago.

WARD: Three *weeks* ago? Then why are you coming to me about it *tonight*?

BEAVER: 'Cause it's due tomorrow.

◆

JUDY: Miss Landers, while we were pledging allegiance to the flag, Beaver was looking out the window. And I don't think that's very patriotic.

MISS LANDERS: Beaver, you're supposed to look at the flag; you know that.

BEAVER: I was looking at the flag outside on the pole.

MISS LANDERS: Well, from now on, we'll all look at the flag inside. Now, as I started to say—what is it, Larry?

LARRY: If we're pledging allegiance outside, do we have to look at the flag inside?

MISS LANDERS: We'll have a discussion on that some other time.

◆

BEAVER: You know somethin', Mom—our lima bean died yesterday.

JUNE: Your lima bean died?

BEAVER: Yeah, our class was growin' it on a piece of blotter in the windowsill. Some of the guys say it died the day before, but I think it died yesterday. We still got our potato, though. It growed a new wart on Monday.

◆

WARD: Well, Beaver, one of these days you'll be in the eighth grade.

BEAVER: Yeah, I guess so, Dad, but I sure will be surprised when I get there.

◆

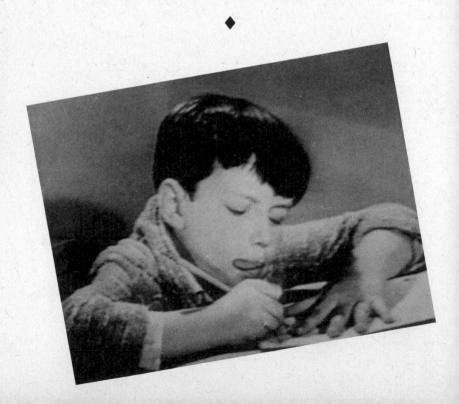

EDDIE HASKELL'S EASY COLLEGE PREP COURSE

EDDIE: Hello, Mrs. Cleaver. Wally and I were just discussing some schoolwork. Wally, you know I really think we should buckle down this year. You know we have college staring us right in the face.

♦

EDDIE: Hold it, Alvin, hold it. I can see you're getting the wrong picture. You don't measure a college by the courses they can give you. It's by the fraternities. Look, pay attention close. You guys can graduate with your Ph.D.s, your B.A.s, whatever, but just let me get next to a fraternity brother whose old man is the president of some oil company, and I got it made.

WALLY: Cut it out, Eddie. It doesn't matter who you get next to. You still have to have an education.

BARRY: That's right; the whole business of who you know instead of what you know is out the window.

EDDIE: Aw, hold it. I can see you guys are going to need some briefing. Look, you're up in the frat house filling up those bags of water to throw out the window. If the guy you're filling up those bags with is a senator's son, he can do you a lot more good than old Professor Glockenspiel in the science lab.

PROPER DRESS

It's almost as great a challenge for Beaver to beat having to change his socks as it is having to take a bath. His socks are subjected to cruel punishment. They can hold his money, his marbles, or the excess water from splashing in a puddle, but once he's broken in a pair, he's reluctant to give them over to his mother. When they get holes, he'll switch feet to get the gaping areas away from key toes.

Other clothes fall into three general categories: play clothes, school clothes, and good clothes. Cuffed jeans are the best for messin' around; the Sunday suit the worst. But in a pinch, any pocket of any shirt or pants or jacket will do to carry fish bait.

WARD: I can never figure it out. The way Beaver looks after he gets dressed, it shouldn't take him more than fifteen seconds.

♦

BEAVER: Bye, Mom, and I'll go easy on my socks today.

♦

BEAVER: How come they make kids' suits so stiff looking?
WALLY: I guess it's to scare you so while you're in them, you won't do something bad.

♦

BEAVER: There's something neat about a sweater with a hole. It makes you look like a tough guy.

♦

BEAVER: Well, if it's not church, it must be girls—those are the only two things heard of that makes a guy shine shoes.

GOOD GROOMING

EDDIE: What's with the nail-filing jazz? Who are you, Cesar Romero?

JUNE: Where's the Beaver?
WALLY: He's upstairs. He's changing his underwear.
JUNE: After he was dressed?
WALLY: He had it on backwards. He said he couldn't walk good.

Soap and water and little boys are far from the eternal triangle, and the Cleaver boys are no exception. They will go to extraordinary lengths not to bathe, including running bath water, dunking in some towels to get them wet, and throwing in some of Beaver's turtle dirt as they unplug the drain so they'll leave a convincing ring.

As Wally gets older and starts paying attention to his personal hygiene and the proper application of hair tonic and "smellin' stuff," he begins to look on Beaver as a little slob whose dirty, soggy socks can only be dug out from their under-the-mattress hiding place with a stick, and it's up to Beaver to carry on the tradition of grubbiness on his own.

WALLY: Beaver, how come you put your shirt on *before* you wash?

BEAVER: I put it on first so I won't wash a lot of me that doesn't show.

◆

WALLY: Boy, Beaver, you better wise up and stop smelling like a kid.

BEAVER: What for? All the kids in grammar school smell like kids.

◆

WALLY: What if Beaver got hit by a truck or somethin', and they took him to the hospital smellin' like that? He'd embarrass the whole family.

◆

EDDIE: Hey, your hair's wet. Don't tell me you took a shower.

WALLY: What's wrong with that?

EDDIE: Who do you think you are—Rock Hudson?

EDDIE: What are you made up for?
WALLY: Well, what do you mean, Eddie?
EDDIE: Well, look at you—you look like Tony Curtis. (Sniffs) You smell like a floorwalker.

♦

EDDIE: (Smelling lilac water on Wally) Man! You got a license to use this stuff?

♦

WALLY: In high school, they make us take a shower after school every day.
BEAVER: Is there any way you can get out of it?
WALLY: Well, it's not so bad once you get used to it, and anyway, the coach says a cold shower closes up your pores.
BEAVER: Oh, I guess we don't have any pores in grammar school.

A TRIBUTE TO DIRT

LARRY: Beaver, how come dirt falls apart when you pull it out of the ground?
BEAVER: I don't know. When you put it on water, it turns to mud.
LARRY: Yeah, and when you have it in your ears, you get hollered at for it.
BEAVER: Funny stuff, all right, but I guess dirt is what holds the world together.

FOOD

Her boys may eat to live, but June Cleaver lives, at least in part, to see that her boys eat a well-balanced diet. No matter what family crisis is brewing, there is a hot breakfast and dinner ready for her men, and on the weekend there had better be a good reason for one of the boys to miss the family lunch, as well. Even washing and drying the dishes becomes a shared experience on many nights.

Breakfast is usually a hearty one of juice, milk, eggs, bacon, and toast; lunches are either packed in a lunch box for Beaver and paper bag for Wally or on the weekends can be any variety of sandwiches—tuna, chopped egg, liverwurst, or baloney.

Dinner is at six P.M. sharp, and it is a multicourse affair, served in the dining room, from which the boys have to ask formal permission to be excused at the meal's end. On a given night, the fare might include soup or tomato juice, pork chops or pot roast and potato pancakes or "loaf of meat," accompanied by a selection of vegetables, and a stack of white bread. On a special night, steak and mushrooms, lima beans, corn on the cob, Waldorf salad, and Boston cream pie. The latter is homemade, of course, as are most of June's desserts, for many an afternoon she can be found whipping up a coconut cake or a batch of cookies. Those cookies are put to good use by the boys during what almost amounts to a Cleaver ritual: the after-school snack. June's kitchen has a cookie drawer *and* a cookie jar, and there's always milk in goblet-size glasses and a basket of fruit to help wash them down. As long as the boys don't eat too much and spoil their dinner.

JUNE: Eddie, would you care to stay for dinner? We're having roast beef.

EDDIE: No, thank you, Mrs. Cleaver. I really must be getting home. We're having squab this evening.

◆

WALLY: (At dinner table) I'm going over to Julie Foster's house for dinner.

WARD: Wally, how could you possibly eat another dinner over there?

WALLY: It's okay, Dad. It's not for another hour yet, and anyway, when you're eating over at a girl's house, you don't want to look like a hog in front of her parents. Hey, Beaver, would you pass the potatoes, please?

◆

Sometimes the family dines out, either for "a dress-up dinner or just an eatin' dinner." At a restaurant or at home, mealtime manners are not the Cleaver boys' strong suit:

WARD: Beaver, would you please chew with your mouth closed?

BEAVER: I can't, Dad. When I close my mouth, there's no room to move my teeth.

WARD: Well . . . do the best you can.

◆

WARD: Beaver, I said fill the water glasses, not the tray.
BEAVER: Water's sort of hard to pour. It's kinda loose.

◆

JUNE: Beaver, breakfast is not a race.
WALLY: Hey, Dad, instead of sendin' him to camp this
        summer, you shoulda spent the money givin' him
        eatin' lessons.
WARD: Thank you, Wally. But I don't think you should give
        advice on etiquette with your mouth full.

◆

Despite June's sensible good taste in food that tastes good,
her boys and their friends are no different from anyone else.
What they really love is junk food, anything from eighteen-cent
Doggie-Burgers at the Chuck Wagon to double-scoop ice cream
cones.

JUNE: I hope Wally gets here in time for dinner.
BEAVER: He will. We're having roast beef. If we were having
        liver or something, he'd come in late and say, "Us
        guys got hungry, so we stopped for a hamburger."

◆

BEAVER: Hey, Larry, how come food always tastes better
        eatin' it outside than inside?
LARRY: I guess 'cause there's nothin' around but dirt, so if
        you spill stuff, no one's gonna holler at you for
        gettin' dirt dirty.

◆

BEAVER: Hey, Wally, where'd you put the hot dogs?

WALLY: In my pocket. We can eat them on the bus.

WALLY: Eddie Haskell and I stopped by the bakery and got
some day-old eclairs to eat on the way home . . .
The whipped cream was a little sour, but after
three or four, you don't notice it.

◆

LUMPY: An apple's no hunk of cake.

◆

WORKING

JUNE: The first day on the job is always the hardest.

BEAVER: That's what you said about school, Mom, and then it got worse.

◆

Although their attitude is not quite as alarmist as Dobie Gillis's pal, Maynard G. Krebs, who cries, "Work!" in the most baleful way whenever the subject comes up in his presence, the Cleaver boys frequently have to be prodded to do their chores. Once they are old enough to earn money for their labors, they show a little more interest in working, especially as another sign to the world that they're big shots.

Among the jobs at which Wally and Beaver are gainfully, if briefly, employed are newspaper delivery, lawn mowing, soda jerking, selling Igloo ice cream bars, candy butchering, working in the Mayfield Dairy, cat sitting, baby-sitting, and sweeping and cleaning cages at a carnival.

BEAVER: You know, working isn't as much fun as I thought it would be. I wonder why older people do it so much?

WALLY: They have to. If they had fun like kids, people would say they were silly.

◆

LARRY: If you let me be partners on your typewriter, I'll let you be partners on my ant village.

BEAVER: An ant village isn't worth as much as a typewriter, especially when all your ants are dead.

LARRY: Yeah, but look at the chance I'm taking—how do I know your typewriter will even work?

BEAVER: Gus can maybe fix my typewriter, but nobody can fix your ants.

MAPLE DRIVE NEWS

EDITOR-IN-CHIEF   BEAVER CLEAVER
EDITOR-IN-STAFF   LAWRENCE MONDELLO
                      (Temporary sick)
                      WALLY CLEAGER
TYPEWRITING
****

DOG FIGHT

There was a dog fight at Vista Drive.
The dogs were Chief that lives at 8718
Lakeview Terrace and another dog who
we don't know his address. The dogs was
not hurt. If you see the other dog tell
him to go home even though you don't
know where he lives.

CORRECT TIME

If you want to know the correct
time call the phone company but
do not talk to the lady because
she is a record.

NOTICE

At 8509 Grant Avenue there is some
boys every day that is throwing dirt
in Linda Thompson and Shelly Thompson's hair. Mrs. Thompson would
like if the boys would throw dirt
in other kids hairs besides Linda's
and Shelly.

EDDIE HASKELL
ON THE JOB

EDDIE: Since they are going out into the jungle world of business, I thought I could pass on some of my invaluable experience along those lines.

WALLY: This I gotta hear . . .

EDDIE: I always know a better way . . . It's quite obvious, my good man, that the kids here don't understand human nature. Follow: When you ask grown-ups if you can do something, before you even get it out of your mouth, they're saying, "No." They gotta be mean to kids, or they lose their respect . . . When I was a kid, I had a very lucrative deal going in the parking lot at the supermarket.

BEAVER: The parking lot?

EDDIE: Yeah, I'd wait until a big, expensive-type car would drive in; then, while the lady was inside shopping, I'd dust the car off.

GILBERT: Without asking?

EDDIE: Sure. Then I'd stand next to the car with the dust rag in one hand and the other hand sticking out for the fifty cents.

BEAVER: And they'd give you the money?

EDDIE: Why not? I rendered a service, didn't I . . . Look, you two—hold out your hand and say, "Lady, we just finished mowing your lawn . . . With your hands stuck out and those two pitiful pusses, you can't miss.

◆

EDDIE: Look, what do you want to get a job for? We could spend the weekends horsin' around.

WALLY: I figured, if I had a job, I wouldn't have to ask my father for money every time I wanted some.

EDDIE: Oh, how square can you get? You know somethin'? *I might have to give you up.*

◆

EDDIE: I was on my way over to the tennis court, but at the last minute, I got sidetracked. I was taking a shortcut behind the florist, and old man Lewis threw out a whole bunch of old chrysanthemums . . . Well, sure I picked 'em up. I made four and a quarter peddling them in a parking lot behind a supermarket.

◆

EDDIE: Come on, Sam, time's a'wastin'.
WALLY: Look, Eddie, I can't go with you guys today. I've got work out in the yard.
EDDIE: Work in the yard? Aw, come off it! We got— Oh, good morning, Mr. and Mrs. Cleaver.
JUNE: Hello, Eddie.
WARD: Good morning, Eddie.
EDDIE: Well, if you've got work to do, Wallace, I don't want to interfere. I was reading an article in the paper the other day where a certain amount of responsibility around the home was good character training. Good-bye, Mr. and Mrs. Cleaver.
WARD: *Good*-bye, Eddie.
EDDIE: (Whispering) Can I talk to you outside, Wally?
WALLY: Okay, Eddie. What's up, huh?
EDDIE: *Come on, Moe, drop the hoe.* Lumpy's out in the car, and we're ready to roll.
WALLY: I told you, I can't. I got work to do.
EDDIE: Come on, Isabel, you gonna let your mother and father push you around? Why don't you read them the child labor law?
WALLY: Hey, Eddie, isn't it about the time of year you're supposed to shed your skin?

MONEY & ALLOWANCE

Hey, Dad, fifty whole cents! If I keep walking
dogs till I'm thirty, I bet you I'll be a millionaire.
—BEAVER

◆

When you're growing up, you may not have much of a grasp
of the world economic situation, but you generally know to the
last penny exactly how much money you own in the world. If
you're Beaver, you might be hiding your funds in your clean-
sock drawer to make sure they're not exposed to the light of
day too often. Your parents have an ongoing campaign to teach
you the *value* of money, which means you get an *allowance*,
which is never around when you need it the most, and you
have to save your birthday money for college, and you can't
touch your savings bonds.

When a couple of dollars seems as unattainable as a billion,
you dream a lot about making a big score, perhaps by sending
away for perfume to sell around the neighborhood or by catching frogs to sell, but most of the time you manage quite nicely
on the universal kid monetary system—swappin' junk. The
going rate for a frog, for instance, is two sticks of gum, five if
it's still wrigglin'.

WARD: I don't like the idea of Beaver handling a lot of money. A boy who's lost three pairs of socks on the way home from school hardly sounds like the banker of tomorrow.

◆

WARD: Well, Beaver, when you're handling money, it's awfully easy to get in trouble.
BEAVER: If you knew that, why'd you give me an allowance? So I'd get in trouble?
WARD: Of course not. I gave you an allowance so you could learn.
BEAVER: Gee, I wish you hadn't let me learn seventeen dollars' worth.

◆

WALLY: Hey, Dad, you think you can get that fixed?
WARD: I will this time, but I should take it out of your allowance.
WALLY: Well, if you took everything out of my allowance that you should take out of my allowance, I wouldn't have no allowance at all.
WARD: How true.

◆

BEAVER: Dad, if a guy tripped on our porch steps, could he sue you?
WARD: Well, under certain circumstances—did someone trip?
BEAVER: Not yet, but Gilbert says if you're insured, it wouldn't cost you anything, and then if he sued you, he could get that neat midget racer he's been wanting.

◆

WARD: Well, now wait a minute, fellows; I just can't give you fifty dollars.

WALLY: We'll pay you back, Dad. I'll cut the grass for the next five years.

BEAVER: And I'll pick up my room for the rest of my life.

◆

BEAVER: I could use my own money, the twenty-five dollars I got in the bank.

WALLY: I thought you were saving that to go to college.

BEAVER: Larry says he never heard of a college you could go to for twenty-five dollars.

◆

WARD: (On phone) Yes, Mrs. Brown, I know Theodore has been selling water to the boys, but I felt—

MRS. BROWN: Well, I for one think it's disgraceful! Why, the idea of a child taking advantage of his playmates! Why, the last time he was here, Beaver got Tooey's penknife away from him. It's none of my business, but I say things like this can lead to juvenile delinquency and . . . communism!

WARD: Well, I really don't feel in this case that democracy is in any immediate danger, but I will speak to the boy. And thank you for your *friendly* advice.

PETS

These here are Beaver's pigeons, which he named after his two teachers, which the cat ate, so he buried them.

—LARRY

◆

WALLY: Boy, Beaver, we got a mess of frogs.
BEAVER: Yeah. I was lookin' in the bucket, and I'm friends with some of them already.
WALLY: How can you be friends with a frog?
BEAVER: Gee, some of them just look at you, and you know they like you.
WALLY: Boy, Beaver—and you give me the business when I get mushy over a girl.

◆

It is altogether fitting that a boy named Beaver have a special place in his heart for animals. Here is a partial listing of the pets and strays that wandered into the Cleaver household—and more than a few times were smuggled in under his jacket—for brief stays under Beaver's care. They never stayed long, since his love for particular animals proved as fleeting as his attention span for most other things in life.

Captain Jack—The genuine Everglades mail-order alligator.

Captain Jack—The terrier puppy who replaced him.

Herbie—The toad.

Smiley and Hoppy—The frogs.

Henry, a.k.a. Henrietta—The pregnant white rabbit.

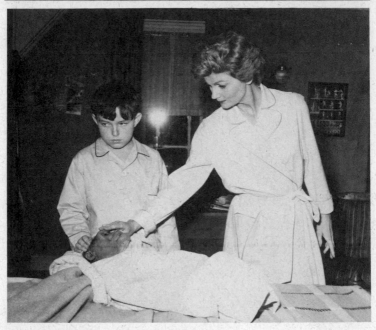

Nick—The carnival horse.

Peter Gunn—The black and white rat.

Sergeant Burke—The talking and singing parrot (a one-day rental).

Pepe the burro—Co-owned by Gilbert and Richard.

Archie—Gilbert's sheepdog, who kept coming around after he helped chase away Bootsie, the cat who kept coming around.

Miss Canfield and Mrs. Rayburn—The pigeons who suffered an untimely passing at the claws of a neighborhood cat.

Stanley—The monkey who caught pneumonia; the recipient of a get-well bouquet from Larry, who, upon presenting them, asked June one of life's most intriguing questions, "Would it be dumb to bring flowers to a monkey?"

Plus a succession of goldfish, hamsters, and even some worms that Beaver planted in the backyard in the hope of growing more worms.

SPORTS

EDDIE: Tennis shoes? Big deal! I guess you wore your old ones out playing hopscotch.

BEAVER: These are for basketball.

EDDIE: Basketball! Who are you going to play with, the Brownies? Some basketball player. You couldn't dribble down your chin.

◆

School sports can mean medals, girls flocking around, your name in the paper, your father in the stands telling everybody around him that you're his boy, and even your mother, who doesn't quite understand what the fuss on the field is all about, squealing for you to "come on!"

One of Beaver's greatest challenges when it comes to sports is living up to Wally's

natural athletic prowess. While Wally is captain of the varsity football team, the best 100-meter man on the swim team, and a hero in the track relays—a three-letter man at Mayfield High—Beaver brings to the sports arena the same kind of generally noncompetitive spirit of friendliness he applies to most of his life.

Beaver even gets a "D" in physical education in school because he can't tumble, and he clowns around on the playing field until the other kids wise him up, and he takes his playing more seriously. As with most other things in life, once he applies himself, he performs reasonably well at most sports. In fact, baseball becomes Beaver's favorite thing in the eighth grade, following a summer at the hot corner, third base, in the Mayfield Pony League. Not bad for a boy who started as the team water boy and the ball chaser and valuables holder for the older boys when they played on the vacant lots. Wally is a fine third baseman, so between them, the Cleaver boys have the left side of the field sewn up.

Football is another good sport for the boys. In his first freshman game, Wally intercepted a pass and scored a touchdown. He went on to play at quarterback and in the backfield. Beaver is usually playing end and manages a week as school hero for scoring a winning touchdown until he gets a swelled head, which then settles back down in time for him to be awarded the Most Inspirational Player Award at year's end.

Basketball and track prove to be Wally's sports to shine alone in. Especially basketball. Wally's game high is 32 points against Taft, but the game and living in the shadow of his brother's ability makes Beaver so nervous he's a virtual spastic at the foul line. Even at that, he's way ahead of Eddie Haskell, who positions himself as manager of most of Mayfield High's teams, the man the coach depends on, if you listen to Eddie tell it; that is, until he's suspended from the teams for hanging the coach in effigy in the locker room or spelling the team name wrong on the jerseys.

BEAVER: Well, I like to wade in big puddles, but I don't think they have a team for that.

◆

WALLY: Hey, Beav, after supper, if you want, I'll show you how to do a real racing start.

BEAVER: No, I can get started all right. I just can't keep going.

◆

JUNE: Wally, after your bath, give me that uniform, and I'll put it in the washing machine.

WALLY: Gee, Mom, it's just getting dirty enough so I look like a real ball player.

WARD: Of course. You can't clean up an old pro.

◆

WALLY: You know, you're making out like you're the only guy in the whole country that ever caught a touchdown pass before. There's thousands of them. The world's filled with guys who are doing a lot bigger things than catching footballs.

BEAVER: Yeah, well, I guess I'm not as big a hero as some of those astronaut guys.

PARENTING

BEAVER: Boy, when I get to be a father, I'm not gonna yell at my kids.

WALLY: Sure you will. The only fathers that don't yell at their kids are on television.

◆

There are days when it seems that Ward and June are locked in a Superman-like battle to instill truth, justice and the American Way in their boys. They are loving and intensely concerned parents, the kind who are the envy of their sons' friends. Ward is empathetic but firm, June is prim yet sympathetic, so they make a well-balanced and tireless parental team.

Ward's capacity for advice and outright lecturing is unmatched. He probably pays more visits to his sons' bedroom for heart-to-heart talks in one week than most fathers do in their children's entire lives. Sometimes Ward and June go overboard and pry into Beaver's diary or poke through the boys' garbage can for clues, or jump to unfair conclusions, but to their credit, they mend their ways. Nobody can say, "We're not prying Wally, we're just curious," and make it sound quite as palatable as Ward.

Thanks to Ward and June, Beaver and Wally are on the road to being pretty good parents themselves.

PARENTS WITH CHILDREN

JUNE: Ward, dear, do you think all parents have this much trouble?

WARD: Just parents with children.

◆

WALLY: That's what a father's for. He's gotta go to work 'n make the money 'n pay the rent 'n buy the food 'n raise the children 'n all that.

BEAVER: Yeah, that's tougher than being a worm.

◆

JUNE: What did your father say?

WALLY: He didn't get a chance to say it yet.

JUNE: Well, don't worry about it. Dinner will be ready in a minute. Maybe my lamb chops will help.

BEAVER: You know, Mom, when we're in a mess, you kinda make things seem not so messy.

JUNE: Well, isn't that sort of what mothers are for?

◆

WARD: Someday I'll come home and find out nothing's gone wrong and the two boys have been perfect, and then I'll discover I'm in the wrong house.

◆

WARD: I think you'd better learn to handle responsibility before you take it.

WALLY: Sure, Dad, but if you don't give a kid responsibility, how can he learn to handle it?

WARD: Well, Wally, I guess that's just one of the things that gives parents gray hair.

◆

''WE'VE EITHER RAISED HIM RIGHT OR WE HAVEN'T''

BEAVER: Boy, Dad, I betcha you're about the smartest guy in the whole world.

WARD: It's nice to hear you say that, Beaver, but I'm far from being the smartest guy in the whole world. But I do think I've had enough experience to give you boys a little advice now and again.

◆

WARD: Why, when you got in trouble, didn't you come to me?

BEAVER: I guess I was a'scared to, Dad.

WARD: What were you scared of? What did you think I would do if you told me?

WALLY: That's the trouble, Dad; we never can tell.

WARD: Wait a minute, boys; let's get something straight. I

don't care what kind of trouble you may get into in life, you don't ever need to be afraid to come to your parents and tell them.

WARD: Well, I thought they would have fun doing things I did when I was their age. I guess you can't wrap your childhood up in a package and give it to your kids.

◆

JUNE: Maybe the Beaver will outgrow being sloppy.
WARD: That's not the modern approach. You can't wait for children to outgrow things. No, you have to send them to orthodontists, psychologists—they've even got experts to teach kids how to play. No self-respecting parent would dream of relying on nature anymore.

◆

WARD: Sometimes I wish I'd stayed single and raised silver foxes.

◆

WARD: I should have concentrated on helping you be yourself instead of someone you couldn't possibly be . . . I really gave you a bum steer.

WALLY: It's okay, Dad.

BEAVER: How come you gave him a bad steer, Dad?

WARD: Well, I guess things like that are just part of being a father. If your boy makes the football team, you have visions of him scoring touchdowns all over the place . . . If he gets a B in mathematics, you see him as an atomic scientist, landing on the moon . . . or you even picture him marrying the banker's daughter.

BEAVER: Gee, I thought only kids got goofy ideas like that.

WARD: No, parents get their share. As you grow older, you realize that a lot of the ambitions and dreams you had are never going to come true, so you try to dream through your children.

WALLY: You mean Mr. Rutherford dreams through Lumpy?

WARD: (Stopping at door) Of course he does. I guess there's not a father around who doesn't want things to be just a little bit better for his children than they were for him . . . Okay, guys?

WALLY: Okay, Dad. (Ward exits)

BEAVER: You know somethin', Wally—when I get big, to make Dad happy, I just might go to the moon and marry the banker's daughter.

WALLY: Ah, cut it out.

◆

JUNE: When they get to be Wally's age, they're not like checkers.

WARD: Yeah, you have to stop making the moves for them. You know, that's something a lot of mothers never learn.

◆

JUNE: You know it's too bad *we* can't pick out a friend for Wally, some nice boy with all the right qualities who always behaves himself.

WARD: The only trouble is, if we did find a boy like that, he probably wouldn't have anything to do with Wally.

◆

WALLY: Is Dad going to go up and belt him?

JUNE: No, Wally, I guess your father's going to go up and teach him a lesson.

WALLY: I think it would be better if he belted him.

◆

WARD: Now when did I ever call you stupid?

BEAVER: Last night . . . when you found the garage still messed up.

WALLY: You really hollered at us, Dad.

WARD: Well, you disobeyed me. What else could I have done?

BEAVER: You coulda hit us.

WARD: (Shocked) Hit you? I wouldn't do that.

WALLY: Yeah, but if a guy gets hit, it goes away. But if a guy's father calls him stupid or somethin', it makes him feel bad for a long time.

BEAVER: Yeah, Dad—once when I was in the second grade, you called me a little boob, and I still feel bad from that.

JUNE: Boys, we don't really mean things like that. Sometimes they slip out on the spur of the moment.

WARD: I'm sorry, fellows. I guess the wrong word can hurt more than a slap. I really should watch what I say when I get angry. But you didn't have to sneak the tire off. You could have waited till I came home and said, "Dad, we had a little bad luck today, and the tire's flat." I would have probably said, "Oh, that's okay, fellows—we'll get it fixed." *(Then later)*

WARD: Sometimes when I talk to the fellows, I don't know who learns more—the boys or us.

JUNE: This time I think *we* did.

WARD: Sometimes I wish I were more like my father. Well, he never got himself trapped trying to be a good guy.

◆

WARD: Look, dear, just because Beaver got himself out on a limb, I can't run out and get him a parrot.

◆

JUNE: I don't like the boys fighting like this . . . maybe it's our fault.

WARD: How could it be our fault?

JUNE: The books always say it is.

WARD: No book's going to make *me* feel guilty.

◆

JUNE: Ward, why did we go ahead and make a promise like that?

WARD: It was very simple. It was the easiest thing to do at the time.

◆

WARD: Beaver breaking windows? That really floors me!

◆

WARD: June, we can't protect Wally forever. I just thought I'd sound him out about the club and then let him make up his own mind. It boils down to this—we've either raised him right, or we haven't. Let's just wait and see what kind of a decision he makes.

◆

WALLY: You know, Dad, sometimes it must be tough having kids.

WARD: You know, Wally, that's the nicest thing you've said to me in a long time.

◆

BEAVER: Thanks an awful lot, Dad . . . It sure is good when your father's a friend.

BEAVER: Boy, my kids are sure gonna think they have a real nut for a father.

◆

''WHAT DID DAD SAY?''

WARD: Beaver you just go on to school today and do the best you can no matter what part you have to sing in the chorus.

◆

WARD: Sometimes when a person's made a mistake or done something wrong, that's the time when they need understanding the most.

◆

WARD: In life, when you don't succeed the first time, you try something, you don't just throw up your hands and say it can't be done. Salesmanship is hard work and sticking to it.

◆

WARD: It might have been their idea, Beaver, but you were the one who carried it out. As you get older, you're going to hear a lot of wild talk from boys. If you're the one who's going to believe it and carry it out, you're the one who gets in trouble—not the boys who do all the big talking . . . Remember one thing: Wrong is wrong even if everyone else says it's right—and right is right even if everyone else says it's wrong.

◆

WARD: Well, very often a boy Wally's age doesn't think he's all right. He's so worried about his appearance, he forgets that people don't judge you by the way you look but by the way you act . . . Why, some of the homeliest people in the world have done the greatest things.

◆

WALLY: What did Dad say?
BEAVER: He said I should hide my feelings and take it like a man.
WALLY: He said the same thing when I had that stiff neck.
BEAVER: Yeah, he uses that for a lot of stuff.

◆

WARD: You can run away and hide from people, but you can't run away from yourself. Why, I'll bet you, when he goes to bed at night, he can't even sleep because of what he did. Chances are he'll be a miserable boy for a long time.

◆

WARD: If you live your life in a dream, you'll wake up someday and realize you never had anything real . . . You think that over, Beav.

◆

WARD: Things like that never work. It's always wrong to lie; and Beaver, you just build up more trouble for yourself by not facing the truth.
BEAVER: Gee, I wouldn't mind facin' the truth if so much hollerin' didn't go with it.

◆

WARD: When you tell one lie, you have to tell another one to cover it up. And that one leads to another and another. Pretty soon you have so many lies to remember, you just can't keep track of them.

BEAVER: Yeah. You know—I don't think I'm smart enough to do all that, anyway.

WARD: That's fine, Beaver. And don't ever think you're smart enough, because nobody is.

◆

WARD: I'm not yelling at you, Beaver. We'd all like to have the most glamorous and exciting parents in the world, but we just have to take things the way God gave them to us.

◆

WARD: Now, Beaver, you just keep your sense of humor and everything will be all right.

VOCABULARY WORDS

anthropoid   high school version of "you little ape"

beaut'   a shiner

because, the   the excuse, the raison d'être

belt   verb, to punch out

blast off   the act of starting a car

blubbering   crying

bomb   a *great* car

business, the   peer pressure, especially teasing, "goofing"

catchy   infectious

chop   to yell at, as in "the coach really chopped me."

clobber   see "belt"

conk out   to croak

constellation prize   given to runners-up in the best contests

crazy   cool or out of one's mind

croak	to die
crook	verb, to steal
ditched me	let me down, left me hanging
eats	food
fee-an-shay	rat engaged to marry your favorite teacher
flaky	goofy
flatted	describing a tire that has been deprived of its air
flip	go out of one's mind, as in "You're gonna flip!"
froggy	the way one smells after playing with toads
gasser	wild
girly	smelling of perfume
golly!	exclamation often interchangeable with "gee whiz!"
goof	verb, to foul up; noun, a young fool, as in "You little goof."
goony	creepy, especially apt to describe girls
goop	that substance used to slick on one's hair
goosh	condition of advanced meltdown, especially ice cream
go ape	to flip, go crazy
go, man, go	encouraging words
guys, the	the gang, the crew, the group, one's pals
haywire	out of control
heck	all-purpose substitute curse word, as in "You'll get heck for fighting."
holy smokes!	exclamation uttered in a pretty bad situation
hunk	a portion, as in "a hunk of milk"
Indian	one who goes back on one's word, as in "Indian giver"

junk	collective noun used to describe just about everything, usually prefaced by "and"
kooky	crazy, as in, weird
losted	opposite of "founded"
mushy stuff	kissing scenes; related verb form, "mushing it up."
neat	real good; even better is "*real* neat"
oar out	to paddle one's own canoe
omelet	secret power charm of hypnotists; can be a washer on a string; also known as an "amulet"
operator	a slick manipulator
owls	kind of girls you wouldn't give a hoot about
slobberin' movies	films containing an excess of "mushy stuff"
slob up	to make dirty
smelly water	cologne or particularly potent after-shave lotion
sore	adjective, angry
'spelled	getting kicked out of school; can occur for not spellin' good
sponge off	take advantage of another, usually monetarily
squirrelly	nuts
squooshed	condition of liquid messiness
suspendered	less severe form of getting 'spelled
tooken	was gypped
'tricity	what makes the lights go on
weepies, the	crying jag
wheels	any old car
willies, the	creepy feeling a girl can give one
yakkin' up a breeze	making up stories

HOW TO TALK MEAN AND DIRTY LIKE THE BEAVER

I guess there aren't any nice bad words.

—THE BEAVER

DIRTY WORDS

chicken	coward
clod	clumsy oaf
creep	miserable creature
crumb	insignificant little creep
dope	stupid individual
globby guy	advanced form of creep
goof	little fool
knucklehead	stubborn dope
kook	nut case
rat	creep, extreme form: "rat, rat, rat!"
runt	short and unappealing fellow, usually preceded by "little"
sap	dumb guy
smelly	advanced case of stinking badly
sneak	fairly formal term for dishonest individual
spook	guy who's creepy enough to haunt houses
squealer	rat who informs on another
sweetheart	suspected girlfriend
wise guy	smart-mouthed clown

FIGHTIN' WORDS

Violet Rutherford, you wanna get *'gressive* with me?

Violet Rutherford drinks gutter water.

I oughta belt you one!

You're a grubby little infant!

I could whip you with one hand tied behind my back!

Linda Dennison, you're a smelly old ape!

You dumb, stupid, creepy sap!

She's ugly and has a face like a cuckoo clock.

You're a dirty, smelly rotten apple!

You creepy-faced zombie!

You dirty little spook!

Bein' a creepy girl is the creepiest kind of creep you can be!

I'd rather kiss a dead lizard than kiss you again!

I burned your picture and spit on the ashes!

You're not only chicken; you're yellow as a skunk!

I hope that crummy Beaver falls in a manhole and a big alligator in the sewer eats him up!

Hey, Judy, is that your own face or are you breakin' it in for a witch?

◆

BEAVER: That Larry's no good. He's a big, dumb, stupid dope with no brains. I'm gonna hate him forever, even when he's a big, dumb, stupid old man.

◆

BEAVER: Boy, if I ever see that Larry again, I'm going to tie him to a tree. Then I'll get an Indian hatchet and scalp all his hair off, and then I'll shoot arrows into his great big stomach.

WALLY: Cut it out, Beaver. People don't do stuff like that anymore.

BEAVER: Then I'll freeze him in a block of ice and push him over Niagara Falls.

WALLY: Wouldn't it be easier just to punch him in the nose?

BEAVER: You know Dad says we're not allowed to fight.

◆

PENNY: You're a stupid little rat.

BEAVER: Yeah, you're a funny-lookin' goon.

PENNY: Yeah, you're a goony hunk of nothing.

BEAVER: Oh, I wish you were a guy so I could sock ya!

PENNY: If I was a guy you'd be a'scared to sock me!

WHITEY: Go ahead and sock her, Beav!

PENNY: I dare ya! I *double* dare ya!

◆

BEAVER: I don't like you, but I'd feel kind of bad if you died.

◆

CAPTAIN JACK

After sending in $2.50 through an ad in the back of their *Robot Men of Mars* comic for a "Genuine Florida Alligator," the boys are surprised when their "Everglade Monster" is only a baby 'gator barely eight inches long. Beav thinks they got "tooken," but they're determined to keep their new pet secretly in their room. They seek professional advice at Captain Jack's Alligator Farm, where Captain Jack himself advises them on how to keep their 'gator happy and healthy. In gratitude they name theirs "Captain Jack." The 'gator outgrows their bathroom and the boys move him into an unused basement laundry tub. For ten cents a peek they show off Captain Jack to the neighborhood kids, which tips June off to the big attraction in their basement, although a doubting Ward has to get his finger bitten before he believes in Captain Jack. The boys are certain they'll be punished but Ward tells them he's proud of their ability to keep an alligator on their own. However, he tells them "you can't hold on to the things you love, eventually you have to turn them loose." The family brings the 'gator to Captain Jack, who promises to introduce him "personal" to the other alligators. Back in their room the boys find a terrier puppy waiting as a reward for their good care of the 'gator.

They decide to name it "Captain Jack," too.

THE BLACK EYE

Beaver shows up at dinner with a shiner which he and Wally have tried to disguise with June's beauty cream. June is horrified that her baby has been fighting with an unnamed opponent, but Ward is more upset to learn that his son ran away rather than return any blows. Wally later uncovers the reason for Beaver's restraint: he was belted by a *girl*, Violet Rutherford. The next morning Ward puts gloves on Beaver, determined to teach him how to stand up to his aggressors. The lessons appear to be less than successful—the plastic boxing dummy actually knocks Beaver to the floor—but Beaver gets charged up and heads over to the Rutherfords' to challenge Violet to "get 'gressive" with him. She's not interested in fighting so the two set off on an afternoon of adventures including charging ice cream sodas to her father. Meanwhile, Ward learns he's practically forced Beaver to beat up a girl and he and Fred search frantically for what they fear will be two bloodied pint-sized pugilists. They finally find Violet and Beaver looking amicable enough until they smile and it looks like they've knocked out each other's teeth, which turns out to be just their carefully placed black chewing gum.

BEAVER GETS 'SPELLED

Beaver's new teacher, Miss Canfield, hands him a note after class. The other kids convince him that a note home means he's getting kicked out of school. Worried that he'll be the first second-grader in the school's history to get 'spelled, Beaver hides the note. The next day Miss Canfield finds it crumpled beneath Beaver's desk and he makes up a quick excuse about the family stove exploding. She insists he deliver the note to his mother, but he loses it for real on the way home. Wally types out an all-purpose reply from "Mrs. Ward Cleaver" assuring Miss Canfield that both she and his father have whipped Beaver for his school offense. Unable to fathom such a severe response to her simple written request that Beaver play Smokey the Bear in the Fire Prevention Pageant, she calls June into school. When Beaver discovers where she's headed, he plays hooky and hides up a tree. When Ward, June, and Wally find him, he insists he is going to stay up there until he dies. June decides to tell him they are going home and will leave him there even if it rains. This gets Beaver to agree to at least come down to earth long enough to get his raincoat. The next day he has a good talk with Miss Canfield and offers to give her some pointers about the second grade if she will call him "Beaver" instead of "Theodore." The following day Beaver carries his most precious possession in his back pocket to show Miss Canfield—a rubber shrunken head.

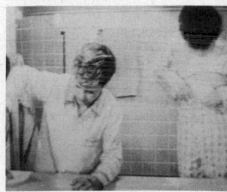

WATER, ANYONE?

Wally, Chester, and Tooey are working hard around their houses to earn money for baseball uniforms. There are no lucrative chores left for Beaver until he hears June scolding Wally for the mess he leaves in the kitchen every time he comes in for a drink, and Beaver gets the idea of hauling water to the boys. Since they all have easy access to their hoses he gets no takers. As he mopes on the sidewalk, Beav meets a crew tearing up the street who inform him that they are repairing a water main and the neighborhood water will be shut off for three hours. Reluctantly the thirsty boys soon pay Beaver six cents a glass for his water—inflated from a nickel. June is more practical; she buys a quarter's worth. Ward lectures Beaver on exploiting his friends when he uncovers his black-market-beverage racket. The boys discover that Beaver has taken most of their uniform money, accuse him of swindling them, and drop him from the team. However, when they learn that as a result of the water-main problems the electricity is going off for the night, Beaver generously donates his water earnings so the boys can corner the market on candles, which of course they sell at exorbitant prices. The boys get their uniforms, including Beaver, the team water boy.

WALLY'S GIRL TROUBLE

Wally double-crosses Beaver on their plan to skip out of dancing school to go fishing when Penny Jameson waltzes into his life. As June predicts, "a girl has come

between Wally and the Beaver and I'm afraid it's going to be awfully rough on the Beaver." Wally forgets boy stuff in favor of sappy phone conversations, "gooping" up his hair, and getting *Rebecca of Sunnybrook Farm* read to him by Penny. Beav mows the lawn for Wally in an effort to win his brother back. In gratitude Wally brings Beaver along on a soda date but Penny has an aversion to "grubby infants." Beaver tries to patch things up and follows Ward's hypothetical advice that the way to make up to a woman is to give her a sentimental gift. Beaver gives Penny his most cherished possession, his gift-wrapped pet frog, Herbie. This quashes the romance for good but the boys console each other. The Beaver says he can always get another frog and Wally decides he can always get another girl.

PART-TIME GENIUS

The boys report they're getting tested at school the next day and Ward tries to drill Beaver in his multiplication tables until they finally get through to Ward that they're having *intelligence* tests for which they're not supposed to study. Ward and June get a shock when Beaver gets the highest mark in the whole school on the exams. Miss Rayburn urges Ward and June to send Beaver to a school for exceptional children. Beaver is upset when Larry, Whitey, and Judy call him a "sneaky genius." Beaver's genius is short-lived, however, when classmate Charles Fredericks steps forward to admit that he switched his paper with Beaver's because he's a new boy in Mayfield and was always an outcast at his previous schools because his parents made a fuss over his excellent grades. Ward and June are grateful that Beaver will remain just plain Beaver after all and promise he will not reveal what Charles did. Beaver is concerned with how the other kids will know he's really not a genius, but Wally assures him all he has to do is "tell them what four times four is."

NEW NEIGHBORS

June sends Beaver to deliver fresh cut flowers to their new neighbor, Mrs. Donaldson, and in gratitude she plants a big kiss on his cheek. Eddie and Wally give him the business about kissing another man's wife. When Mr. Donaldson approaches Beaver with hedge clippers in his hand, Beaver runs away convinced his rival has come to cut him down to size. The Donaldsons merely hope to invite shy Beaver to meet their young niece. Knowing nothing of the niece, Beaver thinks Mrs. Donaldson wants him for his handsome self alone when he arrives all dressed up for Sunday

ice cream. Wally is stationed outside to watch for Mr. Donaldson, but Ward chases him away, causing Beaver to panic and run back home to hide under his bed. Once everything is explained, Mr. Donaldson gives Beaver permission to kiss his wife anytime he wants.

THE HAIRCUT

Beaver has lost three days' worth of lunch money in a row and Ward lectures him about the dire consequences of being careless with money. The next day Ward entrusts Beaver with his haircut money, which he promptly loses as well. The barber won't barter for Beaver's glass doorknob or lead soldiers and Beaver refuses to have the barber call Ward to have his credit approved. Instead he locks himself in the bathroom with a pair

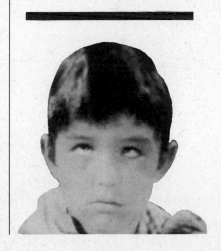

of scissors. Wally looks at his ravaged locks and tries to even things out, leaving Beaver's head an even greater disaster area. They hit on a scheme of showing up for dinner wearing stocking caps, saying they've joined a secret club requiring them to wear the hats nonstop for two weeks. That night June tiptoes in to uncover Beaver's head and discovers her "poor little bald-headed angel!" As the boys await their punishment, June convinces Ward that they have only themselves to blame, that Beaver was warned it was his last chance, then lost his haircut money, so naturally he was afraid to come to them. They decide to go out for breakfast instead of punishing the boys. Beaver even appears in his school play as an angel, stocking hat firmly in place.

BROTHERLY LOVE

June rushes up to the boys' room to separate them during a fierce fight and lectures the brothers on how lucky they are to have each other. She insists they write out a friendship pact promising to start "acting like brothers," doing things together—and enjoying them. Ward is dubious, but the boys agree. However, for Saturday, each boy gets a solo invitation, Wally to a football game, Beaver to go fishing with Gus the fireman in his new dinghy, which only fits a-man-

and-a-half. As Saturday morning creeps boringly into Saturday afternoon for the two new constant companions, each brother tries to get the other to break their pact without revealing his own invitation. When they realize they were both "a couple of sneaks," another fight erupts. Now Ward steps in to enlighten them about brotherhood, assuring them that when they look back on the times they have shared they'll realize the good times far outweigh the bad ones. The next day, Wally apologizes to Gus for making Beaver skip out on their fishing trip and Gus lets the boys have his dinghy for the day, figuring that together they just about equal a-man-and-a-half.

THE PERFUME SALESMEN

A threatening lawyer's letter addressed to the boys tips Ward and June off to their latest money-making scheme: selling twenty-four bottles of Flower of the Orient perfume at a dollar a bottle to win a movie projector. Unfortunately, one whiff wipes out any desire to purchase this "treasured love secret of ancient Persia." Even Beaver says it smells like an old catcher's mitt. So the boys quickly gave up, and all twenty-four bottles lie forgotten in their closet. In order to teach them the value of salesmanship and perseverance, Ward offers to drive the boys around the neighborhood to try again. When they strike out once more, Ward gives them a list of new customers he claims to have picked at random, and urges them to keep trying. The boys suddenly have a complete sellout. Of course, the list comprises members of June's Women's Club, all called in advance by Ward, who guaranteed to reimburse the ladies. When the prize projector arrives, Ward opens the box and sees it's a pathetically cheap viewer, but when the boys get home they find a sharp little machine waiting for them. It dawns on them that Ward has bought them a substitute machine, but they decide not to spoil anything by thanking him for his secret deed.

THE CLUBHOUSE

Eddie, Tooey, and Wally are looking for a way to fill the day and they decide to build a clubhouse. The dues for eighth-graders will be a dollar and Eddie says Beaver can join for the special second-grader dues of three dollars. The fellas set about hammering together lop-sided boards on the vacant lot across the street and Beaver tries to raise money. Sitting on a bench, Beaver meets Pete, a grizzled, lazy gent who is supposed to be walking around wearing a sandwich advertising board. This gives Beaver an idea

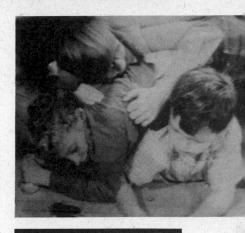

and he makes his own sandwich sign offering space for rent, fifty cents for his front and seventy-five cents for his back. He convinces Charlie the fireman to buy his back sign to advertise the auxiliary fire station, but Beaver's real financial coup comes when he goes to his *spittin'* bridge and paints a sign offering people the chance to "spit off my bridge 10¢." He nets nearly two dollars for the day but he gives it away to old Pete the faker, who tells him an elaborate sob story. Meanwhile the builders have long given up on the club.

BEAVER'S SHORT PANTS

While June's away her Aunt Martha is taking care of Ward and the boys. The boys remember Aunt Martha as their Umbrella Aunt because she always sends them umbrellas for Christmas. Martha has never been married and is rather sensitive and set in her ways but Ward promises he'll make the boys obey her. Aunt Martha takes Beaver shopping for a new school suit in the "Eastern tradition" and to his shock she buys him an Eton jacket, short pants, knee-length

socks, and a cap. At school the other kids really give Beaver the business over his bare legs and he slugs the first kid who calls him a sissy. Wally and Ward empathize but are fearful of upsetting Martha, so Beaver dejectedly dons his suit and heads off for school, even carrying an umbrella, to make things worse. Ward beckons him inside the garage, where he has blue jeans and a sport shirt waiting for Beaver to change into. When June returns home, though, and the family is taking Martha to the airport, Ward is surprised to see Beaver come downstairs in his suit. Beaver tells him he still doesn't want to hurt Aunt Martha's feelings.

BEAVER'S CRUSH

After school Beaver is cleaning blackboards, emptying wastebaskets, anything to prolong his time with Miss Canfield, for whom he has developed a real second-grade-size crush. Larry, Judy, and Whitey accuse him of being a teacher's pet, which Beaver denies. To prove himself they dare him to place a spring–action snake in her desk drawer, which he does. Troubled by his dirty trick, Beaver convinces Wally they have to steal into school that night and grab the snake out of the drawer. When they get to school, they run into the watchman's dog and run right back home empty-handed. The next day in school Beaver's heart is in his mouth every time Miss Canfield reaches toward her drawer, but he manages to stall her each time, even pulling Judy's hair in desperation. After school Beaver opens the drawer but finds the snake missing. Miss Canfield tells him she discovered it before class. She blames herself a little for what he's done, saying a teacher can't favor one pupil for another and that someday Beaver will find a nice little girl his own age. Beaver reluctantly agrees but says, "little girls don't smell as nice as you do."

VOODOO MAGIC

June forbids Wally to take Beaver to a double feature that includes *Voodoo Curse* and suggests they see *Pinocchio* instead. They go to the double bill anyway, when Eddie convinces them how they could get their parents on a technicality. Ward and June find out about the deception, and they make the boys squirm as they ask pointed questions about *Pinocchio*. Beaver spends some especially anxious cross-eyed moments watching the end of his nose when he learns how the puppet's grew the more he lied. The boys are punished when they confess, and Beaver is so angry at Eddie that he concocts his own voodoo curse and sticks a rag doll Eddie stand-in with a pin *and* a nail. At school, Beaver and Wally are surprised to learn that Eddie has been felled by a sudden illness. Suddenly conscience stricken, Beaver pays a bedside call to Eddie, who laughs at the curse and tells Beaver he's just faking to get out of school. But as soon as Beaver leaves, he feels his stomach and yells for his mother. Mr. Haskell demands that Ward get Beaver to remove the curse. Ward draws on his vast reservoir of witch-doctor lore and common sense and sends Beaver over to Eddie with a genuine voodoo curse remover: three worms from the backyard, four hairs from a dog's tail, six toadstools picked by the light of the moon—and two hairs from a small boy's head.

THE PAPER ROUTE

The boys ask Ward for a new bicycle and he suggests they earn their own money. They take jobs delivering newspapers after school. Ward and June promise one another they won't bail the boys out this time, but each secretly pitches in when first Beaver and then Wally is struggling with the workload. While the boys are waiting for their weekend papers to be dropped off, Ward and June discover their neatly stacked pile of leftover papers from the week. Thinking they're the undelivered papers the boys have cavalierly forgotten about, Ward and June decide they must fulfill their sons' obligations, and fold and deliver the entire pile. The boys' customers complain to the *Courier Sun* office for getting last week's papers plopped on their doorsteps and Wally and Beaver are fired. Ward feels terrible about the foul-up and goes to the paper office to get the boys their route back, but the boys have already gotten a new job packing boxes at the supermarket. When they buy their new bike, Ward feels a little left out. He asks which of them will have the honor of the first ride. Beaver tells him they've decided their father should, so with great pride Ward mounts up and rides off.

PARTY INVITATION

Beaver is passed a note in class, an invitation to Linda Dennison's birthday party. Judy teases him that he's got a sweetheart and Beaver suffers even more when he learns that none of the other boys got invited. He conveniently forgets about the party until Mrs. Dennison phones June. Beaver's stuck. Wally tries to help out by impersonating Ward on the phone, telling Linda that Beaver is sick, but Ward catches him, sends him to his room, and drives Beaver to the party. Beaver resists in the car but Ward forces him out, causing Beaver to shout that he's going to "eat so much cake and ice cream I'll bust." Miserable in his suit and party hat, Beaver *is* the only boy, and when the girls announce they're going to play Post Office, he escapes to another room. There he finds Mr. Dennison, who lets Beaver hide out and play with his gun collection. Wally has informed Ward and June why Beaver balked at going to the party, so when he gets home they're afraid he'll hate them, but he claims he had a swell time, thereby really confusing Ward. When he sees Beaver writing a note to Linda, Wally thinks he's now gone soft on girls until Beaver explains he's only asking to walk her home so he can see her father's guns some more.

LUMPY RUTHERFORD

Wally and Beaver have been late from school because big, dumb Lumpy Rutherford has been terrorizing them along the short route home. Ward tells them that he once fixed a bully by carefully placing barrel hoops

outside his house, then calling the bully names until he came out and was ambushed by the hoops. Thus inspired, the boys lay a hoop trap outside the Rutherford home and call out "meathead." Much to their dismay, Fred comes storming out instead of Lumpy, and the boys flee before he can spot them. That night the Rutherfords arrive at the Cleaver home to play cards and Fred melodramatically recounts his vicious attack by "young hoodlums." Ward begins to suspect Beaver and Wally. They confess to Ward and he sheepishly admits to Fred that his sons were the young hoodlums but that they were only trying to get back at Lumpy. Fred promises he'll talk to his Clarence. Ward points out to the boys that the true victory over the bullies of the world comes in not becoming one yourself.

CHILD CARE

Ward has bragged so much to Herb Wilson about how responsible his boys are that when the Wilsons pick up Ward and June for a wedding and have been let down by their baby-sitter, they're certain Wally and Beaver will want to earn some extra money by caring for their little four-year-old daughter, Puddin'. Puddin' is no piece of cake, throwing things from her playpen and demanding to see Mary Jane, which the boys finally discover is her word for the bathroom. To satisfy her they take her to the bathroom, where she locks herself in. The boys take a ladder to the bathroom window, and when Beaver is too big to get through, they recruit little neighbor Benjie. But then the bathroom doorknob comes off in Benjie's hand, which makes the two little ones start to cry. Knowing if they call their father they'll have let him down, the boys call Gus the fireman, who sends a hook and ladder to get the kids safely out of the bathroom. Ward and June arrive home to utter peace

so are quite surprised when a neighbor calls about the fire truck parked outside their home earlier in the day. Ward is about to demand an explanation, but June points out that the boys have proved their responsibility and will tell them what happened when they're ready.

THE BANK ACCOUNT

The boys want new baseball gloves with their piggy-bank stash but Ward tells them they should make do and save their money instead, just as he has resisted buying a new hunting jacket for years. When the boys look at his old jacket in the closet they decide to use their savings to buy Ward a new jacket. They pick out a handsome one at Mayfield's finest sporting-goods store during their lunch period but have to withdraw additional funds from their school accounts to buy it. Mrs. Rayburn informs Ward the boys left school grounds without permission and have not made deposits in their school accounts but have actually taken cash out. Ward is furious that the boys have deceived him and when the box arrives from the sporting-goods store he insists the whole family will decide whether their purchase was a valid one. He is overwhelmed when he unwraps the box, exclaiming it's the greatest hunting jacket he's ever seen. As they prepare for bed Wally suggests the next time they should inform their father ahead of time when they plan to surprise him.

LONESOME BEAVER

Beaver is crushed when he can't join the Boy Scouts with Wally because he's not eleven. Wally goes on an overnight leaving lonely Beaver to entertain himself. Ward and June are busy, Larry's got "swolled glands," even Gus has no time for him. Ward finally finds Beaver singing by an open manhole waiting for the " 'lectric" man to get back. Ward explains that from now on Wally won't always be around to tell him where to go. When they get home Wally is upstairs in bed, where June has sent him after he came home soaking wet from his rained-out overnight. Beaver cheerfully volunteers to keep Wally company, telling him he'd rather do *nothing* with Wally than *something* with anybody else. Beaver figures he can let the Scouts have Wally for one night a week for meetings and in the meantime he'll sleep in Wally's official Scout sleeping bag, getting ready for when he's eleven.

THE PERFECT FATHER

Willie Dennison's father shows the boys a great time at the Sportsman's Show and Ward suffers a twinge of jealousy because he has been busy at work lately and the boys have been spending a great deal of time at the Dennisons'. To teach Mr. Dennison not to try to be a father to *his* kids, Ward puts up a basketball backboard over the garage. The boys and their friends are shooting baskets and when Eddie misses his shot he insists on measuring the hoop and finds out Ward has installed it a foot too low. He leads the guys back to the Dennisons' regulation backboard. Ward adjusts the hoop and buys the boys a new basketball. The next day the guys are over again and Ward comes out and starts showing off some of his hook-shot expertise, driving them all off. At the country club Ward runs into Dennison, who tells Ward that he never hangs around his boys because he realized as his sons grew up they didn't want their old man sticking his nose in unless they asked. That evening Ward tells June the secret of getting close to one's children is knowing when to stay away from them.

CLEANING UP BEAVER

Eddie and Wally are meticulously groomed for an afternoon at the movies but they must wait for a mud-covered Beaver and Larry to get cleaned up. Eddie complains that with the little "creeps" hanging around he and Wally can't talk to any girls in the movies. To encourage Beaver to follow his brother's example, Ward and June praise Wally for his neatness at dinner. Larry warns Beaver that *his* big brother started liking girls and taking baths all the time and his parents made fun of him too, so he fixed his brother good by insisting on his own room. Upset that Wally calls him a pig, Beaver moves into the guest room. When the lights are out a screeching cat sounds like a loose wild animal. Beaver cries out for Wally and runs into the bedroom, claiming he just wants to make sure Wally is all right. Wally understands and suggests Beaver stay in the room with him for the night to save the yelling back and forth. When Wally asks why Beaver moved out, he says that suddenly Wally got neat. They agree that Wally will try being a little sloppier and Beaver will try to be a little neater. June and Ward observe that the boys have taught them that blood is thicker than water.

THE STATE VERSUS BEAVER

Out of old boxes, wagon wheels, and a one-cylinder motor, Ward helps Wally and Beaver build a "real racin' car." Ward tells the boys they must not be reckless with it and they cannot ride off the sidewalk. Larry visits the next day and eggs Beaver on to drive out onto the street. A policeman pulls Beaver over and gives him a ticket for driving without a license. Wally agrees to act as Beaver's guardian in court so he won't have to tell Ward. As he watches the judge sentence people to jail, Beaver gets worried. The judge calls the boys alongside his chair, wipes the Beaver's nose when he starts crying, and states that he's free to go, having been punished enough. The judge leaves it up to the boys whether they tell their parents. When they do tell Ward, he says he doesn't care what kind of trouble they may get into, he doesn't want them to be frightened to come to him. Wally confides to Ward that since their Dad was so nice to help them with the car, Beaver "didn't want you to feel bad 'cause you got a kid like him."

BEAVER AND PONCHO

Under his raincoat, Beaver smuggles in a "bald-headed Mexican," a Chihuahua dog he swapped for with Larry. Ward tells him the dog obviously belongs to someone, but if they run an advertisement in the paper and no one claims it, Beaver can keep the dog. The family grows to like the dog; June even starts to knit it a little coat. However, a Mrs. Bennett calls Ward asking after her "Poncho." Ward gives Beaver the sad news that the dog's owner is coming over to claim it. Beaver sneaks Poncho out of the house and takes him to school. Miss Canfield discovers his companion and reports him to Mrs. Rayburn, who calls an angry Ward. June tries to get Ward to realize that Beaver was only disobedient out of love for his new dog. Ward thinks she's just being soft on Beaver. However, when Mrs. Bennett comes to claim Poncho, Beaver refuses her reward and tells her that since he only had the dog two days, he hoped that if he kept it with him just a little while longer Poncho would remember him better. The childless Mrs. Bennett doesn't understand that, but Ward does, and vows to punish Beaver with a much more lenient attitude.

THE BROKEN WINDOW

Eddie knocks a baseball through the Cleavers' window and Ward forbids further ball-playing near the house. Left on their own the next day, Beaver asks Wally for just one pitch, and by chance he connects—smashing the window of Ward's car. They want to get a new window, but even emptying their piggy bank and selling a wagonload of junk leaves them way short of the money. They follow Eddie's advice and just roll down the window, which they hope will at least get them through dinner. The next day the family piles into the car to drive to a picnic, and when Ward asks him to roll up the window, Beaver almost cries and says

he can't. Wally explains, but June insists he roll up the window anyway. The glass is no longer shattered. Ward reveals that the previous evening he was putting things in the car and slammed the door. He heard glass shattering, thought he broke the window, and got it repaired that morning. Wally says they would have told him the truth eventually, probably after they had done something good that made Ward happy. Ward says they've done something "real good" by telling the truth.

TRAIN TRIP

Returning from a visit with Aunt Martha, the boys convince her to let them buy their own tickets. When their train is delayed, the boys buy a stream of sodas, hot dogs, and candy bars, so when they next step up to the ticket window, they can only afford to go as far as Bellport. They sit hoping some nice rich man will give them a bag full of money, but when the conductor comes around they make up a story about their poor Aunt Martha who lives in a poorhouse and their father who fell out of an airplane and is in the hospital. The conductor doesn't buy their story but he does advance them money for the ticket to May-field and gives them his address. That night George Haskell tells Ward how much he enjoyed the story he heard the boys tell on the train. As Ward is tucking the boys in, he mystifies Beaver and Wally by asking what they're doing about the money—they've already put it in an envelope addressed to the conductor—and by saying they'll be glad to know he's recovered from his nasty fall. Beaver asks Wally how Dad found out and Wally says he doesn't know, but every once in a while parents find out some-thing you know they couldn't find out. Beaver concludes that maybe "it's the same way Santa Claus finds out about stuff."

MY BROTHER'S GIRL

June returns from the Mother's Club meeting announcing that the mothers feel there is a lack of "social awareness" among the eighth-graders. Therefore, they have planned a dance for Satur-day night. June hopes Wally will invite a girl from his class, but he hates girls and plans to go with Eddie. Mary Ellen Rogers

has bigger plans for Wally. She has lunch with Beaver in the cafeteria all week and entices him with her father's electric trains, which he can play with if he brings Wally along. Once Mary Ellen gets them over, she dispatches Beaver in order to get Wally alone and ply him with ginger ale and chocolate-covered doughnuts. She pretends not to want to go to the dance either and suggests she and Wally share this unpleasant task—"like burying the garbage in pairs in scout camp," Wally suggests. When Beaver breaks in on them, "they both looked at each other and told me to drink my ginger ale in the kitchen," Beaver re-ports to Ward. His father says he's afraid Beaver's been used. Mary Ellen gets her Wally, but when she comes to pick up Wally for the dance, Beaver gets back at Mary Ellen by ignoring her.

NEXT-DOOR INDIANS

Beaver is so eager to get the big kids to listen to him that he makes up a story about a big Indian battle that occurred around his house a couple of hundred years ago. That other master yarn-spinner, Eddie, challenges him on his claim and bets Bea-ver a dollar and a half of Wally's money that he can't prove it. Just before the guys come over with their shovels, Wally and Beaver bury some artifacts. Wally pretends to find an arrowhead, but Eddie thinks it looks like the one Wally's uncle sent him once. Then Chester finds a broken arrow and Beaver demands Eddie pay up—until Eddie takes a closer look at the arrow and finds "Japan" printed on it. Tooey, who has continued digging, calls everybody over to examine the shiny stones he has found. They're all excited thinking they'll be "jillionaires," all thanks to Beaver's story. Beaver questions Gus about his stones and learns they are worthless garnets, the kind used for making sandpaper. Ward tells Beaver the risks of making up stories and of being a "make-believe big guy." Wally consoles Beav that the other guys will forget all about losing their instant wealth. They never expected anything that good to happen to real kids anyway.

MUSIC LESSON

Ward and June raise a big fuss over Wally for making the base-

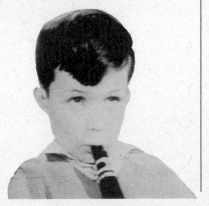

ball team at school. Beaver tried out and was only hit on the head by fly balls. To please his parents he signs up for clarinet lessons with the school band. His first performance for the family is a few barely recognizable measures of "America." His progress isn't swift enough for the music teacher, who dismisses him from the band. Beaver gets to keep the clarinet and still carries it to school each day so his father won't be disappointed over his failure. The night of the band concert, Beaver persists in his charade, getting dressed slowly in his blue suit, still hoping he might get sick in the car. Wally tells Ward and June that Beaver was flunked out of the band three weeks ago and that he kept deceiving everyone because "you got such a kick out of me making the baseball team, he wanted you to like him for something too." Ward tells Beaver that something came up and they won't be able to go to the concert. Later, in his pajamas, Beaver gives Ward a kiss "for pretending that you still thunk I was in the band." Ward tells him not to worry, he'll make it next year.

TENTING TONIGHT

Ward is disturbed by the boys spending their entire Saturday inside the movie house and he promises to take them out in the fresh air the next weekend on a camping trip. On Saturday Ward tells the boys he must cancel their trip so he can go into the office. When Ward comes home that night June tells him the boys decided to go on a camping trip without him—in the backyard. Sure enough, they have pitched their tent and are cooking their dinner. Beaver is even set to protect them with his water pistol. But it's water that causes them their trouble; a big rainstorm. June is worried but Ward assures her the boys will figure something out. The next morning the boys are still outside but June complains about big wet spots on the stair carpet and wants to call the roofers about the leak. Ward tells her he thinks the boys leaked the water when they carried their sleeping bags up to their room in the middle of the night. Eddie tells the boys his father would have dragged him in from the rain and wishes he had a father like theirs, who didn't care what they did. Beaver asks Wally if their dad does too care what they do. Wally says, "Sure, he does, Beav—who do you think left the door unlocked?"

BEAVER'S OLD FRIEND

Beaver, Wally, and Ward are cleaning out the garage when they come across "Billy," Beaver's beat-up old teddy bear. Billy was a present from Aunt Martha when Beaver had the measles. Billy's stomach growls when he's squeezed, and he was practically the first friend Beaver ever had. Ward chides Beaver that he's too big to play with dolls now and dejectedly Beaver tosses Billy in the trash barrel. Before he can return to save Billy, the trash truck makes its pickup. In desperation, Beaver chases the truck for blocks and with the help of a sympathetic trash man retrieves Billy. Beaver asks Wally for a way to "un-smell" the bear and Wally suggests drowning it out with another smell. The next morning June and Ward enter the boys' room, and Ward asks if she isn't wearing a lot of perfume. They trace the smell to Beaver's chest of drawers, where they find Billy resting. June decides to give him the best dry cleaning he ever had. That evening Beaver comes into the kitchen carrying Billy in a shoe box. Little Benjie Harrison is getting the measles and Beaver wants him to have Billy " 'cause he's the best friend a guy could have when you've got the measles." Then when Benjie grows up like Beaver has, he can give Billy "to some other lucky kid that's sick."

WALLY'S JOB

Wally asks if he can paint their two rusty garbage cans and Ward offers to pay him fifty cents apiece. However, when Eddie tells him that *his* father paid a guy three dollars to get his cans painted, Wally loses his eagerness. Beaver leaps at the chance to do the job, brushing right over the rust and getting more paint on himself than the cans. Wally accuses Beaver of stealing his work, and the boys fight. Ward rules that each boy may do one can and receive a dollar. The next day the boys have made up and are painting away when Eddie arrives to announce a raging fire at the lumberyard. Wally and Beaver drop their brushes and rush off. When Ward comes home from the office he's about to finish the cans, until June tells him about the fire, and he rushes off too. When the fire-watchers return home they see the beautifully painted cans awaiting them and Ward detects June's handiwork. Beaver suggests June deserves the two dollars but she declines, noting that her payment will come in the form of the new hat Ward had told her to delay purchasing.

NEW DOCTOR

Wally is "gurglin' " after he wakes up with a sore throat and June makes him stay in bed. Beaver feels left out when he sees that June is waiting on Wally and bought him a model airplane, Ward is bringing home chocolate-chip ice cream, and the eighth grade chipped in to buy Wally an Oriental magic set. Even Dr. Richardson stopped by and gave him pills. The next day Beaver announces that his throat hurts right where Wally's hurt. Things don't go as well for Beaver. It turns out to be only a half-day of school, Wally and Eddie play ball rather than keep him company, Judy brings him homework, and Dr. Richardson is out of town so his associate Dr. Bradley will be looking him over. Beaver worries if Dr. Bradley is a "pill doctor" or the "sticking kind." Dr. Bradley examines him and tells the story of the boy who cried "wolf." Beaver admits he was just pretending, to get the loot like Wally did when he was sick. When they bring in his ice cream, Beaver confesses to Ward and June that he was just crying "wolf" all day but that he won't do it anymore. Ward tells him to eat his ice cream so it won't go to waste.

BOARDING SCHOOL

Johnny Franklin, who used to attend Wally's school, comes to visit during his break from military school. Wally and Beaver are fascinated by his uniform and by stories of a school where you could have so much fun—marching every day, carrying a wooden gun, wrestling, horseback riding, and all men teachers. Wally asks permission to attend Bellport Military Academy and

Ward agrees to send the application. When Eddie hears about Wally's plan, he asks when Ward got this idea, insisting that *his* father tried to get rid of *him* that way but he knows the law and his parents can't throw him out until he's twenty-one. Wally gets cold feet but can't face telling Ward. Beaver suspects Wally has been crying and goes downstairs to ask Ward why he doesn't like Wally anymore and wants to send him to "marching school." Once he learns how Eddie has caused this misunderstanding, Ward talks to Wally and they decide he should go to Mayfield High with the rest of his friends. He's staying home, Wally tells Beaver, because Beaver might get in trouble going down to the lake and catching polliwogs by himself and stuff. But, Wally warns, covering his own relief over not having to leave Beaver, this doesn't mean Beaver can hang around him all the time.

BEAVER'S BAD DAY

In his newly altered gray flannel suit which he forgot to change out of, Beaver is playing on a makeshift seesaw with Larry. Eddie comes by with his dog and pushes Larry off, causing Beaver to hit the ground with a thud. As he stands up, a nail rips a big tear in his good pants. He tells his parents that a dog attacked him but Ward sees the rust on the tear and sends Beaver up to his room for lying. The next day, Beaver tells Wally about Eddie's role in his tear as well as Eddie's claim that he could lick Wally with one hand tied behind his back. Wally calls out Eddie in the presence of several other boys. Eddie pushes Wally when he's not looking, but Beaver butts Eddie in the stomach and knocks him down. Eddie's dog jumps on Beaver and this time it really *is* a dog who rips his pants. Ward and June are quite angry when Beaver offers the same excuse and send the boys upstairs. A phone call from Mrs. Mondello explains the situation and a chagrined Ward goes upstairs to apologize to the boys for not believing them.

BEAVER'S POEM

The night before it's due, Beaver goes to Ward to get help writing a poem for school. Beaver suggests writing about bears, and the two laureates buckle down to find some rhymes. Beaver's concentration flags quickly and he makes excuses about being thirsty and not feeling well. Exasperated, Ward sends Beaver to bed, telling him they'll finish in the morning. Ward gets a sudden inspiration and the next morning Beaver merely recopies the poem Ward finished. June chides Ward for doing his son's assignment and also makes fun of Ward's writing. Ward insists he was trying to sound like an eight-year-old. That evening Wally announces that Beaver is to read his poem at a school program and will get a prize. Ward and June try to make Beaver understand that he cannot accept a prize for a poem his father wrote. Ward makes a special appointment with Mrs. Rayburn to explain things, and she says that even though Ward may have "overhelped" Beaver, many of the parents don't bother to help their kids at all. She gives Beaver another chance to write his own poem. He creates one about a duck and is confident he'll still win a prize because he's the only third-grader who wrote a poem.

BEAVER AND HENRY

Ward and the boys build a trap to catch the gopher that's been eating June's flowers, but they catch a fat white rabbit instead. Beaver names it Henry. After the boys leave, June suggests that Henrietta would be a more appropriate name for a rabbit in *her* condition. Ward delays explaining this development to the boys and Beaver comes screaming that a bunch of little white rats have knocked Henry down and are biting him. June calms Beaver down and tells him his rabbit's had babies. The next day Ward warns Beaver not to pick up any of the babies because the mother will abandon any with the human smell. It's too late, though, and Beaver seeks advice from Gus to save the rabbit he already picked up. Gus suggests putting his mother's talcum powder on all of the rabbits to fool the mother. Ward gets a whiff of the strange scent around the rabbit hutch and questions Beaver. A little hurt, Ward asks why he didn't come to his father for advice. Beaver says Ward's better at telling his sons what they should *not* do than what they should. Ward says he hopes today he's learned as much about children as Beaver's learned about rabbits.

BEAVER'S GUEST

Larry Mondello is Beaver's weekend guest but the coals are barely glowing for the lunchtime barbecue when Ward finds Larry standing on the front porch with his overnight bag and rubbing his eyes. Larry says he wants to go home because Beaver has punched him in the stomach. Ward tries to talk him out of leaving but finally agrees to call him a taxi, since the Cleaver car is in the shop. By the time the cab arrives, Beaver and Larry have gone from sticking out tongues at each other to being best friends again. By this time the hamburgers are burning and Ward starts lunch all over again. In the middle of the night Beaver awakens his parents telling them Larry is sitting in bed holding his stomach. June lifts his pillow and finds the remains of four candy bars. Ward suggests Larry has just overeaten and they turn the lights out. When Mrs. Mondello

picks up Larry the next day, Ward heaves a sigh of relief. Beaver says it was a swell weekend, more fun than he's had in a long time. Next weekend they all have Wally's promised guest, Eddie Haskell, to look forward to.

CAT OUT OF THE BAG

The next-door-neighbor Donaldsons leave the boys in charge of their prizewinning angora cat, Puff Puff. Ward feels they've bitten off too much responsibility and warns them not to come running to him like they did with their paper route if they get in trouble. All goes well until Wally deserts Beaver for a carnival and Eddie's dog comes along and chases Puff Puff. Wally is late for dinner and finds out the cat is nowhere to be found from Beaver during an impromptu under-the-table mid-meal conference. Late that night the boys hear meowing. They take their flashlight and tiptoe outside, where they spot Puff Puff high up their backyard tree. Beaver climbs up but then realizes he can't climb back down. He holds on to Puff Puff, but it's getting cold and he's "a'scared." Wally gets his parents and June pleads for Ward to get Beaver down first before he starts yelling at him, which he does. The next day Mr. Donaldson comes over and says the boys told him their troubles and refused payment for their work; he calls them a couple of little characters. Ward and June have to agree—sometimes they're a couple of pretty *nice* little characters.

WARD'S PROBLEM

Ward promises this will be the weekend for his much-delayed fishing trip with Wally. He even consents to take Eddie along. Beaver comes home excited about Saturday's fathers-and-students school picnic. Ward says he'll be delighted to escort Beaver. Stuck with two commitments, Ward doesn't have the heart to tell Wally that Beaver's school picnic must get priority, and his silent delay convinces the boys that Ward will be going fishing. Beaver makes an excuse to his teacher, Miss Landers, about his father not being able to attend the picnic because he'll be in Washington, and tells Ward the picnic was canceled because all the kids "have epidemics." Miss Landers phones the house and Beaver's "whoppers" are revealed. Beaver explains to Ward that he didn't want the kids "to think I had the kind of father who wouldn't take a kid someplace a father should take a kid," and Ward realizes he put his son in a spot where he just about had to make up the stories. They go to the picnic and win a genuine-solid-gold plastic cup for the three-legged race.

BEAVER RUNS AWAY

Larry persuades Beaver to try out Ward's electric drill. Beaver knows it's wrong but holds a piece of wood against the garage wall while Larry drills, and when the wood is removed there are two holes in the wall. Beaver tries to blame Larry, but Ward tells him his disobedience shows he has no respect for his father or pride in his home. Beaver packs his belongings in a pillowcase and tells Wally that when his father said he was more at fault than Larry, that was being "too mean." At suppertime Beaver lugs his pillowcase downstairs and insists he's running away, hoping Ward will make him stay. Instead, Ward wishes him well and closes the door. Beaver is dismayed and unhappy to be out on the street. He goes over to the Mondellos', where he makes up a story to cover his dinnertime visit. Ward is convinced Beaver will return home shortly, but when he doesn't, June frantically urges that they search for him. Ward stubbornly refuses, but June locates Beaver and brings him home. He apologizes to Ward and asks him how *he* felt when he ran away when he was a boy and *his* dad didn't come after him. Ward confesses that he forgot for a while what it was like when he was a kid. The next day Ward buys the boys their own set of tools.

BEAVER AND CHUEY

Beaver's new friend Chuey Varela comes to visit. Chuey and his parents speak only Spanish, but Beaver says they get along fine—he doesn't understand what Chuey says, only what he *means*. For laughs Eddie uses his level-one Spanish to teach Beaver how to tell his friend that he's a good guy—except he really tells him how to say "you have a face like a pig." Beaver is perplexed when he proudly speaks his line and Chuey runs out of the house crying. The Varelas come to call demanding to know why their son came home crying, and Beaver recites the line again. They too storm out. Wally uncovers what Eddie pulled and Ward dusts off his old Spanish textbook and writes an apology letter explaining what happened. The next day Chuey arrives with

flowers and a note from his parents asking the Cleavers' forgiveness and stating that we learn from our children. That night Beaver says that if he's going to be like Eddie when he grows up he doesn't think he wants to *get* big.

LOST WATCH

Beaver is the stuff-minder for the older kids while they play baseball. After the game, big bully Lumpy Rutherford comes over to collect his wristwatch but Beaver has no recollection of ever getting the watch from Lumpy to hold. Find the watch or else give him fifteen dollars within forty-eight hours—that's Lumpy's demand. After determining that Wally wouldn't be able to lick Lumpy in a fight, Beaver corners Ward the next morning and asks what he would do if he knew about stolen property. When Ward says that such information should be reported to the police, Beaver is really worried. He takes the twenty-five-dollar savings bond his Aunt Martha gave him to the bank, claiming he'll go to jail if he can't convert it to quick cash. The teller refuses without his father's signature and calls Ward when Beaver leaves the bank. Ward gets the truth out of Beaver and calls Fred Rutherford. Fred reports that Lumpy's mother found his watch in his jacket lining weeks ago and they were waiting for their son to come to them to admit he lost it. Fred calls Lumpy downstairs and drives him over to the Cleavers' to apologize. Ward tells the boys that it's kind of hard being a "Lumpy" and states that "when people make a mistake or have done something wrong, that's when they need understanding the most."

THE PIPE

Ward opens a mysterious box from Germany, sent by the Rutherfords, to find a genuine hand-carved white meerschaum pipe which turns brown when smoked. Larry is alone with Beaver and goads him into smoking the pipe. Beaver is reluctant because he's not supposed to smoke until he is twenty-one. They have no "smoke stuff" so they fill the bowl with coffee grounds. Even though Beaver is not supposed to drink coffee or light matches, they fire up the pipe and get such a rank smell they quit. The next day Larry brings over real tobacco emptied from ashtrays. The boys light up and get a little sick. Beaver scrubs out the pipe and sprays pine deodorizer. Ward notes the smell, then sees the now brownish pipe and concludes that his son has been smoking. Except he thinks it's Wally. Ward tries to get him to confess by an elaborate telling of the Pandora myth. Wally un-

derstands just enough of it to know he's supposed to have a guilty conscience about something, but he doesn't know what. Later, when he learns Ward is yelling at Wally for smoking, Beaver breaks down and offers that "you can lock me in my room and I won't do anything bad until I'm twenty-one." Wally isn't angry. He figures he never got a bawling out for leaving nails in the driveway which resulted in a flat tire for Ward, so he had one coming to him anyway.

WALLY'S PRESENT

It's Wally's birthday and Ward and June know that Beaver is planning to buy Wally a $6.98 camera. Beaver asks Wally if he can go with him and Eddie to the movies for his birthday, and Wally refuses, saying he promised Eddie they'd mess around together. When Beaver and Larry go shopping for the camera, they spy a nifty bow-and-arrow set for $6.50. Larry rubs it in about what a mean brother Wally has become and pressures Beaver into buying the bow and arrow for himself and a small toy for Wally with the leftover money. On the way home Larry bends the bow until it breaks. Wally has changed his mind and plans to take Beaver to the movies. When the presents are opened, everyone is embarrassed by Beaver's meager gift, especially Beaver. Ward calls the store and learns about the bow and arrow and he is disturbed over Beaver's apparent selfishness. Beaver explains his reasons and Ward suggests he return the bow and arrow in exchange for the camera. Beaver walks around the block with the box under his arm until Ward calls him inside and finally gets the truth. He sends Beaver upstairs to apologize to Wally, and Wally tells him he understands how it is, much to Beaver's relief.

HER IDOL

Beaver is walking through the park to meet Larry and Whitey when Linda Dennison calls down to him from a tree. Surprised that a girl would climb a tree, Beaver joins her to look at a bird's nest. When they climb down, the guys spot them and tease Beaver about Linda being his girl. In school, Beaver gets the business about Linda, and in order to stop it, he agrees to call her a really mean name—a "smelly old ape." Linda runs off crying and in frustration Beaver hauls off and hits Larry in the stomach. The fight lands Beaver in the principal's office. Beaver explains his mess to Ward, who promises to straighten things out at school. The next day, Miss Landers gives her pupils a little talk about how boys and girls should have mutual respect and learn to get along together. As Beaver walks home from school, he sees Linda up in the tree with Larry. That night Beaver asks Wally why he feels bad about that and Wally says that *he* feels bad when he sees other guys talking to Mary Ellen Rogers. They wonder if that bad feeling is what makes people get married.

THE GRASS IS ALWAYS GREENER

Beaver overhears Ward complaining about the monthly bills and remarking that at this rate they might end up in the poorhouse. Wally explains that the poorhouse, like in *Oliver Twist*, is where you have to wear old clothes and never go to school, which sounds pretty neat to Beaver. Beaver is still musing about poor people when he carries a wastebasket out to the trash man. The trash man tells him he lives next to the junkyard and Beaver accepts his invitation to visit his two sons. Ward reluctantly grants him permission and Beaver comes back late but exhilarated. June envisions the trash man's sons to be rough and grimy and agrees to have them come to visit Beaver rather than his returning to their home. Beaver complains that there's nothing fun to do around his house. When Pete and Chris arrive, they are neatly groomed and polite. They are thrilled with the Cleavers' backyard, with trees and grass they don't have at home. They admire the garage workbench and toolbox Beaver and Wally have always taken for granted. They think Ward is "an all-right guy" and June is as pretty as a movie star. June and Ward are glad they had the trash man's kids visit after all.

BEAVER'S HERO

Beaver learns that his father was in the same war with President Eisenhower, so when they are discussing the war in his class, he brags about Ward being a hero. Judy calls him a liar but Beaver says he'll bring in some of his father's mementos. He and Wally open Ward's chest and find only old letters to June, some drawing equipment, and a surveyor's transit. Ward interrupts their rummaging and disappoints the boys by telling them he was in the Seabees and the extent of his heroism was in building bases. Beaver gets Wally to write a letter purportedly from Ward to June describing a dangerous mission, but they discard it. Ward finds the letter and decides to call the teacher before Beaver gets in too deep. In class, the subject of the war is avoided. When Beaver gets home he tells Ward that he fig-

ured that if his father was in the war he must have been a hero. Ward explains that since he had been an engineer he could accomplish more with tools than with a gun. That night Wally tells Beaver his composition about his "most exciting experience" sounds so dull he should "jazz" it up. Beaver says that after his experience the last two days he doesn't think he'll be "jazzin' stuff up" anymore.

WALLY'S NEW SUIT

Wally needs a new suit for an upcoming dance and Eddie talks him into asking Ward for permission to buy the suit on his own. With great apprehension Ward agrees to let Wally go to the Prep Shop with Beaver and promises not to criticize the suit he buys. At the Prep Shop the only suit that appeals to the boys is a loud plaid number with a lot of pockets. June stifles Ward's criticism and Eddie and Tooey drop by and rave about how S-H-A-R-P it is, vowing to buy suits just like it. Ward tries to talk Wally into exchanging the suit, unsuccessfully. June tries another tack, saying the suit sleeves are much too long and they should all go down to the store to have them shortened. The salesman, primed by a phone call from June, says the sleeves cannot be shortened without ruining the drape of the suit, and besides, this suit was meant for

a boy who needed padding to make him look big and strong, which obviously Wally doesn't need. He suggests a normal suit, which all of Wally's classmates are now wearing. Wally takes it. The night of the dance, the guys show up in normal suits too, making excuses, and Wally thanks his parents, saying he would have felt like a "creep" wearing the plaid suit. Beaver says he still likes the plaid better, since it had more pockets.

THE SHAVE

Wally is upset because the other guys claim they're shaving veterans and he hasn't even thought about starting. Before supper Wally practices with Ward's razor. He admires his smooth shave until Beaver points out there's no blade in the razor. With blade in place his hand shakes so that Wally nicks himself. Seeing his adhesive-spotted face, Ward lectures Wally on how beards get stiffer when you shave, which means Wally will have to shave all the time if he keeps it up. He thinks this will discourage Wally, but it only inspires him to shave every day. A week later Ward storms into the boys' bathroom looking for his razor and bawls out Wally in front of Eddie, saying he shouldn't be shaving until he has a beard. The next day, thanks to Eddie's big mouth, Wally gets called "baby-face" by the guys. When Beaver tells Ward what happened, Ward realizes how thoughtless he was in bawling out Wally. He learns that the next day Wally will be getting his hair cut at the same time as several of the fellas and calls the barber ahead of time. When Wally gets into the chair the barber tells him he needs a shave—and gives him the works, much to his friends' envy. Wally thanks Ward and Ward reminds him that shaving is "just an *outward* sign of being a man."

THE VISITING AUNT

Tooey has free passes for the last day of the carnival and the boys make plans for Ward to drive the guys over that afternoon. Then June tells them that Aunt Martha has just called. She is driving through town with her friend, Mrs. Hathaway, and June has invited them to lunch and promised the boys would be there to greet her. The boys get into their aunt-greeting finery but worry that Aunt Martha's visit will spoil their carnival junket. The boys are polite to the ladies but clearly insincere and keep nervous eyes on the clock. In the middle of lunch Wally's friends come by. Wally asks them to wait, and as lunch drags on, has to tell them to leave for the carnival on their own. At two o'clock the women finally leave. Ward offers to drive the boys to the carnival, but they are sulking and refuse to go. Ward reminds them that the Cleavers are the only family their Aunt Martha has and that they have made their mother very unhappy by the way they acted. The boys apologize to June. The whole family then decides to spend the evening at the carnival.

THE TOOTH

While Beaver's awaiting the results of his oral X rays, Larry frightens him by describing the dentist's big drill that makes

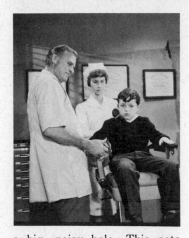

a big, noisy hole. This sets Beaver's imagination on edge and on the way home he watches a pneumatic street drill and becomes terrified. Beaver awaits the call from the dentist's office and tries telling the nurse the Cleavers moved to Alaska. Upset by the Beaver's behavior, June asks Ward to take him to the dentist the next day. In the office Fred Rutherford is waiting with Violet. As usual, Fred brags about his child, extolling his little trooper's courage. Ward firmly tells Beaver he is expecting him to be a good soldier and not let his father down. Trying to be brave, Beaver enters the inner office—and is soon heard screaming, before he even gets in the chair. The dentist promises Beaver he will give him every toy in his toy box if his drilling hurts. It doesn't hurt. The dentist and Beaver thank each other for their mutual trust and Beaver gets some toy sol-

diers anyway. At home Ward realizes he expected too much of Beaver and should have offered reassurance instead of pressure. He apologizes, and Beaver replies that his father would have to do a lot worse than that before he would stop liking him.

BEAVER'S RING

Beaver is presented with a surprise from his Aunt Martha, a family heirloom ring. Ward makes him promise not to wear it to school where he might lose it. And Beaver doesn't wear it exactly; he ties it to a string that he wraps around his belt loop and whisks past Ward the next morning. As he proudly shows off the ring, Judy Hensler challenges Beaver—it couldn't be his ring; otherwise, he would be wearing it. To prove it is his, Beaver jams the ring onto his finger, where it remains stuck. Miss Landers sends him to the school nurse, but no simple procedures will pry the ring loose. June arrives with Wally and is told that the only solution is to cut it off. Beaver is terrified, because he interprets this to mean it's his *finger* rather than the ring that will receive radical surgery. When Wally corrects him, Beaver's relieved, until he considers the yelling that will ensue, which leads him to believe he'd be better off with the amputation. The ring is cut, and

Beaver gets a lecture from Ward and an assignment to write an apology to Aunt Martha. The letter turns out to be so painful that Ward feels it's punishment enough and rips up the letter. He even tells Beaver there might be a way to get the ring fixed.

BEAVER GETS ADOPTED

Wally wins a trophy in the discus throw at the school Field Day and Beaver is a little jealous. Wally warns Beaver not to touch any of his stuff before he leaves for Chester's. While Larry's over, Beaver examines the trophy, and even though they put it back carefully, it topples from the dresser and breaks. They try to glue the pieces back together, unsuccessfully. As he feared, the family thinks Beaver broke the trophy on purpose. Beaver tries to explain, but Ward and June scold him, leaving him feeling his family doesn't love him anymore. Ward adds that if Beaver thinks he can improve on his parents, he's welcome to try. So Beaver heads for the Margaret Manning Adoption Society, where he is interviewed by Mrs. Brady, and states he wants new parents—and *soon*, because he's hungry. Mrs. Brady is very understanding, says she has the perfect parents in mind for him, and goes to make a phone call. As he waits, Beaver begins to worry that he won't like his new

parents. Just then the door opens and a very relieved Ward and June walk in. Mrs. Brady asks Beaver what he thinks. He answers, "I'll take them."

EDDIE'S GIRL

Eddie brags to Wally that he has a girl, Caroline Cunningham, and wants Wally to go with him to her house. When they get there, Caroline warms up to Wally and almost ignores Eddie. That evening Caroline calls Wally and invites him to the club dance. Wally thinks she's looking for Eddie and hangs up, but Mrs. Cunningham calls June, who accepts for Wally, even though, as Ward points out to her, she should have consulted her son first. When Wally finds out what his mother has done, he angrily tells her she's ruining his life by dating him up with Eddie's girl, and he refuses to go. Eddie comes over and complains of a sore throat to Wally, then asks him to do a favor and take Caroline to the dance. Wally agrees. Later, Eddie confesses to Beaver that he never had a sore throat. He found out Caroline had asked Wally to the dance and knew, since he was his best friend, Wally wouldn't take her, but since he had only made it up about Caroline being his girl, and Wally was a pretty good guy, he pretended to be sick so Wally would feel free to take her. Beaver's not sure, but he thinks it sounds like Eddie actually did something nice for a change.

THE PRICE OF FAME

Larry cautions Beaver about Mrs. Rayburn's automatic spanking machine she keeps in her office. Beaver stays behind one afternoon to check out her office, where he satisfies himself there is no such machine, but ends up getting locked in the principal's office by the janitor. His only escape source is the lever of a fire alarm. He is quite excited about riding home in a fire engine until Ward lectures him about the expense to the city of his foolishness and about how conspicuous he made himself and the family. Later in the week Beaver is looking for four-leaf clovers in the park and manages to get his head stuck between the bars of the park fence. He nixes Wally's suggestion of calling the police or fire department, so Wally goes to get Ward. He tells Ward to go easy on Beaver because Beaver has told him he would rather starve to death than let his father know what a mess he's in after the escapade in the principal's office. With the park gardener's help Ward gets Beaver's head out. Ward once more tells Beaver he wants him always to feel that his parents are the first ones to come to in time of trouble. Beaver replies that he will probably be using them for a lot of things while he's growing up.

SCHOOL PLAY

The challenging role of the yellow canary in the third grade's upcoming musical will be played by Beaver. Judy teases him, saying he won't keep the part

because he can't remember lines. To Ward's surprise, Beaver is excited by his costume and the role. His teachers are less than pleased by his thespian ability; however, they allow him to stick with the part. The night of the show, Ward and Wally talk so much about ways Beaver could goof up on stage that he works up a mean case of stage fright. As the curtain rises on the class's sketch, it appears as if Beaver's nervousness has flown, for the "canary" gives a fine performance, flitting gracefully from flower to flower. Backstage, June gives her boy canary a big hug, and the family heaps praise upon him until the headpiece is removed and they see Whitey inside. It seems Miss Landers switched the boys' parts so that Beaver was a mushroom that just squatted on the side of the stage. Beaver is unhappy about losing his big

part, but after a consoling soda with his parents, he concludes, "I guess a guy oughta do what he can do—not what other guys can do," to which Ward adds, "In life, it just doesn't work when a mushroom tries to fly."

THE BOAT BUILDERS

Wally, Tooey, and Chester build a makeshift boat out of barrel staves, boards, oilcloth tablecloths, and a water bucket for the seat. Ward warns the boys not to do anything reckless, but they head for Miller's Pond. Chester wins the chance to be the first boatman, but they soon realize that only Beaver can fit. When they shove Beaver off in the boat, he capsizes. After they rescue him they bundle him in a blanket and rush back to the garage, where they try to think of a plan to get him inside the house without his parents find-

ing out what happened. Tooey gets the bright idea of going to his house to telephone June as a distraction, and it's good enough to get the boys inside—with a little help from turning on the garbage disposal to get Ward and June into the kitchen. Wally hangs Beaver's wet clothes and boots over the furnace vent pipes to dry. During lunch Ward smells smoke and discovers the clothes. Beaver admits he fell out of the boat. After sending them to their room, Ward gives them a serious talk about what the tragic consequences might have been and grounds the boys for the weekend.

THE HAPPY WEEKEND

Ward comes home with cabin reservations at Shadow Lake for a weekend family fishing trip. He is first bewildered and then angered over the boys' disappointment that the trip will mean they'll miss seeing *Jungle Fever* at the movies. Ward denounces comic books, movies, and ready-made entertainment and declares the boys will have a wonderful rustic weekend like he used to enjoy. Not quite in the spirit of things, the boys forgo the cabin for the nearby town and have breakfast at the drugstore. Ward takes them out on the lake and they catch several fish but are embarrassed to discover they have to pay for each fish because the lodge stocks the pond for the convenience of its guests. That evening the boys take off with fieldglasses and Ward thinks they must be looking for deer, but finds them looking down at the nearby drive-in theater, which is playing *Jungle Fever*. He gives up and has June pack up the next morning, stating that you "can't wrap up your own childhood in a package and hand it over to your kids." Then Wally and Beaver burst into the cabin, all excited. They have found some logs and are going to tie them together and make a raft and take a picnic lunch to an island in the lake, pretending they're pirates. Ward is pleased.

BEAVER PLAYS HOOKY

By the time they finish watching a mechanical street digger and having their books and lunch boxes run over by a truck, Larry and Beaver are late for school for the third time in a week.

They're afraid Miss Landers and the principal will "kill" them so they decide to hide, and find a big billboard where they hole up. They get hungry and go to the supermarket, hoping for free samples. They enter a big tent where a televised promotion for Chocolate Rockets is about to start with TV star Marshal Moran. Wally, who is home sick, is amused when he sees the marshal interview Beaver and Larry, whose excuse for not being in school is that their classroom is flooded. June is upset at seeing Beaver on TV but she's waiting for the doctor to call on Wally and so she phones Ward at the office and sends him to retrieve the boys. He finds them and drops Beaver off at school, instructing him to speak to his teacher. School is over when Beaver approaches Miss Landers's desk. He tells his story and apologizes and she explains the importance of attending school each day. Beaver absorbs the message and then thanks her for not "killing" him.

THE GARAGE PAINTERS

It's raining and the television is broken so Ward suggests the boys read a good book. He selects *The Adventures of Tom Sawyer,* which he tells them is fun to read, and that when he was young, he used to do some of the same things Tom did.

When Ward is called to a Saturday meeting just as he is getting set to paint the garage door, the boys ask permission to do the paint job for him just like Tom. Their hopes of their friends actually paying them to paint soon turn out to be just book fantasies, however, as neither Lumpy nor Larry will take the brush bait. The only boy who's interested is little Benjie Bellamy, who ends up pouring a can of paint down his front. Mrs. Bellamy is horrified, blaming Beaver and Wally for painting her boy. Sent to their room, the boys wish their father had grown up on another book than *Tom Sawyer.* Ward comes home and calls Benjie's mother to apologize. He points out to the boys that Tom Sawyer's world was less complicated than theirs. Beaver thinks it sure must have been easier being a kid in those days.

BEAVER'S PIGEONS

Beaver, Larry, and Whitey have formed a pigeon club with the purchase of two fifty-cent pigeons apiece. Beaver has two females picked out and has named them Miss Landers and Miss Canfield after two of the most important women in his life. However, when Ward brings the pigeons home from the pet store, June tells him that Beaver has come down with chicken pox, and since Wally and Ward have never had the disease, they are barred from contact with Beaver. Wally is assigned to care for the pigeons in the garage. Larry asks to board his pigeons with Beaver's while he's away for the weekend, and Wally agrees, even though Larry's look a little mangy. It turns out they have lice, and Ward has to take the pigeons to be sprayed. The next morning Wally reports that a cat must have knocked over the pigeon cage and eaten two of the birds—and as luck would have it, it's Beaver's who have "conked out." Beaver takes their demise philosophically and watches from the window gratefully as his fellow members of the pigeon club give his birds a proper burial. The next day Ward asks if Beaver wants something new from the pet store, like a couple of pigeons perhaps. Beaver replies, "No more pigeons! Not for a while, anyways."

WALLY'S PUG NOSE

All is going smoothly during Wally's first conversation with Gloria, a pretty new girl in school, until she says she didn't realize he had a pug nose. Desperate for a more Roman profile, Wally sends for a nose harness, which is nothing more than a ridiculous-looking metal cup and a strap. Ward tries to find a way to build Wally's confidence in his appearance and tells him of his own distress as a boy when he was called "elephant ears" until he looked in his history books and saw all the famous men with big ears. Instead of feeling relief, Wally goes to bed that night with nose harness in place *and* his ears taped down. The next day, Wally tries to hide from Gloria, but she asks him to be her escort to an upcoming gym dance. He asks why she chose him, and she says maybe it was his cute pug nose. For the first time in days, he's happy, as he realizes he badly misinterpreted her first nose comment. Ward and June are pleased to see the nose guard in the waste basket and explain to Beaver that teenagers frequently feel the whole world is looking at them and forget that people judge them by their actions, not their looks.

THE HAUNTED HOUSE

Larry and Beaver are certain that they have the only school with a genuine haunted house en route. As they pass the old, empty Cooper place they see a newly returned Miss Cooper come out carrying a broom, wearing an old smock, her hair tied in a bandanna. The boys

run home convinced they've seen a witch. Ward thinks Beaver will be eager to earn the money when Miss Cooper happens to arrange with June for Beaver to walk her dog, but when he learns whose dog it is, he refuses. June has committed him, however, so he has to go. Beaver enters the foreboding house shaking in his shoes at every step and odd sound. When he sees his own reflection in a clouded mirror he runs out of the house before Miss Cooper appears. A puzzled Miss Coop-

er stops by the Cleavers' and Wally tells Ward that Beaver imagines her to be a witch, so Ward tries to explain the situation to Miss Cooper. When she leaves, Ward calls Beaver downstairs and tells him Miss Cooper is a very pleasant lady. Beaver retorts that she probably only changes into that disguise for grown-ups. By the next day Beaver has met Miss Cooper in the pet store and discovered for himself that she is nice, and he is now happily taking care of her dog.

WALLY'S HAIRCOMB

June is shocked; she feels it looks like an oil mop and makes Wally seem like a gigolo, a tango dancer, and a gangster. It's the absolute latest haircut, a wild "do" inspired by Eddie: hair combed up at the sides, flat on top, with crossed ducktails in back and all smothered in grease. Ward is convinced it's just a passing fad, but his subtle plea for individuality leaves Wally concluding it's for the "squares." Wally then decides to skip the swim-team tryouts, since Eddie says they'll make him cut his hair. June even talks to Wally's principal, but he tells her that as long as the students' hair is neat and clean, it would be wrong for the school to stifle their self-expression by outlawing any style of grooming. Fred Rutherford calls to complain that

his "strapping boy came home looking like a rather ugly girl," because Lumpy's aping Wally, but the last straw comes when Beaver adopts Wally's haircomb. June demands Wally wash and comb out his hair, because he has been embarrassing her. She reminds Wally of how awful he felt to be seen with Beaver when he took it into his head to wear one of her old hats to Sunday school. Wally clearly remembers and says it's too bad Eddie isn't lucky enough to have parents who yell at him.

BEAVER AND GILBERT

According to Larry and Whitey, Gilbert Bates, the new boy who moved in across the street, is a "dumb kid" because he carries a briefcase to school. Ward sends Beaver over to introduce himself to Gilbert nonetheless. That evening Beaver returns home filled with stories about Gilbert's father being in the FBI, his brother being a famous ball-player, and Gilbert being the youngest Eagle Scout in America. Wally tells Beaver Gilbert is just making up stories, but Beaver is loyal to his new friend. Beaver refuses to go to the movies with Larry and Whitey because he is waiting for Gilbert. Gilbert stands up Beaver and goes to the movies with Larry and Whitey. When they're all playing ball, Ward sends Beaver outside to join in and act as if nothing had happened. Reluctantly Beaver tries, but soon comes back crying because he feels the boys have ganged up on him. Ward sends him back out to solve his own crisis, and Beaver calls Gilbert over to his lawn, where he tackles him and starts pounding away. Ward separates the boys and sends them home as Mr. Bates appears. He explains to Ward that he's a musician and has had to move around a great deal. Since his son can't make a hero out of a flute player, Gilbert tells exaggerated stories to interest the other boys. Beaver now sees him in a more understanding light.

THE BUS RIDE

Beaver gets an invitation to spend the weekend with a former schoolmate, Billy Payton, who now lives about ninety miles away in Crystal Falls. Ward and June have a previous commitment so Wally offers to escort Beaver on the bus, drop him off in Crystal Falls, and return home. Ward decides to trust Wally. When the bus stops at Elmhurst along the way, the boys get off for refreshments. Beaver insists on getting some comic books while Wally returns to the bus to wait for him. In confusion Beaver asks for directions to the bus to Mayfield instead of Crystal Falls and doesn't realize he's on his way back home until the bus is rolling. At Crystal Falls Wally explains things to the Paytons. They call the Cleaver house, where Beaver answers, having arrived safely, via taxi from the station. Mr. Payton agrees to drive Wally back to Mayfield and pick up Beaver. When June and Ward finally arrive home, they praise Wally for responsibly taking care of Beaver. With a guilty conscience Wally pulls Ward aside to tell him the full story, saying he didn't want to embarrass his father in front of June. Ward appreciates that and they agree they will keep this to themselves for the time being. The next day Beaver agrees, saying the secret's okay with him, as long as he's not in trouble.

A HORSE NAMED NICK

Wally and Beaver get work doing chores at the carnival. Ward cautions them that carnivals have a long history of skipping town without paying wages. The boys come home on the last night announcing they've gotten something even better than the twenty dollars they're owed: the carnival man gave them Nick, a tired old circus horse, for payment. Ward says they can't keep a horse and a Board of Health man sent around by a neighbor confirms that. An ad is placed and a Mr. Johnson arranges to buy Nick. When the boys find he's from a rendering plant, they demand their horse back. In desperation Ward calls Billy Payton's father in Crystal Falls. He agrees to board Nick for ten dollars a month. Without telling the boys about the money arrangement, Ward and June tell them Nick is going to the Payton farm and Mr. Payton will let them come to visit Nick anytime they want. Beaver even gets to call Nick on the phone and talk to him through Billy, who has been talking to horses all his life and will translate Beaver to Nick.

BEAVER SAYS GOOD-BYE

Ward makes an offer on a house in Madison, so Beaver tells his classmates that he's going to move. Miss Landers makes the class tell Beaver they're going to miss him—even Judy. The next morning Ward gets the disappointing news that another offer was accepted for the Madison house. Beaver doesn't know how to break the news in school.

Before he can do anything about it, his class surprises him with a party and farewell gifts. Embarrassed, Beaver takes the presents home without saying anything. Larry drops by the house to look at the swing Beaver had promised him once he moves. Ward tells Larry they're not moving and Larry leaves convinced that Beaver made up the story just to get the presents. Ward asks why he let his class give him a farewell party. Beaver answers that he would have felt dumb because everyone was singing and having fun and he didn't want to spoil it for them. Beaver promises to return the presents. The next day "Beaver Is a Crook" is written on the blackboard and Judy says Miss Landers should expel him. Instead Miss Landers tells the class Beaver brought all of his presents unopened to the principal's office, where anyone who wishes can reclaim them. No one volunteers.

BEAVER'S NEWSPAPER

Beaver and Wally are cleaning out the garage and find the old typewriter Ward had given to Wally, which had stopped working when Wally dropped it. Beaver and Larry take it to Gus, who fixes it, and the boys decide to type out a daily newspaper, *The Maple Drive News*. Wally now wants his working machine back but Ward says they must share it. The next day Wally is still angry at Beaver but June asks him to try to get along with his brother to make her happy. He finds Beaver laboriously typing his paper with all the carbons in backward and takes over at the typewriter. He tells Beaver he's still mad at him but doesn't want people reading the paper to think he has "a little goof" for a brother. The boys distribute all twenty-four copies except for two that fell in a puddle, and Beaver has already gathered news and ads for the next edition. Wally can't help him the next day because he has a baseball game, so June types the paper. She tells Beaver she realizes she was wrong to force the boys to work together, since Wally is growing up and has other interests. Ward tells Beaver that even June will not be able to help him as much as she wants because she has other duties around the house. Beaver understands the newspaper may be too big a job but doesn't want to be a quitter. Ward solves the problem by typing "Final Edition" at the top of Beaver's paper.

BEAVER'S SWEATER

At dinner Beaver says he wants an "Eskimo" sweater he and Larry admire in a store window, but Ward says he shouldn't spend his savings on a whim. June gets Ward to change his mind and Beaver gets the sweater. The next day, he no sooner places his sweater in his locker than he sees Judy wearing the identical sweater. Larry teases him that he's bought a girl's sweater. "Yeah," answers Beaver, "and with my own money, too." Beaver realizes his parents would yell at him after he spent the money on the sweater if he didn't wear it, so he wears it over another sweater so he can take it off and hide it once he leaves the house. On Saturday he comes home from the mov-

ies without the sweater and tells his parents some boys took it from him. The theater manager calls and says he found the sweater stuffed behind the candy machine. Beaver tells them the truth. June reasons he made a mistake but that it would have taken more maturity than they should expect for him to admit it to them. They tell him they will give his sweater away to someone who can get some use out of it. When Beaver asks why they let him·go ahead and buy the sweater if they knew it was wrong, Ward says that "often parents love their children so much that, to make them happy, they sometimes let them do the wrong thing."

FRIENDSHIP

Beaver and Larry have a fight and Beaver claims he never wants to see Larry again. Ward tells him the story of the friendship between Damon and Pythias and how they were willing to die for each other. At school the next day Beaver tells Larry the story and says that's the sort of friends they should be. They take an oath that Larry will be Pythias and Beaver will be Damon and they will be friends forever. Larry seizes the opportunity to cement the pact by insisting Beaver give him his homework, which he forgot to do. After hesitating, Beaver agrees. Miss Landers collects the homework and Beaver tells her he did his but won't tell her what happened to it, "even if you kill me." Beaver takes home a note and tells Ward it all happened because of the Damon-and-Pythias story. Ward points out that Larry apparently didn't understand the story—and Beaver comes to the conclusion that Larry is a "crummy Pythias." The next day as the children are being dismissed for recess, except for Beaver, Larry puts up his hand and confesses to Miss Landers. Beaver and Larry become friends again and, arms around one another, they walk out of the classroom.

THE COOKIE FUND

The class's new co-chairboys of the Cookie Fund, Beaver and Larry, are putting the goods away on a closet shelf when an older student, Roger Delacy, gives them a hand. The next day, Roger comes by again, only this time he asks the boys for three dollars for food for his starving little sister until his father's paycheck comes through. The cookie monitors swallow every bit of his tale and hand over part of the fund. On the following day, the boys try to collect, and Roger not only denies ever borrowing the money, he tells them he'll get his gang to "fix" them if they don't stop bothering him. Mr. Preston, the cookie-company representative, comes to settle up the boys' account and tells them theirs is the wildest excuse he's ever heard. He does give them until the next day to replace the money without reporting their shortfall. They get the money from their parents. The boys tell their trials to Miss Landers and suggest they resign their responsibilities and give them over to Judy, someone who would never be swayed to give money to a hungry child. Miss Landers, however, tells them that they made a mistake trusting someone, but she won't make the mistake of not trusting them.

DANCE CONTEST

Mary Ellen Rogers, who has blossomed into quite a fetching lass while away at school, invites Wally to be her escort at the Mayfield Cotillion. She has even entered them in the cha-cha contest, although Wally is too embarrassed to tell her he doesn't know how to cha-cha.

He buys an instruction record, and Beaver catches him practicing with a canoe paddle for a partner. Wally gets so angry at Beaver, when he walks in on him, and at Larry, mimicking his "choo-choo," he breaks the record and tells Ward and June he's not going to the dance. Ward learns the cause of his son's distress and calls a professional instructor to arrange a cha-cha crash course. The night of the dance, Ward and June anxiously await their terpsichorean's return. They are pleased to hear he has won honorary mention until he informs them that everyone who didn't win first or second prize got similar honors. Ward reminds Wally that while it may be awkward to say you can't do something, it's a lot worse when you say you can and someone finds out you can't, adding, "Just be grateful you learned this on something as harmless as the cha-cha."

FORGOTTEN PARTY

Beaver is so busy shooting pictures with his new camera, he forgets all about his former schoolmate, David Manning, calling to tell him he's the only friend from his old school invited to David's birthday party on Saturday. On Saturday, Beaver is off watching a road get tarred when Mrs. Manning calls wondering why Beaver hasn't come to the party. The search

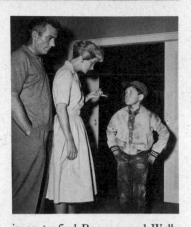

is on to find Beaver, and Wally brings him in covered with tar from having slipped in the new road. Ward takes Beaver to bathe and dress while June rushes off to the toy store to buy a present. Beaver is truly bewildered by the fuss but is advised by Wally to keep his mouth shut. Beaver is miserable when he sees the present June bought, a plastic float with a horse's head, which he says is a "baby present." He's sent on his way. That night June is surprised when Mrs. Manning calls to thank them profusely for David's gift, which is one of the nicest he ever received. Ward calls Beaver downstairs and he explains that he gave David the new camera for which he had saved so long and bought for himself. David had told his new friends that Beaver was his great pal, so Beaver didn't want to mess him up by giving him a baby toy. Ward and June apologize for misjudging him.

BEAVER THE ATHLETE

Ward is upset with Beaver's report-card D in physical education. He tries to instill the competitive spirit in his son. At school the coach begins training for the annual boys-versus-girls baseball game. Beaver steps up for batting practice and swings so badly he decides to clown around. Everyone is amused by his antics except Judy. A few days later the boys' team is fed up with his clowning because they fear Beaver will lose the game, but he still claims that "anyone can beat the girls"— until Judy steps up to the plate and smacks a home run. That night the family is worried when Beaver is late for dinner. Wally and Ward finally find him practicing his batting against the playground screen. A shivering Beaver tells Ward that he wasn't doing it because Ward accused him of a lack of competitive spirit but because of Judy's home run, saying "it's only fun doing stuff wrong if the guys know you can do it right." At the big game against the girls, Beaver is the star because he gets the most hits with men on base and Judy only hits a solo home run. When Beaver worries that he might not be able to match these feats during the next game, Ward reminds him that even Ted Williams strikes out sometimes.

FOUND MONEY

Beaver is out of spending money, so Larry invites him to be his guest at the carnival. However, Mrs. Mondello denies Larry his allowance for charging candy and sodas at the drugstore. His mother does absentmindedly say before leaving that Larry can go to the carnival if he *finds* money, giving him an idea. He takes his mother's "pin money" from her sewing basket and throws it out the window. When Beaver arrives they pick up the change, which Larry tells him was dropped from a passing airplane. Mrs. Mondello calls June upon returning home, saying she's afraid Larry has stolen her money. June is certain Beaver wouldn't have anything to do with taking it, but she tells Mrs. Mondello to do nothing about it until Ward returns home. Beaver comes back from the carnival all smiles and laden with prizes. He sticks to his story about the money falling out of an airplane, as does Larry when Mrs. Mondello brings him over for Ward to get the truth out of him. Ward tells Larry that Beaver is being punished for lying. Larry speaks up, saying Beaver really believes the airplane story, and asks Ward not to blame Beaver because "when we were picking the money up, I almost believed I was finding it myself."

MOST INTERESTING CHARACTER

Beaver's class is assigned a hundred-word composition on the subject of "The Most Interesting Character I Have Known." Judy Hensler says she's going to write about her father, who, she claims, once shot fifty wild elephants in Africa. That afternoon Ward hears Beaver tell Wally how dumb Judy is for writing about her father. Wally notices Ward's disappointment, and after Ward leaves, he suggests that Beaver write about his father. Ward is delighted with Beaver's choice. Beaver tries unsuccessfully to gather interesting things about Ward by observation, and even gets help from Wally to liven up his piece, but is still not satisfied. The next afternoon Beaver is still struggling with his assignment. June suggests he try writing what his father *means* to him, instead of trying to list interesting things Ward has done. At breakfast on Monday Ward asks to read Beaver's composition. It is simply wrought and expresses Beaver's love and respect for his father. Ward is deeply moved. That night Beaver reports that he got a B for his efforts and Judy had to stay after school for what she made up about her father. Just before they go to bed, Ward and June burst in to say that they have sold the house and they will be moving.

SCHOOL BUS

Soon after the family move into their new house, the school sends home the rules for riding the school bus. Within a week, another letter arrives saying that Beaver has been suspended from riding the bus for conduct unbecoming to the fourth grade. It seems somebody hit Beaver and Beaver hit him back, but only Beaver got caught. Ward and June order Beaver to write a letter of apology to the driver of the school bus. Beaver takes his best turn at a letter, but Wally tells him it's not good enough and helps him write a cute letter. It works—the driver calls to say Beaver can ride on the bus again. A few days later Judy gets suspended from the bus and seeks out Beaver to learn his secret for getting reinstated so quickly. Beaver lets Judy have a copy of his letter. Wally asks him why he helped out Judy, the meanest girl in his class. Beaver explains that now when she feels like being mean to him she'll remember that she did something nice for her. Judy is allowed back on the bus. As Beaver is dropped off, the guys call out their good-byes and Judy is back sticking out her tongue at him. Good Samaritan Beaver shrugs and goes into the house.

BEAVER'S TREE

Inspired by Miss Landers's moving recitation of a poem about trees, Beaver tells her about the tree his parents gave him for his birthday, which he planted in the side yard of their old home. Miss Landers asks if he's taking good care of it, and Beaver realizes he misses his tree and becomes determined to regain possession of it. He drags Larry and a red wagon to the old house, now owned by a Mr. Benner, digs up the tree, and brings it back to the new house. Mr. Benner gets in touch with Ward and reports the tree theft. Ward and June discover Beaver and Wally transporting the tree across the yard and send them to their room. Later, Beaver explains that he took the tree because it was a friend he loved and it was his tree to care for. June and Ward are understanding and Ward straightens things out with Mr. Benner.

WALLY'S PLAY

Wally is voted into the high school letterman club, "The Crusaders," and gets a part in their satire of a western play for their annual Follies. He is most embarrassed when he gets his costume and learns he is to play a dance-hall girl—in a dress! Ward suggests he get into the spirit of the satire and have fun with the role. Wally still hates the part so Ward suggests he take it up with the other performers and try to get one of them to switch with him. Wally pours it on thick to Eddie, who has a two-line, strictly masculine role. Soon the club president asks Wally to do a favor by switching parts with Eddie, who is now pleading for the role of the dance-hall girl. Wally readily complies. However, on show night, Eddie is a big hit and gets a lot of laughs for hamming it up in his dress, and Wally regrets not holding on to his old part. Ward points out that it wouldn't hurt Wally if he were just a little bit more like Eddie. June quickly adds that it certainly wouldn't hurt Eddie if he were a *lot* more like Wally.

BLIND-DATE COMMITTEE

Wally is appointed chairman of the blind-date committee for a Saturday-night dance, which, according to Beaver, means he has to get dates for "girls nobody wants to be seen with."

Beaver's prediction turns out to be true when Wally cannot get any of his friends to take Jill Bartlett and gets stuck with her himself. He's never seen Jill; she's "some new strain of girl," he learns from friends, not at all talkative. Eddie makes Wally more miserable when he describes Jill as a "gopher." The night of the dance, Ward tries to cheer up Wally by telling him about the college prom when he was stuck with a "wet blanket" and paid off his friends to dance with her. Armed with this ray of hope, Wally borrows a dollar from Beaver. After the dance Wally and Jill are having sodas and Jill reveals that she knows Wally has been buying her dancing partners all night. Although Wally denies this, she is grateful and did enjoy herself. Wally tells her that he doesn't see anything wrong with her and she says she wants to be popular but just doesn't have the knack for getting boys to talk about themselves. She does sincerely tell Wally that she would like *him* to talk about himself because he's one of the nicest boys she's ever met.

BEAVER'S FORTUNE

"Today is your lucky day," predicts Beaver's penny fortune, but it's only bad luck when he and Larry run into Sonny Courtwright, Larry's latest fifth-grade adversary. Larry issues a chal-

lenge to Sonny but passes the gauntlet to Beaver, figuring there's no reason for him to fight on Beaver's lucky day. Refusing to cower, Beaver agrees to fight Sonny, and they set up an afternoon match. All of Beaver's confidence is built on his fortune, but it collapses when Wally points out the pitfalls of counting on luck. As the hour of the showdown approaches, Beaver gamely marches off with his seconds. Wally lets the story of the bout slip out to June, who insists Beaver be saved. Ward sends Wally over but instructs him to use his judgment before interfering. Beaver, the battler, returns, announcing that Sonny never showed. Guiltily, Beaver admits that he was afraid. Ward says fear is not a bad emotion, because it keeps us from doing hazardous things. Larry later gets his just reward when he calls Sonny a coward and gets a big fat sock in the stomach.

BEAVER TAKES A WALK

Rescuing his pedometer from a box of junk, Ward presents it to the boys, bragging how, when he was their age, he used to walk over twenty miles a day. Beaver flips for the "real neat walking machine" and walks to school the next morning. While showing the pedometer to his friends, he tells them of his father's feats. Whitey doesn't believe him, so Beaver bets him that he will walk twenty miles himself, staking his new fielder's mitt against Whitey's three-cell flashlight. However, as dinner time approaches, Beaver is crushed to see he has only walked three miles "and a hunk." The next day, Beaver hands over his mitt but still defends his father. Ward finds Beaver sulking and tries to cheer him up by offering to play catch with Beaver's new glove. In anger, Beaver locks himself in the bathroom. After Wally fills him in, Ward confesses to Beaver that he exaggerated the distance he used to walk in a genuine effort to share his enthusiasm for the pedometer. Beaver understands, asking Ward not to stop telling stuff he used to do even if he does take some liberties. Ward buys Beaver a new glove, telling June, "It makes you feel good when your son backs you up with his favorite mitt."

BEAVER FINDS A WALLET

The Grant Avenue gutter yields a real find for Beaver, a wallet filled with the small fortune of $89 cash. Ever honest, he brings it to the police station, where a sergeant tells him that if the wallet is unclaimed after ten days Beaver can collect the money. Beaver makes at least one phone call per day to the station for the next nine days, dragging Wally and Larry into service when the sergeant begins to tire of his queries. He also draws up a long list of purchases, which includes hip boots for himself and silk pajamas for his entire family. On the tenth day the sergeant calls him to the station, but while Beaver is waiting, he meets a Miss Tomkins who turns out to be the lady who lost the wallet. She is grateful and promises to send him a nice present. Ward is impressed that, after four or five days, Beaver has still not given up hope of receiving her reward, and sure enough, the next day's mail brings a $16.95 radio "with a clock in its middle." June is not fooled, and gets Ward to admit that he bought it, since he felt it was a small price to pay to maintain Beaver's faith in human nature.

BEAVER TAKES A BATH

Wally volunteers to care for himself and the Beaver overnight when the woman who is supposed to watch them calls to cancel just as Ward and June are ready to leave. While he is massacring hamburgers for their dinner, he sends a reluctant Beaver to take his bath. When Beaver gets the dinner call, he forgets that he left the bathwater running until water starts leaking through the kitchen ceiling, having already seeped through the bathroom floor. They mop up the water and Wally uses a hair dryer on the ceiling water stain. Wally threatens to tell on Beaver until Beaver points out it will reflect poorly on Wally as a crummy baby-sitter. Wally agrees it will be for the best for them both to keep their mouths shut. "It always has," Beaver adds. After Ward and June return, there is a crash from the kitchen during lunch, which turns out to be plaster from the ceiling. The boys keep silent. That evening Ward thanks Wally for his excellent care of things while they were away and pays him the same amount he would have given the woman who was to watch them. With lights out but the money lying there, Wally can't sleep, and the boys decide they must tell Ward what happened.

BEAVER'S PRIZE

For leaving the cap off the bottle of ink Ward has spilled on his hand, Beaver is ordered to stay around the house on Saturday. Left alone, Beaver is reconciled to his sentence, but Larry's lure of a western and jungle film double feature proves irresistible. After the second feature the manager holds a prize drawing. Despite his efforts to hide, Beaver has the lucky ticket, and he steps up to the stage to claim a fancy racing bicycle with a "guaranteed leather seat." Beaver knows he cannot bring the bike home because it will signal his disobedience, so Larry suggests he can keep the bike until the next day, when Beaver can say he won it at the theater. Larry's mother quizzes him about his new bike and learns why he is keeping it for Beaver. She calls Ward, who is grateful and waits to see how Beaver will extricate himself from this latest ticklish situation. The next day, Beaver confesses, but surprises his parents by telling them that since he knew he couldn't keep a bike he won improperly, he left it on the steps of a church with a note attached asking that the bicycle be given away.

BORROWED BOAT

A very strained relationship develops between Beaver and Wally

when Wally arranges for Beaver to ride on the team bus to the varsity football game but Beaver turns him down because he's promised Larry he'll share a picnic at Friend's Lake. At the lake Beaver and Larry are offered the use of a rowboat by two older boys, who then leave, neglecting to inform them it is stolen. A police car arrives and Beaver and Larry are hauled off to the station house, where they are accused of breaking into the boathouse and taking the boat. Their explanation is given little credence. Larry is released to his mother's custody but everyone at the Cleaver home is at Wally's football game. Finally Beaver gets Wally on the phone and asks him to come and free him. Wally arrives and manages to name two older boys who fit Beaver's description of the real culprits, so Beaver is released. Wally agrees to say nothing to their parents. Later, Wally receives a call from the sergeant that the other boys were picked up and Beaver is cleared. Ward and June are very suspicious of Wally's side of the conversation and demand the truth. Beaver enters and explains. June is concerned that Beaver didn't come to them for help, but Ward says in this case it's better that the two brothers realized they had a stronger bond than any feud could destroy.

BEAVER'S LIBRARY BOOK

Ward lends Beaver his library card so he can borrow a copy of *Treasure Island* for a book report. It's a one-week loan with a nickel-per-day fine. Beaver loses the book after reading only thirty pages. He also manages to bury the overdue notices in his drawer until the "20 days—$1.00" fine has arrived and Eddie discovers his cache. Eddie paints a rather terrifying portrait of a library cop who is bound to come to the Cleaver house and haul Ward to the clink for not paying the fines on his card. Beaver seeks out the head librarian, Mr. Davenport, who assuages his fears about imprisonment but does insist the book must be replaced and suggests Beaver talk to his father. Ward is somewhat taken aback by Beaver's much-rehearsed formal apology: "I am truly sorry, Dad, I lost a library book on your card and made a fine and you can take it out of my generous allowance." Ward tells Beaver that he can't go through life doing things wrong and hoping they'll turn out right or telling elaborate lies to cover up the truth. The next day Beaver's library book is found hidden in Larry Mondello's locker and he returns it, even though it smells like a bologna sandwich.

BABY PICTURE

For a class project, Miss Landers asks each student to bring in a baby picture of himself to enter in a beauty contest. June sends a picture to school without showing Beaver; however, Wally sees the leftover pictures from which June made her choice and shows them to Beaver. He is horrified. The shots were snapped of Beaver lying naked on a white bearskin rug. Wally cautions him against complaining about his embarrassment to June, since she thinks the photos are cute. Beaver turns to Ward but is vague about his problem and so gets only vague advice. Early the next school day, Beaver tells the whole story to Miss Landers, who lets him off the hook by giving him back the unopened envelope containing the picture. Now Beaver must get a second photo without offending June's feelings. Ward solves his predicament by cutting the photo down to just a head shot of Baby

Beaver. After the contest is judged, Beaver merrily announces that he lost. Ward tells Beaver that there was nothing wrong with the original picture, that, like beauty, ugliness or embarrassment is in the eye of the beholder.

TEACHER COMES TO DINNER

"She's the neatest teacher in the whole school," Beaver tells his family about Miss Landers. To do something nice for her, June invites her to dinner that night. In school Miss Landers takes Beaver by surprise by mentioning the invitation, but he is excited. He tells Larry in confidence, making him promise not to divulge the news to anyone, lest they accuse Beaver of being the teacher's pet. Beaver gets all spruced up for dinner and even leads Miss Landers by the arm out to the steak barbecue on the patio. All goes cordially until Beaver spies something in the tree overlooking the patio. It seems Larry hit on the money-making scheme of charging Gilbert and Whitey for the privilege of seeing a real-live teacher eating dinner. Miss Landers also spots the boys, and when the others have left the table, she calls them down from their spying post. The three intruders are scared when Ward returns, but Miss Landers is quite nice about the whole thing

and says they've only dropped in for a visit. She wisely realizes that children sometimes can't realize a teacher is also a "real" person, and that their embarrassment over the whole affair is punishment enough. Ward invites them all to stay for dessert.

JUNE'S BIRTHDAY

Shopping at only the finest emporiums for a gift for his mother's birthday, Beaver heads for the variety store where his design consultant, Larry, picks out an atrocious print blouse that the shameless saleslady promotes as the "exquisite La Parisienne Model," complete with sixteen authentic Paris landmarks, including the Eiffel Tower and the repeated phrase "Oooh, la, la." When she opens the gift, June is stunned by the gaudy blouse but, in her sweet way, tells Beaver it is beautiful. He asks her to wear it to the Mothers' Club tea the following day. June is trapped. She puts on the blouse

until Beaver leaves for school and then changes before she goes to the meeting. June didn't count on Beaver's class making a special appearance at the tea to sing their rendition of "Old Macdonald." Beaver is terribly hurt to see that his mother is not wearing her new blouse. June explains her "double cross" by admitting that while it was wrong to tell him she would wear the blouse and not do so, there are times when it is impossible to be honest without hurting someone's feelings. Beaver forgives her, for he now sees she acted out of motherly kindness.

PET FAIR

On the day their class is to report what pets they will be bringing to the upcoming "pet fair," Beaver and Larry stop at the pet store where they spy Sergeant Burke, an old parrot that served in the Rainbow Division in World War I and has a fifty-word vocabulary and the ability to sing "Over There." In class, Beaver is upset to be the only kid without a pet, and so he claims he will bring in his parrot. Everyone is impressed, but Beaver is *de*pressed when he discovers the parrot costs two hundred dollars. Ward brings home a hamster to fill the pet bill, but Beaver feels his father has only played a "dirty trick." Wally tells Ward about Beaver's untruth, but Ward sees no way to help out his son this time. June reveals how she was once deeply hurt when her mother showed her no understanding when she was caught in a stretch of the truth. Touched by her story, Ward manages to rent Sergeant Burke for the fair. The bird is a sensation and wins first prize. When the others are dismissed, Beaver approaches Miss Landers and confesses his deception. That night, Beaver asks Ward why he helped him cover up his lie. Ward acknowledges that sometimes parents love their children so much they'll do almost anything to protect them, even if it means making some mistakes.

WALLY'S ELECTION

Against his wishes, Wally is nominated for sophomore class president, running against Lumpy, among others. Irritated by Wally's lack of "gumption," Ward throws down a challenge to his son: "Are you going to try for this thing and be proud of yourself on election day? Or are you going to slouch around and be a nothing?" Ward advises Wally to wade into the campaign aggressively, introducing himself to students he doesn't know. Completely out of character, Wally wades into the glad-handing like a seasoned politician. He's so slick that his friends, who always saw him as so "natural," begin to resent him for trying to be some big-time, "swingin' " operator. Even Ward fears he might have gone too far, so he's not surprised when Wally loses the election, as he and Lumpy are both beaten by a candidate nicknamed "the Horse." Ward apologizes to Wally for his advice giving, noting that sometimes parents "go off the deep end" when they grow older and realize that the dreams and ambitions they had for themselves are never going to come true and so dream through their children instead. Wally may have lost the election, but he wins a better understanding of parents.

SCHOOL SWEATER

A query from Ward as to why Wally is not wearing his high school letterman's sweater brings the response that it's "sorta at school." His parents are puzzled and tell him to bring it home that evening. Actually, a flirtatious girl, Frances, has "borrowed" the sweater from Wally after a basketball game. Eddie urges Wally to go up to her and reclaim the sweater, but Frances exercises her giggly female charm and postpones the return until the following Monday. That night, Ward and June are still concerned about the whereabouts of the sweater, and they're really shocked when, at the drugstore, they see it wrapped around Frances, who is bragging to her girlfriends about how she has Wally tied up. Ward takes Wally aside and informs him that he knows about Frances. Wally storms over to Frances's house and in terse, no-nonsense terms demands his sweater. He also warns her to watch what she says about him in drugstores. The sweater smells kind of "girly," but Wally figures a few days in his gym locker will wipe that out. Ward tells him that he has learned a valuable lesson. "Women never want a sweater just because they're cold."

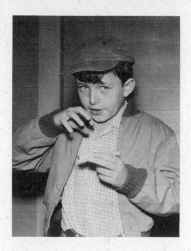

BEAVER, THE MAGICIAN

Aspiring prestidigitators Beaver and Larry quickly realize their best audience is little Benjie Bellamy, so they work out a routine: Larry holds a blanket in front of Beaver, who places a rock on the ground, then crawls into a wooden box. When Larry drops the blanket, they tell Benjie that Beaver has been turned into the rock—and they have him absolutely convinced. So convinced that when Larry is called home before he can change the rock back to Beaver, Benjie carries the rock away in his wagon, certain that it's Beaver. He becomes increasingly worried about Beaver the rock, and Mrs. Bellamy brings him over to see that Beaver is all right, but Beaver is at his Aunt Martha's. No amount of adult reasoning will comfort Benjie, nor does speaking to Beaver on the phone, because he thinks Beaver is talking from heaven. Wally repeats the trick with Larry before Benjie's eyes, but this only makes Benjie more adamant that Wally change Beaver back. Finally, Beaver must be brought home early to ease Benjie's troubled young mind. Beaver realizes that "if you've been a'scared yourself, you shouldn't go around being a scarer of other kids."

BEAVER MAKES A LOAN

Ward expects seventy-five cents' change back from Beaver's notebook money, but Beaver lends a quarter to Larry who manages to get the rest of Ward's dollar confiscated by the storekeeper, to whom he's in debt. So Beaver can learn not to let people take advantage of him, Ward holds back his movie money, advising him to get Larry to settle up if he wants to go to the show. Larry calls Beaver to tell him he's bringing over *his* movie money to settle up, but along the way he is persuaded by Gilbert and Whitey to forget about Beaver and go along with them to see *The Iron Fiend*. Afterward, in the drugstore, a stoodup Beaver finds Larry drinking a soda and happily reviewing with Gilbert and Whitey the highlights of the monster crunching up people in the neat movie. Larry won't accept Beaver's challenge to fight, so Beaver calls him a "rat" and vows never

to speak to him. The feud is serious for a while until Larry guiltily makes a peace offering to Beaver of his cherished goods, things he won't need since he's planning to run away to the Foreign Legion and get himself shot. Won back over by Larry's show of self-sacrifice, Beaver relents. The legion's loss is friendship's gain.

TIRE TROUBLE

Beaver and Wally plan to go into the chinchilla business, so they decide to begin by building a cage for the furry creatures. When he arrives home from work, Ward is angered to find the garage a mess of lumber, nails, and tools. Ward orders them to have the garage in inspection shape the next day. Their school activities keep them from the cleanup, and Ward tells them that leaving the garage in such bad shape was a "stupid" thing to do. On Saturday, they turn to their task, and Beaver discovers that a nail-studded block of wood is stuck in Ward's tire. As he pulls it out, the tire goes sickeningly flat. Wally tries unsuccessfully to inflate it with a hand pump. Eddie suggests they remove the tire and roll it to the gas station, get it repaired, and then sneak it back on without their father's knowledge, which they do. Ward finds out when Eddie calls and asks how Wally made out with "that crazy flat tire," not realizing he's speaking to Ward. The boys tell Ward how bad they felt when he called them "stupid" the night before and so didn't want to get condemned again. Ward assures them he spoke in the heat of anger and will watch what he says in such circumstances in the future.

LARRY HIDES OUT

Mrs. Mondello catches Larry laughing over his sister's diary with Beaver, and she yells at him and sends Beaver home. Larry decides to run away to Mexico, then adjusts his exile sights to Beaver's house. A frantic Mrs. Mondello calls Ward, but Beaver is able to avoid telling his father that Larry is holed up in his bathtub. Beaver sneaks food up to the fugitive by asking permission to eat his dinner in his room to pretend he's ordering room service in a hotel. Wally agrees to help the boys raise Larry's suitcase from the bushes via the Cleavers' window and a rope. Just as Mrs. Mondello comes to call, hoping to get a lead on Larry, Ward spies Larry's luggage getting airlifted. He flushes Larry out of the tub and marches him down to his mother. Larry explains to his mother that he ran away because she bawled him out in front of his best friend. Acting as a peacemaker, Ward sympathizes with Larry but tells him

he should have thought about the anxiety he caused his mother. Larry apologizes, and they head home. For their role in the drama, Beaver and Wally are stuck with weed-pulling detail. They agree they should have gone to Ward and let him put runaway Larry on the right track right away.

WALLY'S TEST

Instead of horsing around with Eddie and Lumpy, Wally is forced by Ward to study for Mr. Gannon's History II midterm. His scholar pals feel they don't have to worry. Eddie is writing key dates and names on a paper towel they will plant in the bathroom, so all they have to do is get excused during the exam and clean up with all the answers. The morning of the mid-term, Wally's pen leaks, and while he washes the ink off his hands, he finds a towel that reads, "To thine own self be true—Polonius and Mr. Gannon." When Eddie and Lumpy pay their cramming visit to the bathroom, their answer towel is nowhere to be found. They begin to suspect Wally double-crossed them. Their suspicions are confirmed when the grades are posted and Wally's name is in the top group and theirs are below flunking depth. To fix Wally, Eddie sends an anonymous letter to Mr. Gannon, accusing Wally of getting his knowledge from the towel dispenser. Mr. Gannon assures Wally he knows who the real guilty party is, because the crib sheet and the letter are in Eddie's scrawl. Wally is furious, but Ward calms him down, so Eddie is not pulverized when he comes to apologize. Eddie tells his regained friend that he might even take a crack at the studying bit himself.

BEAVER AND ANDY

Beaver's newest friend is Andy, the garrulous old handyman Ward hires to paint the trim on the house. Ward and June choose not to tell the boys about Andy's drinking problem, which he insists he has licked, and they refer to it only as "Andy's trouble" and "you-know-what." But Andy has not overcome his need for liquor. While Beaver is left alone with him, Andy runs out of his own supply and tells Beaver he's a little shaky and needs a drink. He turns down water and Honolulu punch but brightens considerably when Beaver leaves him Ward's bottle of special brandy before going off to Larry's. Andy gets completely bombed and has to be driven home by Ward. He later calls to apologize for slipping back to his old ways. Beaver discovers what happened and reveals his innocent role in pushing Andy off the wagon. June and Ward are taken aback but realize that in trying to shield the boys, they have locked out knowledge they needed to cope properly with one of life's evils. As Wally states, "Somebody's got to tell a guy about all the bad junk in the world," and his parents say they hope they will always be the ones to do it. The next day, Andy tells Beaver he has taught him that an empty bottle and an empty life go pretty much together.

BEAVER'S DANCE

The Pink Room at the Mayfield Hotel is the site of a series of six dances conducted by Miss Prescott that are making Larry and Beaver miserable, since both their parents have enrolled them for a forced feeding of the social graces. Larry is prepared to make a break, having brought

along two baloney sandwiches, and convinces Beaver they should sit out the dance behind Anderson's barn. They encounter a young girl on horseback who offers to let them ride on her "Whiskers." Unable to pass up such an opportunity, the boys mount up for a long ride. They return from the "dance" rumpled, dirty, and smelling very "horsy." After 'fessing up, the equestrian schemer is deodorized by Wally and then censured by Ward for deliberately disobeying his parents. Beaver offers that the dancing was an awful experience for him. Ward counters that he and June will have to make many demands of Beaver that he will not like. But, he adds, in years to come, Beaver will be grateful to his parents and should trust them and carry on with as much grace as possible. Beaver and Larry agree that with only a lecture and an extra bath, they got a light sentence for ditching dancing class and that for their parents' sakes they will put up with the rest of the sessions.

THE HYPNOTIST

The Mad Hypnotist is the "educational," "scientific" movie Beaver and Larry have most recently enjoyed. The ancient amulet-toting master of hypnosis so inspires Beaver he decides to give it a mad whirl himself. Unable to find a sympathetic subject in his

family, Beaver starts to work on the neighborhood cat. Eddie views part of this and suggests to Wally they pretend to be under the squirt's dark power. Wally refuses, but Eddie can't resist. Beaver goes through the motions and is amazed when Eddie is mesmerized. Beaver gets scared, however, when Eddie refuses to snap out of his spell and trudges off zombielike toward home. The next day, Eddie still addresses Beaver as his "master" and dramatically cries out, "Slave . . . slave kill for Master . . . slave steal for Master." That night, Beaver is awakened from a nightmare by Wally, who hears him pleading with Eddie in his sleep. Wally explains that Eddie is only giving him the business and decides to fix the wise guy for playing such a cruel trick. The next afternoon, Wally catches Eddie obeying one of Beaver's orders and shoves him in the mud, which ends Eddie's "slave" days for good.

LARRY'S CLUB

Beaver is sworn into "the Bloody Five," a secret club newly "thunk up" by Harold, one of his classmates. Larry is not deemed a neat enough guy to join, but Beaver succumbs to member Whitey's grade-school truism "What's the use of havin' a secret club if you can't keep other guys out?" Larry feels so left out that he shows up at Beaver's door dressed in the costume of *his* club, "the Fiends," a paperbag prototype for velvet hoods and an armband with a skull. "The Fiends" sound like an even neater bunch of guys than Harold's, so Beaver gets himself "unsweared" from the first club and goes to Larry's basement to try to get initiated. Larry blindfolds Beaver and tries to explain his silent meeting by saying his members are voting by secret hand signals, but Beaver is not fooled and is furious when he removes his blindfold and sees that Larry is the only Fiend. Unhappy about Beaver's joining any kind of exclusive club, Ward tells him a bedtime story about villagers who splinter off to build a series of castles and wind up isolated from one another and unable to cope with an invading army. Ward shows Beaver that the *worst* reason to form a club is to keep people out.

WALLY AND ALMA

Wally draws Alma Hanson's name for an upcoming school picnic. Mr. and Mrs. Hanson want to check out this new boy and invite him to dinner. Wally "seems like a nice safe boy" to Alma's mother, and so she proceeds to arrange a whole host of dates for Wally and her daughter. Ward objects to such blatant matchmaking on Mrs. Hanson's part and urges Wally to turn down some of the engagements in favor of dating other girls. Wally would like to but doesn't want to hurt Alma's feelings. Reaching back to his college days, Ward recalls that he had a girl who was similarly hard to get rid of until he started bringing along one of his fraternity brothers each time, one of whom finally interested the girl and got him off the hook. Wally tries the approach with Eddie

and Lumpy to no avail and is beginning to run out of friends when Ward and June are visited by the overbearing Mrs. Hanson and husband. She comes right to the point, claiming Wally is demanding too much of Alma's time and that he always manages to be there when other boys come to call. She asks the Cleavers to keep Wally at bay for a few days to give Alma a chance to see the others. Resisting a big grin, Ward agrees. Wally's Alma problem is solved.

WARD'S BASEBALL

Babe Ruth, Lou Gehrig, Lefty Grove, and Bill Dickey are among the baseball giants whose autographs Ward is proud to have gathered on an old ball. Beaver shows the special memento to Larry, who suggests they have a game of catch with it. Larry throws a high one over Beaver's head, and they both watch it land in the middle of the street where it is squashed by a passing truck. To make amends, Larry donates his new ball, and the boys try to recreate the signatures of the greats. They fall way short of the mark when they sign "Baby Ruth" and otherwise mangle the names. That night, Fred Rutherford stops by, and Ward takes the ball down from the shelf to show off. Fred thinks it's a joke. A furious Ward calls Beaver into the den. Beaver is sent to the showers and

is denied company and television during all his free hours for an entire week. The following night, Ward decides he lost his temper and will relax his too-stiff punishment. Wally disagrees with his father's decision, saying that once Ward backed down on a similar punishment to him and it was a serious blow to his respect for his father. Ward realizes he would be letting Beaver down if he went back on his word now, so Beaver must serve the full term.

BEAVER'S MONKEY

When Beaver brings home a mouse, Ward tells him he cannot keep a pet that is used to living in a wild state but could keep a "regular pet." So he has no choice but to accept Stanley, a monkey Beaver brings home that has been raised in captivity. Stanley is an instant hit with Beaver; however, he escapes from his cage and makes a shambles of June's bridge game before scampering off. Beaver is heartbroken until Stanley scratches at his bedroom window that night. The monkey is cold and wet from a soaking rain and appears to be quite sick. The veterinarian checks him over the next day and reports that Stanley has come down with pneumonia, having been made susceptible so far from his South American homeland. During the next anxious days, Stanley hovers between life and death, surrounded by hot-water bottles, but pulls through. Beaver wants to send him to South America to keep him out of further jeopardy. He is disappointed to learn the plane fare would cost eighty dollars. Ward is pleased by Beaver's caring and suggests an alternative. He gets Stanley placed in the Mayfield zoo's steam-heated monkey house. Beaver visits Stanley and is delighted to see the monkey has his own tree and his own tire swing.

WALLY'S ORCHID

For the spring dance, Wally has a sophisticated date, Myra, who is used to dating older boys and expects him to buy her an orchid. The passionate flower is way out of his price range and Ward's, too, since his father refuses to fund the purchase. Beaver helps out by getting a sympathetic Mrs. Rayburn to donate her orchid, which was given to her in honor of twenty-five years of teaching. Wally puts it in the refrigerator vegetable bin until the day of the dance to keep it fresh, but it turns brown around the edges and then falls apart

completely when he tries to pull off a bad leaf. Wally is quite upset and asks Beaver to call Myra to say he's sick and can't take her to the dance. Beaver is uneasy about telling such an untruth and talks to June. She asks Ward to relent. He holds firm until June shows him the orchid, pressed in a book, that he gave to her when she was sixteen. Wally gets his orchid. The dance is ultimately a disappointment to Wally, who complains that Myra spent most of the time dancing with older boys who messed up his orchid. June remarks to Ward that it's a shame that all the worrying and expense were wasted. Ward disagrees, because he feels now *Wally* knows it wasn't worth it.

BEAVER'S BIKE

Beaver is able to convince Ward that he shouldn't be the only kid with a "no-bike father" and gets permission to ride his new bicycle to school. After class on his first bike day, Beaver and Larry allow his prized possession to be "borrowed" by a young stranger, who never returns. Saddened by his loss, Beaver returns home and gets yelled at for his carelessness. However, when a policeman comes to investigate the theft, Ward discovers that he, too, is guilty of a little carelessness. He neglected to properly register the bike with the police, nor has he had the bike insured. The bike is recovered in poor condition by the police several days afterward. Ward promises Beaver it can be repaired. Beaver says he regrets that the police didn't catch the boy who stole it so he could be punished. Ward assures Beaver that the boy's conscience will punish him. Every time the boy steps outside, he will live in fear of being spotted by Beaver or Larry or that the police will be after him. Indeed, Larry does see the boy, and the boy runs from him, which makes Beaver realize that Ward knows his consciences.

MOTHER'S DAY COMPOSITION

In honor of Mother's Day, Beaver's class is assigned a composition about what their mothers did before they were married. Beaver interviews June and is disappointed when her life as a

Bronson seems so uneventful. When his classmates read their compositions aloud, all of their mothers sound pretty interesting. Beaver manages to postpone reading his for a day. That night, Beaver is fascinated by a television interview with a famous actress who tells of her valiant struggle to the pinnacle of success. Beaver takes notes and the next day delivers a composition that is now revised to depict June's younger days as a glamorous show girl who got her big break thanks to a gangster. Mrs. Rayburn recognizes that it bears no resemblance to the facts of June's life. She calls June to the office and gives her the piece. June shows it to Ward, who is amused and tells June that they should not be too hard on Beaver, who was clearly motivated by love and a desire for June to be the most exciting mom in the whole world. Ward tells Beaver that everyone would like to have parents who lead charmed lives, but we have to take things, and mothers and fathers, the way God gave them to us.

BEAVER AND VIOLET

Fred Rutherford organizes a joint family picnic outing with the Cleaver clan that begins badly for Beaver when Violet Rutherford has to sit on his lap in the car. It gets worse when Violet is sent to drag Beaver away from his fishing to pose for one of Fred's famous photos. Before Beaver knows it, Fred calls out for Violet to give her little friend a big kiss just before he snaps the shot. Beaver is stunned to see the picture in *print*—Fred has submitted it to the house organ down at the "salt mines" where it ran with the caption "A Future Merger?" He feels even worse about it when Whitey tells him it proves Violet is in love with him, drawing that logical conclusion from the fact that "all the people in movies who kiss each other are in love." Beaver dodges Violet in school, but she finally corners him and tells him not to worry, that she only kissed him because her father told her to and she still can't stand him. Beaver in turn claims to have burned the picture and spit on the ashes. With those pleasantries behind them, the two are able to part by admitting that the other is not so bad.

THE SPOT REMOVERS

Thanks to the dead minnows Beaver left in the pocket of his jacket in the closet, Wally's Saturday night party suit smells "fishy." It's rushed to the dry cleaners, and upon its return, Beaver neglects to hang it back safely, so it is in a perfect spot to get a perfectly awful spot when Richard spills a bottle of baseball glove oil. Richard's helpful household hint is to remove the stain the way his mother does, with bleach. When they remove the bleach-soaked towel, Beaver and Richard are shocked to see the oil gone and a big white blob in its place. Beaver tries to paint over the trouble site with his watercolors. Eddie breaks in on him, sees Beaver is truly scared, and recommends to Wally that they play it casual for the party by wearing their sports jackets. Beaver is temporarily spared. That night, Beaver starts crying when Wally simply asks how he looks. Later, Beaver tearfully confesses to Ward and June, and they show understanding and let him know the suit can be dyed. As for Eddie's rare act of mercy, Ward suggests that Beaver not say anything to anyone about it, since it is part of Eddie's character not to let people know he ever does nice things.

BEAVER, THE MODEL

Having sent his picture to a magazine-advertised modeling agency, Beaver receives a letter declaring him a top prospect and inviting him to get his photo placed in a model's directory. Beaver has visions of flashing lights down the runway to fame, but Ward warns Beaver it's all a come-on and he must ignore the letter. Beaver agrees, but his sometime career counselor, Eddie, encourages him to send in the form. Sure enough, Beaver soon gets another letter requesting the agency's thirty-dollar fee. Beaver decides to follow Ward's advice and ignores this and future letters that threaten legal action. In terror, Beaver seeks his own attorney and goes to the office of George Compton, a lawyer friend of his parents. Beaver relates his entire grim story, including his disobedience, and offers his accumulated personal fortune, forty-six cents, to hire Compton to handle his case. Compton says he will straighten the matter out and does take Beaver's money to prove to him that any time he gets himself in a position where he cannot go to his father for help, it is going to cost him something. When Ward hears the story from Compton he feels Beaver has gotten the best forty-six cents' worth of experience he will ever get.

WALLY, THE BUSINESSMAN

The new neighborhood "Igloo Bar" salesman, Wally, has gotten an advance from Ward to cover his start-up expenses. Imprudently, Wally extends credit to a number of friends and customers, so after the first week he is nearly four dollars short. His boss, Mr. Nibling, will be collecting the next day, and Wally is nervous. He seeks a loan from Beaver, who is still bitter about Wally's chasing him away from his cart and now refuses to help him out. Wally tries to get his friends to make good their debts the next day but is unable to make a dent in the deficit. That evening, Wally timidly asks if his boss has come around yet, and June tells him Beaver brought down the money from Wally's top drawer for Mr. Nibling, who said he would speak to Wally later. Wally starts tearing into Beaver for interfering, since Mr. Nibling will fire him when he discovers he's short. Beaver interrupts to show Wally a receipt marked paid in full. Beaver made up the difference from his own savings. Wally is supergrateful and apologizes for screaming and for telling his brother to "get lost," giving him full license to hang around the Igloo Bar cart anytime.

BEAVER AND IVANHOE

For his book report, Ward suggests Beaver read a *real* boys' book, *Ivanhoe*, a childhood favorite of his. Beyond the knights' getting to kill a lot of guys and eating like pigs, Beaver is fascinated by Ivanhoe's penchant for always defending women in distress. Identifying with his new hero, Beaver steps in to help a girl who is being pushed around by a boy at the bus stop. He winds up in a tussle that has to be broken up by the bus driver, and much to Beaver's dismay, the girl accuses Beaver of starting an unprovoked attack—on her brother. Ward suggests Beaver mix some caution with his chivalry. Beaver decides to form a brotherhood of knights by pronouncing an oath for ten cents per dubbing. Whitey is the first new knight, and classmates ask these defenders of the weak to vanquish the notorious neighborhood bully, Clyde Appleby. Whitey bows out, and Beaver begins to wish he had read something safe like *Happy the Kangaroo*, but with his honor at stake, Beaver confronts Clyde and gets unceremoniously clobbered by the bigger boy. That night, Ward tells Beaver that Ivanhoe's virtues are still good in modern-day Mayfield but his violence isn't; after all, discretion is the better part of valor.

BEAVER'S TEAM

Wally agrees to coach "the Lightning Eleven," the seven-man football team Beaver has formed to take on Richard's "Grant Avenue Tigers." he gives them a secret play, "old number 98," a bootleg end around. After practice, Beaver meets up with Penny, a loyal supporter of the Eleven, and he stupidly divulges the secret play to her. Penny then runs into Richard and, in the course of defending her squad, describes their big surprise. In a tough match, Beaver's team manages to hold the opposition to a scoreless tie. After keeping it in reserve, Wally gives permission for Beaver to use "old 98," but the Tigers are waiting for it and throw him for a major loss. With just a minute left in the game, Beaver trots out the play again, and this time he is hit hard. The ball flies out of his hands and is grabbed by Richard, who runs

for the winning touchdown. A deflated Beaver learns from Penny that she told Richard about "old 98," and he is disgusted with her. He tells Ward he doesn't see how she could be so dumb, and Ward reminds him that he wasn't exactly a strategic genius telling her in the first place. Beaver has learned a valuable lesson for the playing field of life.

LAST DAY OF SCHOOL

For a term's-end present for Miss Landers, June decides on some nice handkerchiefs and phones in the order to the local store, adding a nylon slip for herself but giving explicit instructions for the handkerchiefs to be gift wrapped. The next morning, when he is alone, Beaver peeks at the gift and is shocked to see a nylon slip inside. To save himself the acute embarrassment of presenting an undergarment to his teacher in front of the whole class, Beaver decides to give her another gift, a postcard June received of the Capitol. Judy makes a point of announcing to everyone that Beaver is the only student who gave the teacher a crummy gift. Miss Landers graciously dismisses the matter, then treats the class to ice cream. After the party, Beaver approaches Miss Landers and explains his actions. She is understanding and kindly accepts the gift, which

Beaver has waiting in his locker. At home, June discovers the wrapping mistake made by the store and explains it to Beaver. He is pleased to hear that his mother didn't pull such a wicked trick on him. However, when June and Ward offer to call Miss Landers, Beaver assures them that he and his teacher have already straightened things out.

BEAVER'S HOUSE GUEST

Chopper Cooper, one of Beaver's camp pals, comes to spend the weekend. The Cleavers soon learn Chopper comes from a broken home. His father, a wealthy sporting goods manufacturer, has remarried, following two divorces, and his mother is dating a man known to Chopper only as Uncle Dave. Each parent vies for Chopper's affections with presents, trying to outdo the other. Beaver is fascinated by Chopper's exotic life: the gifts, shuttling between parents, a half sister and half brothers, and a lot of independence. In fact, Beaver asks June and Ward if they're thinking of dissolving their marriage. Chopper has a wonderful weekend, but it's cut short by a call from his mom. Listening to Ward talk to his mother on the phone, Chopper sadly tells Beaver he'll have to return home to his mother because she has "the weepies" again. While he packs, Chopper tells Beaver what it is *really* like to be in his position and how lucky Beaver is to have parents who love one another. Chopper confesses that *he* often gets "the weepies," too, something all the presents in the world can't make up for. Chopper has shown Beaver that his little world is a comforting and good one.

BEAVER BECOMES A HERO

While fishing with Wally, Beaver wades out to retrieve a drifting canoe, and the boys return it to its grateful owner, W. J. Watson, who says his daughter probably didn't tie it tight enough. The boys make no mention of the incident to their parents. At school, Beaver embellishes the canoe story, and by the time it finishes making the rounds, Beaver has made a daring rescue of a rich man's daughter trapped in a runaway speedboat. Beaver has never heard himself in such a neat story before, so he doesn't correct the facts. After class, Judy suggests to Miss Landers that they give Beaver's tale to the local newspaper, which offers twenty-five dollars for interesting news items. That night, the puffed-up story appears in the paper, and Ward and June are delighted with the congratulatory calls they receive. Beaver, however, is quite upset to read the account of his "adventure" and bravely tells the truth at school the next day. Miss Landers tells the class they

should write to the paper and explain what happened and how, in the end, Beaver stood up and told the truth and in essence *was* a hero. Mr. Watson sends Beaver five dollars with a nice note asking him not to reveal the amount, since it might ruin his newly acquired reputation as a millionaire.

BEAVER'S FRECKLES

Lumpy Rutherford crushes Beaver's feelings by nicknaming him "Freckles." Self-conscious, Beaver asks some general freckle questions at home, but his parents are unaware what a sensitive topic his freckles have become and make Beaver feel worse when Ward talks about a movie character whose freckles made the audience howl with laughter and June relates his freckles to the fair "Bronson skin" like that of his Aunt Martha, who hides under a parasol in the sun. Beaver is determined to eliminate his trouble spots. He even tries sandpaper and comes to dinner, with his face covered by a heavy layer of June's makeup. In an emotional outburst, Beaver shouts that he hates his freckles and runs from the table. Ward makes a frustrated attempt to put the freckles in their proper perspective. After school the next day, Beaver consults another befreckled boy, Clyde Appleby, for advice. Clyde says that he likes them because they attract other people's attention to him. This refreshing point of view from a freckles survivor eases Beaver's mind. When Ward returns home, June informs him of their son's new profreckle policy, and Ward remarks that one of the great advantages of being a kid is that the biggest problems in your life seldom last more than twenty-four hours.

BEAVER WON'T EAT

June issues an ultimatum: Either Beaver eats his dreaded Brussels sprouts, or he doesn't get to go out to dinner and the football game the following night with the family. Beaver is shaken but still doesn't move his fork in the direction of the deadly cabbage balls and so gets sent to his room. The next day, Ward arranges a compromise: Beaver can go out with them if he promises to eat the Brussels sprouts the very next time they're served. At the pregame dinner, Beaver is shocked to see that the restaurant's vegetable du jour is a generous helping of Brussels sprouts. Refusing to eat them, Beaver says, "I think I can find my way home alone." June will not back down, and the ensuing scene causes a great commotion in the restaurant. Finally, Ward asks Beaver to try just one sprout. He puts one in his mouth but makes no attempt to swallow. Wally gives

Beaver a little back slap for encouragement, and the force of the blow causes Beaver to gulp down the Brussels sprout. Suddenly, Beaver smiles as he realizes it's going to stay put in his stomach, and he works his way through the rest of them. Later, he apologizes for being difficult when his parents were only insisting he eat his sprouts for his own good.

BEAVER'S BIG CONTEST

For every book of benefit raffle tickets he sells, Beaver gets a free ticket for himself. Eddie tells Beaver that even if a kid was allowed to win, his father would take the prize away from him. Beaver does win third prize, a $3,500 red sports car, and is walking on air. The night before the prize is to be presented, Ward undertakes the difficult task of telling Beaver that he will not be able to keep the prize but that it will be sold and the money put in Beaver's savings account for college. Eddie's forecast of trouble comes back to

Beaver, who gets angry and unreasonable. He knows his father is right but can't apologize, and so he tells Wally that he presumes that he and his father will just not speak to one another for the rest of his life. The next day, Beaver begins his silent treatment toward Ward, who who chooses to ignore it. Before leaving for school, Beaver gives June his rather self-pitying "for sale" ad to run in the paper, stating his father is making him sell it for his own good. Ward is puzzled by the wording, but Wally explains that this is Beaver's way of saying he's sorry for his behavior the night before. Ward places the ad verbatim and gets immediate results. That night, father and son get back on speaking terms over some math homework.

WALLY, THE LIFEGUARD

Wally gets a job as weekend lifeguard at Friend's Lake. Ward and Beaver are so proud of him they decide the family should drive up on his first day to see him in action. Wally leaves early and is disappointed to be told that he is under the minimum age required for lifeguard duty and accepts a job selling candy, cold drinks, and hot dogs on the beach instead. The Cleavers arrive at the lake with Gilbert and Whitey in tow so that Beaver can show off his brother. Beaver is stunned when he sees

Wally hawking hot dogs and spirits his friends away before they spot him. Soon, however, Wally comes barking his dogs right past the Cleavers' picnic table. Beaver is so embarrassed in front of his friends he refuses to talk to his big brother for the rest of the day. That night, Ward talks to the still-pouting Beaver. Beaver says he's mad because he feels that for the first time Wally has let him down. Ward points out that actually Beaver has let Wally down. Beaver has tried to use Wally to look like a big shot to his friends and now won't speak to his brother because he got a bad break. Feeling like a heel, Beaver starts talking to his brother, the intrepid candy butcher, once again.

BEAVER'S IQ

After a lecture from Ward about his apparent lack of interest in school and homework, Beaver begins to worry about his educational potential. At school, Mrs. Rayburn tells Beaver's class that on the following day they are going to have an intelligence test. This is a new type of test for Beaver, and he is obsessed with the fear of failing. He is further rocked by Penny, who tells him that if you flunk the test, they send you to "dumb" school and won't let you go to college. Ward discovers Beaver wading through volumes of the encyclopedia way past his bedtime. Ward explains that you can't study for IQ tests and tries to give him self-confidence in his abilities. The next afternoon, June tells Ward that Mrs. Rayburn has called and that Beaver ranked in the top ten of his class on the test. Ward breaks the good news to Beaver, who is relieved and plans to go outside and "goof around," since a guy in the top ten can do homework anytime. Ward disabuses him of this notion real fast, stating that IQ tests merely indicate potential, that now he must live up to it by buckling down to his schoolwork. Accepting this challenge, Beaver glumly remarks, "Yesterday I was worrying that I'd fail the test, and now I gotta worry 'cause I passed it."

BEAVER GOES IN BUSINESS

All of the lawnowners in the neighborhood seem to have existing arrangements, so Beaver and Gilbert's latest moneymaking business venture, grass cut-

ting, is going poorly. Entrepreneurial wizard Edward Haskell tells them of his old scheme he pulled in the supermarket parking lot, dusting off ladies' cars first, then asking them for the money. Beaver and Gilbert pick a house where the occupants are not home and mow the lawn. Just as they finish, the man of the house arrives and rather than pay them threatens to sue them because he has a professional gardening service care for his greenery. The boys take off, and Gilbert quits the business altogether. Fortified by encouragement from Ward, Beaver tries again and gets a commission from a "real nice lady." She gives him a five-dollar check that bounces, dealing a severe blow to his enthusiasm and trust in adults. Ward informs the lady of her rubber check, and upset over what turned out to be a mistake, she brings cash over to the house for Beaver. This restores his faith in free enterprise and in adults, especially after he holds the bill up to the light to make sure it's genuine.

WALLY'S GLAMOUR GIRL

June is aglow because Margaret Bannerman, an old family friend, and her daughter, Kitty, are returning to Mayfield for a visit. Wally is to escort Kitty to the country club dance. Hearing the news, Wally looks odd and quick-

ly begs off, claiming extra basketball practice that night. Beaver later uncovers the reason for Wally's being upset: The previous summer at camp, Wally's friends were getting letters from girls, so Wally invented a rich fantasy life to impress Kitty, which elicited the kinds of return letters that made him look like a "swinger." Kitty is *really* loaded and sophisticated, and now Wally is afraid that she will clobber him when she finds out he doesn't own a tuxedo or a sports car and that Frank Sinatra isn't a family friend. Ward and June force Wally to keep his date. They learn the reason for his reluctance, and Ward advises Wally to tell the whole truth about himself, no matter how awkward that might be. Before Wally can get out his story, however, Kitty sits him down and confesses how nervous she's been, since her lavish life also exists solely in her letters. The date they've been worrying all week would be the worst evening of their lives might turn out to be one of the nicest.

EDDIE'S DOUBLE-CROSS

Quite full of himself, Eddie tells Wally that he is going steady with pretty Caroline Shuster. He and Wally run across Caroline at the soda fountain, and she does seem to be spellbound by Eddie's dubious charms and even calls him "Peachy." However, Wally later overhears a conversation between Caroline and her girlfriends in which she admits that she really can't stand Eddie at all but is accepting his attentions temporarily while her true boyfriend has been grounded for two weeks. In fact, Caroline thinks Eddie is a "conceited creep." Wally is dismayed by this two-faced deception. Seeking Ward's counsel, Wally is advised to set his friend straight. When he tells Eddie what he heard, Eddie becomes angry and accuses Wally of making it all up so he can move in on his girl. He storms off, vowing never to speak to Wally again. After he has cooled off, Eddie lets down his guard somewhat to Beaver. He explains that he knew Wally was telling the truth but couldn't stand for his best friend to know that other people think he's a creep. Beaver agrees to talk to Wally about making up with Eddie, figuring it won't hurt to be nice to Eddie just this once.

MISS LANDERS'S FIANCÉ

As Beaver and Whitey are raking leaves for Miss Landers, Tom Brittingham arrives to pick her up for a tennis date. Miss Landers introduces him as her fiancé. That night Wally tells Beaver what a fiancé is and that leaves him with a bad case of crestfallen crush, made worse when Whitey brings over a newspaper clipping officially announcing her engagement. The next morning Wally informs June that Beaver is sick. Beaver tells her that he feels like he did the time his turtle died. Later Miss Landers calls to inquire about Beaver and offers to drop by with his homework assignment. When she arrives, Beaver is vowing to Wally that he might return to school but he will never look at Miss Landers again. She senses that something is bothering Beaver and he produces the clipping. After a long talk she does convince Beaver that teachers have as much right to fall in love and get married as anyone else. Beaver says he wants her to be happy, but wishes there was another way. Miss Landers assures him that he will like Tom, and she adds that she will still want him to rake her lawn after she's married. She also agrees to Beaver's request to make Tom stop calling him "Teddy."

CHUCKIE'S NEW SHOES

Little Chuckie Murdock's mother comes by to ask June to take Chuckie to buy shoes while she drives her husband to the airport, but Wally and Beaver are alone in the house. She asks Wally to escort Chuckie, and he agrees. Eddie comes by to go skating with Wally, so Beaver volunteers to take over. Chuckie immediately proves to be a spoiled little brat and more than a handful for Beaver. In the shoe department Chuckie threatens to throw a tantrum until Beaver buys him sandals in addition to the shoes he was sent to buy, so Beaver buys both pairs. After he signs for the purchase, he and the clerk discover that Chuckie has disappeared. They search the store without any luck. Unbeknownst to them, Chuckie wanders off and meets a friend of his parents',

who takes the lost boy home. Beaver calls home, where Wally intercepts the call. Before Wally can explain anything to Ward and June, Mrs. Murdock and Chuckie arrive at the house. Ward is quite put out with Wally passing on his responsibility. Beaver calls back and tells Ward he's never coming home because "you can't come home when you lose a whole kid." Ward assures him Chuckie is safe and goes down to the store to pick up a much-relieved Beaver.

WARD'S MILLIONS

After a chat with Ward, who's going over the monthly bills, Beaver decides he'd like to see Ward become a millionaire so he needn't worry about expenses. For $2.98 Beaver purchases a book, *I Became a Millionaire in Twelve Months*, as a gift for his father. Ward is taken aback by the gift but pleased by the thought behind it and tells Beaver the book will have an honored place in his library. Later he asks June to put it away somewhere, and during a distracted moment she sticks it in the cookie drawer. Beaver staunchly defends his book to Wally, who tells him it's dumb, but when Beaver finds it in the drawer covered with cookie crumbs, he is let down and runs off. That night Ward finds him high in the backyard tree. Ward gets him to come down and

points out the error in believing that anyone could become a millionaire by reading a book. He notes that he only told Beaver it would have an honored place in his library so that he wouldn't hurt Beaver's feelings. Beaver admits he really didn't think Ward would become a millionaire, but he did want to dream a while longer before the bubble burst. They walk into the house together, each realizing this experience *has* made them richer.

TEACHER'S DAUGHTER

Wally has been seeing a lot of Julie Foster, whose father teaches English at Mayfield High. Eddie can't understand how he can date a girl whose father can't help him get ahead in the world. Wally says he's taking her out because he *likes* her. Then when the new semester assignments are made, he gets the business from Lumpy and Eddie because he is assigned to Mr. Foster's English class and they think he's merely being an operator, dating the teacher's daughter for an easy A. A concerned Wally asks Mr. Foster to transfer out of his class, but the teacher assures Wally his social relationship with his daughter will have no influence—positive or negative—on his English grade. Wally is still worried about the whole matter when Ward asks him to stop "going steady" with Julie, saying it isn't fair for them to monopolize each other's time at their age. Wally complies by dropping her over the phone. Eddie advises him that breaking up with Julie will now mean he's a cinch to fail English. The next day, Wally tries again to transfer, and again Mr. Foster refuses. But when Wally sees Julie walking down the hall with Lumpy, he's convinced Lumpy will ace English and he will fail. The fear is short-lived. When Mr. Foster returns tests to the class, Wally gets an A-minus and Lumpy gets a big fat F.

BEAVER AND KENNETH

Miss Landers tells June after a parents' meeting that things have been disappearing at school. The class has not been told, but so far the missing items are a baseball glove, a lunch box, and a cap. Later that day while cleaning under Beaver's bed, June discovers those exact items. After school, Beaver is confronted by Kenneth Purcell, a lonely boy who has been giving Beaver the stolen items as gifts. That night Ward and Beaver have a closed-door session at which Beaver tells the truth. Ward decides they must go to the Purcells' house to confront Kenneth. However, Kenneth denies Beaver's charges and his father backs him up. The next day, Beaver reproves Kenneth at school for having lied. He threatens to tell Miss Landers himself, but Kenneth comes clean to her. She

asks why he stole things and he says he has no friends and wanted more than anything to win Beaver as a friend because he's so popular. Miss Landers points out his error: he's not friendless, *she* is his friend and she's sure Beaver is too. She urges him to realize that the way to make friends is not by giving them things but by "giving them a little of yourself."

BEAVER'S ACCORDION

Ward discards a letter from the World-Wide Academy of Music stating that Beaver is eligible for a free five-day trial delivery of a stereophonic accordion. Encouraged by Eddie Haskell, who says Ward is trying to stymie his chances for fame and fortune,

Beaver sends in the certificate of acceptance without telling his parents. Wally warns Beaver the five-day trial will pass by quickly. Beaver has good intentions to return it but winds up hiding it in the hall closet. Weeks pass and Ward and June get a visit from a Mr. Franklin, who represents the academy, inquiring about the accordion. They assure him there is no accordion in their house, but just before he leaves, June pulls open the closet and the accordion tumbles out and down the stairs. Ward strongly censures Beaver for having sent for the instrument behind his back. Beaver will have to pay for the forty dollars of damages incurred by the accordion in its fall, and Beaver notes that "accordions don't bounce downstairs too cheap." Ward adds that if Beaver can't quite make it, he'll help out; he remembers what it was like to be taken in by an enticing offer through the mails when he was young.

THE DRAMATIC CLUB

Encouraged by Ward to participate in school activities, Beaver tries out for Miss Landers' dramatic club. She announces the cast assignments in the club's first production, *The Little Dutch Boy*. Beaver is given the male romantic lead, the part of "Hans," and classmate Vickie is cast to play his sweetheart, "Gretchen."

While Ward and Wally help Beaver memorize his part, he learns that he will be required to give Vickie a *kiss*—onstage. Beaver refuses, insisting he would rather leave school or "croak." He even locks himself in the bathroom, but Ward coaxes him out and tries to explain the insignificance of a stage kiss. Beaver agrees to play the part on one condition, that his family not attend the performance. At school Beaver has a talk with Vickie, who, it turns out, is just as repulsed by kissing as Beaver. She too raised a fuss at home, but will sacrifice herself for her parents. She tells Beaver she'll pretend she isn't kissing him, and Beaver says he'll pretend he's kissing his Uncle Billy. The night of the play, all goes smoothly. As for the kissing, Beaver says he's pretty sure he'll never get to the point where he'll enjoy kissing as much as Wally does.

UNCLE BILLY

Ward's Uncle Billy arrives for a visit and Ward and June are apprehensive about the boys' swallowing his tall-tale-telling. Ward still remembers his disappointment over Billy never taking him for a promised fishing trip. Billy promises to send Wally a rifle and to take Beaver to the sporting-goods store to pick out a fishing outfit. Beaver is so excited he goes down early to the store to await Uncle Billy's arrival. As lunchtime approaches, there is still no sign of Billy. Beaver locates Billy in the barber shop of his hotel. Beaver is embarrassed for Billy when he silently observes the barber and the manicurist rolling their eyes over his stories. Beaver has discovered for himself what Billy is really made of. Dejected, Beaver comes home and tells Ward what he saw in the shop. June tells Ward Billy is on the phone. Ward thinks it's time Billy knew how his exaggerated promises can hurt people, but Beaver asks him not to "holler" at Uncle Billy. He says there are kids at school who are always making up things so the other kids will like them. Ward is impressed by Beaver's observation of Billy's character and just wishes his uncle a good trip home.

BEAVER'S SECRET LIFE

"Writer" is Beaver's answer

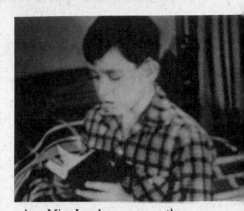

when Miss Landers surveys the class about the vocations they hope to pursue. Ward is pleased and suggests Beaver follow in the footsteps of Somerset Maugham, who kept a diary of his daily experiences. The next day Ward brings him his very own genuine-imitation-leather diary with a lock on it to ensure the privacy of Beaver's thoughts. At first he puts down a strict record of his quotidian activities, but soon begins to fabricate more elaborate happenings. Sometime later, June and Ward become worried when Beaver fails to come home for supper. All leads exhausted, Wally suggests they might gain a clue to Beaver's whereabouts by reading his diary. Ward pries open the lock and they are shocked to read Beaver's adventures, including handstands on State Street Bridge and hitchhiking to Bellport. Beaver comes home while they're reading, and they decide not to confront him with his "secret life," but the next day June reads the latest entry—in which Beaver and Whitey paddle out into deep water. Ward decides to level with Beaver. Beaver is not upset about their breaking into his diary. When he admits he made up his adventures, Ward admits that he was much too quick to believe that Beaver did something wrong without giving him the benefit of the doubt. Despite the kind of trouble a writer can get into, Beaver sticks to his literary ambitions.

WALLY'S TRACK MEET

Just after Coach Henderson gives the track team a lecture about horsing around in the locker room, Eddie and Lumpy pull a sneak towel attack on Wally and he fires back at them just as the coach comes back. Result, Wally is suspended from the team. Ward and June are disappointed, since they had planned to turn the weekend meet into a nice family outing, but his horseplay *really* disturbs them. Beaver, who knows the full story of the locker-room tussle, bravely pays a visit to Lumpy the next day, urging him to tell the coach the truth, making a play to Lumpy's conscience as well as to his fears about the rest of the school finding out the track team will get creamed without Wally because Lumpy and Eddie got him suspended. Lumpy does get a Beaver-inspired belated conscience attack

and asks his father to call the coach for him. However, Wally is not exonerated by Lumpy's confession. Instead all three boys are banned from the meet. Ward tells the boys that Wally was wrong to seek revenge in a way he knew was breaking the rules. Wally has learned that lesson the hard way.

BEAVER'S OLD BUDDY

Beaver is all excited about a weekend visit by his friend from the old neighborhood, Jackie Waters. He has planned a full schedule of activities, all the stuff they used to love doing. Jackie arrives and he too is keenly looking forward to messing around with Beaver like in the old days. But somehow the tire swing, army men, and buried-treasure-hunting don't pack the same wallop for the two buddies. They're bored by each other's company. Ward and June realize that Jackie's having a miserable time, so Ward gives up his golf date and Wally his visit to Eddie's in an all-out effort to help entertain Jackie. Darts are a bust, and Ward plans a movie triple feature as a last resort, but Jackie has already called his parents to pick him up. That night Ward talks to Beaver, who is feeling bad about his weekend of high hopes that turned out so unhappily. Ward tells him that he and Jackie went through an experience that happens to everyone at one time or another. Beaver is somewhat reconciled to this fact and after a pillow fight with Wally feels almost back up to snuff.

BEAVER'S TONSILS

Dr. Kirby looks into the latest of Beaver's sore throats and notes that his tonsils are inflamed. He says he will keep a close watch but he believes the tonsils should come out. Beaver is scared and would much prefer the tonsils just "rot out by themselves," but Ward cheers him up by telling him about all of the presents, care, and ice cream he got when he had a tonsillectomy. "Tonsils are almost as good as Christmas," Beaver decides. He tells all of his friends about his impending surgery and has gifts preselected for them to bring him

during his recuperation period. Sometime later, though, Dr. Kirby changes his mind and tells Beaver the tonsils can stay in place. Beaver is crushed and June is puzzled. Ward points out to her that they have gotten Beaver so worked up about the operation that he has become like a fighter who trains for months and then has his bout canceled. He suggests they buy Beaver the postoperative telescope they promised him to help him cope. The telescope much improves Beaver's mopey condition and he squares things with his friends, but he still asks Wally to take a good look at his tonsils in case he spots a sudden flare-up.

THE BIG FISH COUNT

Parker's Pet Store is holding a big contest in which the contestants guess how many fish are swimming around in a big aquarium in the front window. First prize is a puppy, and Beaver sure wants to win it. Eddie is working at the store and he smugly tells Beaver and Gilbert that he knows the answer to the contest. Gilbert is positive Wally could get it out of him, but Beaver doesn't think it's quite cricket to get the answer from Eddie. The next day Lumpy is about to write his entry when Eddie tells him he's way off, and after swearing the Lump to secrecy, gives him the right number. On his way out of the store, Lumpy runs into one of his classmates, Kathy, and blurts out the answer in order to impress her. From there the word spreads all around town. On the day of the big fish count, Mr. Parker announces the correct number and is confronted by a veritable army of winners. He guesses who leaked the total and fires Eddie on the spot. Beaver's honest guess was way off, but he still comes home a winner, since Mr. Parker gave out "constellation" prizes to all entrants—a pair of fish.

MOTHER'S HELPER

June tells Ward how fatigued she is from the daily housework, so Ward suggests she get Mrs. Manners to come in a couple of days a week to help out. Mrs.

Manners has been quite busy, though, so the next day she sends her daughter Margie to the Cleavers'. Wally comes home from school and is instantly attracted to Margie and offers her his own helping hand with the chores. June is a bit concerned over this infatuation, but Ward is certain that with track practice and exams coming up Wally will have little time to pursue the "mother's helper." However, the next afternoon Wally cuts track practice in order to assist Margie, doing cleaning he would never dream of doing on his own

around the house. When June learns he got a C-minus on his English exam, she decides it's time for her to speak to Mrs. Manners and clean up the situation between her son and Margie. The next afternoon, Wally again arrives home from school early to help Margie wax the kitchen floor. June tells him to go right into the kitchen, his assistant is waiting. The assistant is not Margie, though, but her *mother*, who thanks Wally for his offer to help and hands him a wax applicator.

BEAVER'S POSTER

Miss Landers asks for volunteers to paint posters for the class project on the colonial period. Beaver raises his hand, as do Penny and Gilbert. There will be a prize for the best poster. Beaver is convinced Ward will paint him a prize-winning poster, but Ward refuses to do his assignment for him. Beaver is left to draw on his own artistic talents, and his first poster is a paint-clotted disaster. Ward offers him some pointers and Beaver tries again to do justice to his subject, Paul Revere, using his friend Harry as a live, though somewhat unwilling, model. Wally inspects the second poster and declares it an even worse mess than the first attempt: it has no proportion, at least one leg too many, and all of the colors run together. At school, Beaver's poster looks even worse when displayed next to Penny's and Gilbert's. However, in awarding the prize, Miss Landers suggests it would be best to judge the posters on the basis of original effort. No one contests Beaver's claim that he did his all by

himself. Miss Landers gives him the prize and Beaver proudly gives the ribbon to his father to thank him for *not* helping him.

WALLY AND DUDLEY

June gets a call from a childhood friend, Ruth Macmillan, who has moved into the neighborhood. June arranges for Wally to escort her son, Dudley, to high school and introduce him around. The next morning, Wally is shocked when Dudley arrives in black raincoat and fuddy-duddy hat, carrying an umbrella. Beaver asks him, "Who died?" and even Ward pegs Dudley as rather a square. On the way to school they run into Eddie and Lumpy, and Dudley is too naive to realize that it's only for laughs at his expense that Eddie introduces him around and invites him to a party at his current girl Christine's house. A few dance lessons and some rules about

giving and getting "the business" are the best Wally can manage in his crash course on being one of the guys. At the party Eddie and Lumpy play some pretty rank pranks on Dudley and he is really out of the swing of things. That is, until the hi-fi goes on the blink. During the lull, Dudley sits down at the piano and starts tickling a pretty mean set of ivories—much to everyone's surprise. Suddenly Dudley is the center of attention, as a pretty square peg has managed to dig a round hole all his own.

BEAVER'S REPORT CARD

Arithmetic is proving too great a challenge for Beaver so Ward tutors him a little each evening, hoping to see a marked improvement. On the day report cards are passed out, Beaver is at the dentist, so Gilbert brings it over to the house. Eddie and Lumpy manage to intercept the report card and just for kicks take a pen and change Beaver's D-minus in math to a B-plus. Beaver is taken aback by this unexpectedly high mark but on Wally's advice says nothing about it. Ward and June are so pleased by the improvement in Beaver's math grade that they decide to reward him with the new train set he has been asking for. On the evening Ward brings the train, June is the hostess for a meeting at the school, where

Miss Landers mentions Beaver's D-minus in arithmetic to her. When questioned, Beaver admits to knowing nothing about the change. Ward and June are troubled by this apparent lie. Wally finally gets to the source of the trouble and forces Eddie to call Ward and confess to tampering with the Beaver's report card. Ward and June hope Beaver will give them extra credit for apologizing for their error in judgment.

EDDIE SPENDS THE NIGHT

Even though Eddie always seems to cause trouble when he's around, Ward allows him to be Wally's overnight guest. It proves an impossible task to find a Friday-night date for Eddie, so the boys decide to stay home and play chess. Beaver catches Eddie cheating, which leads to an argument and a near-fistfight. Eddie heads for home, stopping to tell Ward and June on his way out that Wally and Beaver were *mean* to him. After Eddie is out the door, his father calls to thank Ward for having Eddie over while his parents are out of town because Eddie tends to get a little "edgy" when he's left alone. Ward convinces Wally that they have to retrieve Eddie, whom they find alone in his house with all of the lights on, obviously afraid but refusing to admit it. He agrees to go back with Wally, telling June it was "the mature thing to do." The following day, Beaver has a little talk with Eddie in the kitchen, during which the wise guy lets down a little of his guard. Later Beaver tells June he thinks he might have seen the nonobnoxious side of Eddie she has told him probably exists. Not to worry, though—soon after their enlightening talk, good old Eddie rubbed a candy bar in Beaver's hair.

WALLY'S DREAM GIRL

Wally starts neatening up his act and wearing after-shave lotion to school. June smells a rat. Ward thinks it's an innocent high school crush. A crush it is—Ginny Townsend, a transfer student a year older than Wally, and quite a vision. Wally confides in Beaver that he has romantic dreams about Ginny even though he hasn't worked up the nerve to ask her out. June decides to aid her shy son. She calls Mrs. Townsend and invites Ginny on a family picnic. Ward admonishes her that "dream girls don't go on family picnics." Wally is horrified when he's told and is on the verge of being violently ill the night before. At the picnic, Ginny is as gorgeous as ever, but when she announces that she can't eat because she's gained two whole pounds and is allergic to chicken,

can't play volleyball because she has a sun allergy and breaks out in lumps, Wally's dream just about rolls over and dies. He even falls asleep in the car on the way home. June apologizes to Wally for meddling, but he thanks her. As he tells Eddie, he might have continued thinking Ginny was "the absolute most," and "who wants a sunburned, allergic dream girl with lumps?"

MISTAKEN IDENTITY

The deserted McMahon house is a great temptation, but Beaver knows his father would not like him going along with Gilbert and Richard. Beaver goes home, but Gilbert and Richard disregard the "No Trespassing" sign on the property. Richard even heaves a rock through the one remaining window. A police car pulls up just as the rock shatters the glass, and Richard is caught by the cop. When the officer asks for his name, a frightened Richard gives Beaver's name and address. That evening the chief of police—whom Ward has met with that very day on the committee for the new youth center—pays an embarrassing visit to the Cleaver home with the arresting officer. Ward is shocked to hear what Beaver is accused of, since it involves disobeying not only his orders but also the law. He calls Beaver downstairs, but the arresting officer lets him off the hook since he is clearly not the "Beaver Cleaver" he apprehended. Although he knows it must have been Richard who broke the window, Beaver refuses to squeal on a friend, but the name slips out. The mess is cleared up when Richard calls Ward and apologizes for using Beaver's name to try to cover up his wrongdoing.

THE SCHOOL PICTURE

As the fifth grade is lining up for the official yearbook picture, Gilbert convinces Beaver that they should make real goony faces for posterity. As the shutter is snapped, though, Gilbert has wised up, and only Beaver's ridiculous expression is immortalized on film. According to Mrs. Rayburn, who examines the photographer's proof, nothing this disgraceful has happened at the school since Eddie Haskell's time. Ward is called in and concurs that Beaver has shown a

disturbing lack of respect for his school and his classmates by this act. Upon returning home, Ward finds Beaver locked in his room, but Ward doesn't let that stop him. He lectures Beaver and punishes him by making him come straight home after class for an entire week. When the yearbook is issued, Beaver is relieved to discover his embarrassing expression covered by Myrtle Jarvis's hair ribbon, thanks to a creative photographer who airbrushed the ribbon high enough to save Beaver's face—by hiding it.

BEAVER'S FROGS

Ward agrees to put up half the cost of the twenty-five-dollar canoe Beaver covets if Beaver will earn the other half. Richard tells Beaver he knows a man who will pay twenty-five cents for each live frog brought to him. Early the following morning, frog hunters Beaver and Wally head for Miller's Pond where they have a wet, slimy, smelly time but manage to catch more than six dollars' worth. Beaver plans a return trip to catch the remaining frogs, and in the meantime he boards the first batch of creatures in the portable swimming pool and in June's large washbasin. Soon Beaver has befriended most of his frogs and has even given pet names to some, including his favorite, "Smiley." When Richard tells Beaver that his contact collects the frogs in order to kill them and preserve them for laboratory experiments, Beaver makes up a sudden excuse to postpone selling his frogs. Forced to choose between paddling his own canoe and having his frogs croaked, he returns the amphibians to their home pond. Ward offers to let Beaver polish his car for $12.50 so he can buy his canoe. Beaver realizes Ward's car doesn't need polishing and appreciates his father's understanding about canoes and about frogs.

COMMUNITY CHEST

Reluctantly June allows Beaver to make her rounds collecting for the Community Chest. The can is "jingling pretty good" as Beaver and his companion Gilbert take a break to enjoy ice cream cones, and enjoy them so much they don't realize Beaver has stopped jingling, since the can fell out of his back pocket while they sat on a bench. They retrace their steps but can't find the can. After some deliberation, Ward offers to replace the money if Beaver will return to every home where he collected and find out the exact amount of each contribution. Beaver and Gilbert go knocking on doors once more, and much to their delight, people are most understanding, giving them another contribution as large as and in some cases larger than their previous one. When Beaver gets home Ward tells him the original can was turned in and since he got second donations only because people felt sorry for him, the money must be returned. This time Ward goes through the unpleasant task of contacting all of the donors and begins to see what Beaver went through. June decides that the following year, if she is unable to collect for the Community Chest, she will let Ward replace her—and let him lose the money.

BEAVER'S RAT

After Beaver makes his latest bad trade of a new sweater for a cheap magnifying glass, Ward admonishes him for not knowing the value of things and always getting the worst of his deals. The following day, Beaver comes home with his latest swap, a fifty-cent black and white domesticated rat he's named "Peter Gunn." Although Ward believes Beaver got a bargain this time, June is so repulsed by having a live rat in the house that Beaver is ordered to get rid of Peter. He unloads him on an eager Violet Rutherford, who pays him three dollars. Fred visits Ward about his little "gyp artist," and Ward agrees to speak to Beaver about his pretty sharp deal. Beaver returns home with the rat, since he couldn't find anything worth the three dollars he had to trade back to Violet. Fred pays another visit to the Cleavers, this time offering to buy back Peter for *five* dollars, since his wife, who has always had a weakness for animals, developed quite a fond feeling for the rat in just the short time Violet had him. Beaver will only accept his original fifty-cent investment for Peter but asks his father why an adult like Mr. Rutherford would make the kind of silly trade offer Ward had said only kids make. Ward admits we never get too old to do "goofy stuff."

KITE DAY

Father and Son Kite Day is coming up at Metzger's Field and Ward agrees to help Beaver build a real competitor, telling him that as a boy he was known as the greatest kite-maker in Shaker Heights. They build a real beauty. Beaver is warned to leave the kite in his room to allow the glue to dry properly.

The day before the contest, Gilbert convinces Beaver to give his kite a trial flight. It soars magnificently and then plummets to the sidewalk. Beaver is terrified to think of Ward's seeing the busted kite. Wally tries to help him repair the kite, but it's a hopeless task. Beaver's only salvation could come in the cancellation of the contest, and in desperation he pays a visit to Judge Henderson, who is part Indian, in the hope he will perform a rain dance, but to no avail. Finally Beaver is forced to tell his father about the kite. Ward is furious, pointing out to Beaver his selfishness in ruining something they worked on together. But Ward does forgive his son, and with only a few hours left before the competition, they rush out to buy a new kite. With this second kite, father and son bring home a third-place ribbon in the intermediate class.

IN THE SOUP

Wally is having a bunch of the guys over for a party on Friday night. Beaver is supposed to spend that night at Whitey's house, but on their way there they are fascinated by a big billboard featuring a woman holding what appears to be a steaming cup full of Zesto Soup. Whitey wonders how they keep the soup hot, and Beaver says there's no soup in the cup. Whitey dares him to prove it—if he's not *chicken*. Beaver works his way over the lady's hand and climbs into the cup and proves conclusively there's no soup—just before he falls in. He's too short to climb out of the cup, and a smirking Whitey has to go home to get his father. Meanwhile Wally is wondering what's keeping his guests. Lumpy arrives all excited to tell Wally that the gang is all over watching the billboard. Ward goes with Wally to help drive the guests back. When they arrive on the scene, a big crowd has gathered. Lumpy thinks they should get a psychiatrist to talk the unseen kid down, but someone calls the fire department. Beaver wishes he was dead instead of having a lot of people watching him get fished out of a soup bowl by a fireman. Wally threatens to slug any of his guests who make any cracks in the car.

JUNIOR FIRE CHIEF

Miss Landers' students groan when she announces the beginning of "one of our interesting civics projects," but her news that they will be electing a junior fire chief for Fire Prevention Week piques their interest. A number of his classmates approach Beaver to win his vote. When he discusses the election with his parents that night, Ward and June encourage him to run for something for a change. In a switch, the class elects Beaver, thinking that he is a "nothing" they can shove around. But Beaver throws himself into giving out citation slips around the house for fire violations. Then he turns his attention on the neighborhood, with many neighbors calling Ward to complain about their citations. Ward is afraid Beaver is making out like too much of a big shot. Beaver brags to Gus that he's handed out fifteen citations and yelled at a lot of people threatening trouble. Gus tells Beaver that little was ever accomplished by yelling at someone and that he would get better results if he were nice to people. Beaver rips up his citations and in class he reports what Gus has told him. Convinced that he has learned a valuable lesson about being a fireman, Miss Landers is proud of the junior fire chief.

BEAVER'S DOLL BUGGY

The crude coaster racer Beaver buys from Eddie for two dollars needs wheels, and Penny Woods, one of his classroom enemies, seems not so "creepy," since he learned that she has serviceable wheels on her old doll buggy. He visits Penny and actually enjoys talking to her. Beaver leaves his tools at home, so instead of removing the wheels, he is forced to push the doll buggy through the streets of Mayfield. He gets more and more self-conscious with each quizzical glance he gets from passersby. Wally goes to look for his brother, realizing that "a thing like this could put a curse on the whole family." Beaver spots Gilbert and Richard coming his way and shoves his buggy down into a weed-filled incline. When he sees the abandoned carriage, Gilbert claims the wheels for *his* coaster. Beaver doesn't have the nerve to contest it. To make Beaver feel better, Ward buys him a new set of wheels in the hobby shop. Penny finds out Gilbert wound up with her wheels, and she accuses Beaver of selling them to him, and the two return to their usual bickering. Beaver tells Gilbert he still might try talking to a girl again sometime. Gilbert warns him he's "goin' flaky."

SUBSTITUTE FATHER

Ward is away in St. Louis on business, and Wally is taking his role of man of the house quite conscientiously. Beaver is deliberately tripped by an older boy, Arthur, and he responds by calling him "a big dumb . . . ," a terrible word that Miss Landers makes out over the blast of the school bell and finds shocking and intolerable. This is "sendin'-for-Dad kind of trouble," and when he brings home her note, Beaver is afraid and embarrassed to repeat the word to June, so Wally has to try to deal with the matter. He decides to substitute for Ward before Miss Landers. Wally insists that he has listened to his father yell for years and is certain he can make Beaver see the error of his ways. Convinced that the brothers are not trying to get away with something, Miss Landers accepts Wally as the substitute father this time, and Beaver promises not to say so much as "ouch" the next time somebody trips him. June finds out Wally paid a visit to Beaver's school, but Beaver assures her he's ashamed of what he did, and "Wally made me even ashameder," so she lets the matter drop. That night Wally checks Beaver for hand washing and teeth brushing and gets a big thank you in return for being such a good brother *and* father.

WALLY'S WEEKEND JOB

Eddie is annoyed when Wally sets the bad example of getting a weekend job at the soda fountain. On the first day, decked out in his white shirt, bow tie, clerk's coat, and cap, Wally is a big hit with the customers. As Lumpy notes, not only has Wally got the neatest job in town, he's got all the girls," so Eddie decides it's time Wally was cooled off. Mary Ellen Rogers is having a big slumber party that night, and her father has forbidden any boys to come near the house. Lumpy calls the drugstore, impersonating Mr. Rogers, and asks Wally to bring six quarts of ice cream to the party. When Wally arrives, Mary Ellen's father throws him out, claiming to be "wise to the tricks of a young pup" trying to bother his daughter. Wally leaves in embarrassment and sees the perpetrators laughing outside. He gives chase but temporarily loses them. Still angry, he takes two quarts of now-melted ice cream and dumps them over Eddie's and Lumpy's heads. Ward understands but does not condone Wally's unusual loss of self-control. Wally reassures his father by saying that when he "really went ape," he went too far.

WALLY'S CAR

For twenty-five dollars, Wally buys his first jalopy, a wreck that lives just long enough to collapse in the Cleavers' driveway. About to leave for the evening, Ward and June convince Wally that since he doesn't have his license yet or the money saved to pay for insurance and running costs, he should get rid of the car. However, the immediate concern is moving the jalopy out of the way of Ward's car. Wally's coupe moves slightly and comes to a loud, grinding halt. Ward calls a taxi and leaves with orders to get the driveway clear. Wally calls in his board of auto experts, including Lumpy and Eddie, but after several hours, the car's innards are strewn all around the driveway and the car has moved no farther than the lawn. The others take off, leaving Beaver and Wally with a "big old greasy jigsaw puzzle." The car is becoming a neighborhood eyesore, and Ward will not allow Wally to store it in the garage. Wally and

Ward hit on two independent solutions simultaneously: Ward calls up the local junk dealer and offers him the wreck for fifteen dollars just as Wally finishes selling off the parts of the car—for more than his original purchase price, enough to cover the junk dealer's price for hauling off the shell of his coupe.

ONE OF THE BOYS

Eddie claims it's "the best thing that's ever happened to us in our entire career as teenagers" when he and Wally are invited to join the school's most exclusive club, "the Barons." At first, Wally and his parents are impressed by the fact that the Barons dress sharply and drive sporty cars. After checking with the vice-principal, who has nothing to say either for or against the club, Ward cools on the Barons, because they apparently have no interest in either academic or athletic performance. He tells June that Wally is now too old for them to influence his decision about the Barons, that they will have to count on having raised him properly. Wally is not satisfied with what he observes about the Barons. Their leader jests that their purpose is "to improve the social status of this moth-eaten educational institution." He agrees to go to the big Friday night meeting with Eddie, though, because Eddie has promised to recruit Wally in

order to get himself welcomed. Both boys are disappointed when all the Barons do is hang out in a big house, playing pool and knocking the other students and school. Much to Ward's and June's delight, Wally has made the right decision, that the Barons are spoiled and pretending to be a little too sophisticated for their own good.

BEAVER'S FIRST DATE

For two years, dancing school has presented a test of Beaver's imagination to think up new excuses for trying to get out of going. So Ward, June, and Wally are amazed when Beaver comes home from class quite happy because he has made a new friend, even more surprisingly, a *girl*, Betsy Patterson. He actually asks for a new suit to take Betsy to the Junior Cotillion. With help from Wally, Beaver survives asking his first girl on his first date. Everything goes well until Betsy agrees to dance with another boy, thereby freeing Beaver, who never thinks to ask another girl to dance. He seeks out Whitey and Gilbert, who are similarly unattached for the moment, and the three adjourn outside to hear Beaver's new repertoire of funny noises and to look at Whitey's baseball cards, which he's brought along. Upon his return, Beaver tells Wally he doesn't think he'll soon feel like going through all that junk he had to go through that night for a date. Ward admits to June that he would have been disappointed if Beaver had truly liked the dance, and June concurs that "while we're making ladies and gentlemen out of them, we shouldn't forget they're children."

WALLY'S BIG DATE

Mayfield High is having an exchange dance with a nearby high school. Wally draws Marjorie Muller, whom he's never met, but Eddie knows her and offers to swap the girl he chose, Gail Preston, with Wally. Wally is suspicious until Eddie shows him pictures of the two girls. Since Gail looks okay, he accepts the deal. Ward is convinced Eddie has once again put one over on gullible Wally, and he's proven correct when Wally has a predance date and discovers that Gail is several significant inches taller than he is and will make him look like a "dwarf." He tries all sorts of methods to increase his height, including cardboard boosters in his shoes, but considers himself doomed. Gail arrives for the dance and she is suddenly no taller than Wally, having worn flats and combed her hair down. They start to dance, when Lumpy stops them with an urgent phone message from Beaver that his mother is sick and Wally is needed at home. Wally ignores him and

stuns Gail with his callousness. Wally explains that his brother is just trying to give him an emergency excuse to duck out of the dance, but he doesn't want an excuse after all. They go on dancing and end up seeing eye to eye all night.

NO TIME FOR BABY-SITTERS

Beaver brags to his friends that at twelve his parents feel he's too old to need a baby-sitter, but at the last minute Ward and June decide he still must have one for Friday evening. On short notice they have to use a new girl, Judy (Barbara Parkins), and force Beaver to be civil to her, which he is—barely, trying to ignore her by pretending she's a lamp. As they threatened, Gilbert and Richard arrive to check out their skepticism about Beaver's being allowed to stay by himself all night. Beaver pleads with Judy to ignore the doorbell. She catches on and hides in the kitchen. Beaver passes the no-supervision inspection by putting his feet up on the couch and shouting, and when June calls asking to check in with Judy, he hangs up on her. Gilbert and Richard are almost convinced, until Beaver panics when they try to get into the kitchen. They race past him and Beaver expects the worst, but the room is empty. Judy, who has a younger brother of her own, is outside the back door, and doesn't come back inside until Beaver's envious friends have left. Beaver pays Judy the ultimate compliment, saying he doesn't mind a baby-sitter like her.

WALLY GOES STEADY

Ward is shocked when one day in the golf-club locker room Bill Boothby broadly hints that they may be hearing wedding bells soon, since his daughter Evelyn and Wally are going together. He and June can barely place the girl. Wally is defensive when they raise Evelyn's name casually at dinner, claiming they show interest only when something is wrong. When Wally and Evelyn play tennis with her sister, Judy, who is married to a young acquaintance of Wally's, Tom Henderson (Ryan O'Neal), Ward and June are concerned that Wally and Evelyn will be carried away by the apparent glamour of marrying young. Wally and Evelyn

are invited over to the Hendersons' for dinner. When they arrive promptly, the small apartment is a mess, dinner is nowhere near ready, and Tom and Judy are soon quarreling bitterly. Tom reveals that Judy's father has to pay for their apartment, since he's always got money pressures, and Wally quickly sees that the married Tom is a much more harried person than the Tom who plays touch football with him. He returns home and Ward and June are relieved that Wally has learned that marriage is nothing to fool around with while a guy is still having fun.

BEAVER'S BIRTHDAY

Beaver decides he's outgrown birthday parties, and Ward and June celebrate this new maturity by giving him money, as do several relatives. Ward and June tell Beaver he's old enough to make his own decisions about the birthday money, but they suggest strongly that he save it. Beaver is willing, even though he has his heart set on a model car. When he's home alone with Gilbert, a registered letter containing ten dollars from Uncle Billy arrives. Gilbert convinces him his parents will never know about this bonus birthday money and leads him past the toy store, where he gets Beaver to buy the model, explaining that if Beaver hands him the package, then they can truthfully say he "gave" the car to Beaver. June finds Beaver's thank-you note to Uncle Billy, and Ward sees the car, which leads them to deduce what Beaver has done. To Beaver's surprise, they tell him that if he had come to them to ask permission to buy the car, they would have granted it. Ward points out that Beaver is big enough to make decisions, even though he might mess things up sometimes. Beaver decides he'll tell Gilbert his plan didn't work, and he decides to tell him "while I'm sitting on him."

BEAVER TAKES A DRIVE

Pretending to be driving Ward's parked car, Beaver accidentally releases the emergency brake, and he, Gilbert, and the car roll down the driveway out into the middle of the street. They cause a horn-honking, shouting, traffic-blocking mess. Gilbert takes a powder but runs into Wally, who comes to Beaver's aid. He recalls that Ward keeps a spare ignition key under the mat and drives back up the driveway. A policeman sees him and demands to see his license. Of course, Wally has none, and he is slapped with a ticket. Ward is annoyed at Wally until the true facts emerge. He agrees to appear in juvenile court with Wally and Beaver. The judge is made aware of the extenuating circumstances

and lectures the boys but directs the brunt of his heat at Ward about his parental responsibilities in regard to driving. Early one morning, the boys decide to wash the car. They awaken a sleepy Ward to move the car out of the garage for them. Ward is reluctant to go outside at that very moment, so the boys offer to release the brake and roll the car out themselves. A moment later, Ward snaps awake and rushes past them in his robe and slippers. Beaver wisely observes that the judge really got through to Ward.

BEAVER'S CAT PROBLEM

The boys are unnaturally quiet, and when Mrs. Prentiss calls asking if anyone has seen her large, expensive silver Persian, "Precious Bootsie," Ward correctly deduces that Beaver has the cat in his bedroom. Before Mrs. Prentiss arrives to claim Bootsie, Beaver has given it some salmon from his dinner, not realizing that cats have a tendency to return to where they have been fed. Mrs. Prentiss gives Beaver reward money, but Bootsie soon returns. Although Beaver knows it's wrong, he hides the cat for the night. Then he returns it a second time and gets another reward, but this time Bootsie almost beats him back home. Mrs. Prentiss is begining to get annoyed, and Beaver decides to borrow Gilbert's dog, Archie, who effectively discourages Bootsie from hanging around the Cleaver house. Unfortunately, as a reward for chasing away the cat, Beaver feeds Archie, and now the dog is a repeat guest. Luckily Beaver is able to sit down and have a good firm talk with Archie, who proves to be a lot easier to send home than a poor cat saddled with a name like "Precious Bootsie."

WEEKEND INVITATION

Wally is invited by his classmate Scott to spend a weekend at a lake cottage with a bunch of the guys. Ward and June don't know anything about Scott or his parents and so are not inclined to let Wally go, but Scott assures Ward his parents have given their permission, so Ward agrees. The next day, Wally learns the key fact about the weekend that Scott has neglected to reveal: his parents will not be supervising the trip. Wally tries to decide whether

he should tell Ward and June, but while he delays, Ward finds out just before the guys are about to gather, and he refuses to let Wally go. He points out that the whole weekend has been built on each of the boys telling their parents that "the other guys can go, so why can't I," which he considers a weak reason. Scott and Lumpy arrive and Lumpy gloats about his parents not treating him like a baby, but Ward has called Fred, who puts the reins on Lumpy in a hurry. Scott is sympathetic, admitting to Wally that he wishes his parents cared enough about him to refuse him permission for something. Wally digests this and concludes that in the long run his parents still know what's best for him.

BEAVER'S ICE SKATES

Ice-skating season has begun and Beaver is thrilled to get permission to buy his own skates without his parents. At the sporting-goods store, Beaver's proper size is sold out, as are the next two larger sizes. The salesman brings him a pair that are way too big, claiming they'll fit perfectly once he puts on the three pairs of wool socks all the professionals wear. Beaver falls for it, and when he gets to the rink, he keeps falling every time he tries to skate. Unwilling to let his parents know he's done a dumb thing, Beaver hides out every afternoon in the library, where Wally finds him. Sympathizing with his younger brother, he takes him back to the store but has no luck getting the skates exchanged or Beaver's money refunded. Beaver perseveres with his deception until Ward reads in the paper that the rink has been closed for several days while Beaver has been leaving the house with his new skates. Under questioning Beaver admits his sorry tale. Ward has to threaten to go to the Better Business Bureau, but he gets Beaver a refund. Beaver says he wants to let his parents make his mistakes for him in the future, since they can afford it better than he.

BEAVER'S ENGLISH TEST

Beaver gets a "stupid note" about his English marks and Ward wants to help him study but has to go out for the evening, so he asks Wally to tutor his brother and Gilbert, who got a similar warning. Wally is frustrated when the two scholars cannot grasp the crucial differences between adverbs and adjectives. In a last-ditch effort to wise them up, Wally gives them one of his old exams, which has the correct answers underlined. The boys memorize it, hoping some of the knowledge will rub off. The next day they cannot believe their luck as their English teacher gives the class the identical test. Beaver is a little troubled, but Gilbert convinces him they did nothing wrong. Beaver is still not sure, but his parents are so thrilled when he tells them he got a 96 on the test that he doesn't want to spoil it. He does finally tell Ward, who suggests Beaver should talk to his teacher, who appreciates Beaver's honesty and understands what he has been going through. Several days later Wally asks Beaver why he hasn't seen Gilbert around much. Beaver says that Gilbert's father laid down the law that if Gilbert could get a 96 once he should be able to get it more often and has been forcing him to stay home every night to study.

WALLY'S CHAUFFEUR

Wally's first white-dinner-jacket dance is coming up at the country club, and he and Evelyn Boothby have planned to pile into Lumpy's car along with three other couples, but Ward tells him to find a safer, less cramped mode of transportation. None of his other friends have room in their cars, and Wally rejects Ward's offer of a lift. He has no choice but to tell Evelyn of the situation, and she tells him not to worry. The night of the dance, a car pulls up for Wally, who gets sick when Evelyn gets out—from the driver's side. "Having a girl drive you is worse than riding with your father," Wally groans, but he's stuck. Sure enough, Wally takes a sound ribbing, especially from Lumpy, who asks Wally why he's "not wearing the corsage?" The joshing simmers down, and Wally has fun at the dance. Lumpy still wants to have some fun, so when everybody's leaving, he pulls his heap around to block Evelyn's car. His prank backfires, though, when a policeman arrives, giving him a ticket for parking in a red zone and having only one headlight and illegal pipes. While he's detained, Evelyn and Wally give the gang a lift to the hamburger joint.

FAREWELL TO PENNY

Penny is the creepiest girl in Beaver's class and he's always getting into heated name-calling sessions with her. Which makes both Penny and Beaver very upset when they find out her mother has invited Beaver to her farewell party when her family is about to move. Wally advises Beaver that the fact he and Penny hate each other so much must mean they really like each other, and Penny's mother tells her something similar. Beaver winds up having a good time at the party, and afterward Penny gives him her pencil box and they mutually agree that they not only like each other a little but also will actually miss each other. But that night Whitey gives Beaver

the awful news that Penny will be able to stay the school year. Beaver is crushed, fearing Penny will blab all over school that he likes her. The next day he rushes up to her in the corridor and calls her a "spook" and all sorts of names, and she gives back as good as she gets. Things are back to normal, but Wally still makes Beaver uneasy by assuring him that this new round of bickering is even more conclusive evidence that he likes Penny.

WARD'S GOLF CLUBS

Ward not only has a bad shooting day on the golf course, he's broken his driver so that the head has come loose from the shaft. Gilbert brings Beaver a whole box of golf balls he picked up outside the driving-range fence, and they borrow Ward's driver to whack away at them. As Beaver is showing off his duffing style, the boys watch the club's head sail into the bushes. Beaver sticks it back on and replaces it in Ward's bag. Wally catches him at it and advises Beaver to come clean right away to Dad. Beaver intends to, but when Wally gets yelled at about leaving his father's things alone after wearing one of his father's shirts, Beaver figures this is not a good time. Instead, Beaver substitutes a new driver he could buy on the installment plan. In examining the wounded driver, Ward discovers his club has mysteriously healed itself and calls the boys down for an explanation. Under direct questioning, Beaver breaks down, and Ward tells him not to worry about the rest of the payments. However, he instructs Beaver to be more careful about letting friends talk him into doing things he knows are wrong.

BEAVER'S ELECTRIC TRAINS

June decides that Beaver's electric trains, which have been unused for two years, should be given away to eight-year-old Jimmy Battson. Beaver is agreeable until he takes them out to get them cleaned up and gets totally drawn back into the fun of playing engineer with Gilbert. The trains are slated to be picked up the following day, but Beaver gets Wally to agree to stall Jimmy so he and Gilbert can have some additional playing time. However, it's Jimmy's pretty sister, Georgia, who comes to get the trains, and when Wally answers the door, he is spellbound and

cannot refuse her Beaver's trains. Beaver thinks this is all a big "gyp," and he resorts to something else from his little-boy days: locking himself in the bathroom. Wally and June cannot get Beaver out, but Ward issues a direct order which acts like an "open sesame." As they discuss Beaver's feelings, he tells Ward he doesn't know when a kid is supposed to stop acting like a kid. He is reconciled to the loss of his trains but asks for a new set for his next birthday, then later realizes he'd rather have a new, bigger bike.

BEAVER THE BUNNY

It's school pageant time and under the duress of school spirit Beaver is talked into portraying an animal, but since he's at the end of the line, the neat animals are spoken for and he has to play a bunny. His friends call him "Bunny Boy" and "Cottontail," and Beaver becomes more miserable when he sees his silly bunny suit. When Ward is delayed at the office on the night of the pageant, Beaver is sent on ahead in Lumpy's car with Wally—in costume. One of Lumpy's retreads blows out and Beaver has to walk through the streets to school. Wishing he was a real rabbit so he could crawl into a hole and die, Beaver suffers all kinds of stares from passersby and even tries hiding in a garbage can, but faces his greatest challenge when he is chased by a pack of dogs. He takes refuge in a phone booth, where he calls the police. Much to his nervous teacher's relief, Beaver arrives just before curtain time, the only bunny in school-pageant history to make an entrance with a police escort. Afterward Beaver concludes that he might be better off being a real animal, because no one would ever force him to portray a human being in a pageant.

NOBODY LOVES ME

Looking at the plethora of popular parenting psychology books in a store window, Beaver is disturbed to hear Richard's explanation that they are at the "awkward stage." When he arrives home, Ward, June, and Wally manage to yell at him almost constantly for being messy and clumsy. In getting ready for bed, Beaver tries to clean up his act, but his parents don't notice, and he is convinced he is ugly and unwanted. The next day, even Gus and Miss Landers, the two adults he can usually rely on to put things in perspective for him, can't comfort him. Wally recognizes what his brother is going through, and when Beaver locks himself in the bathroom, Wally believes he's crying. He urges his parents to make a big fuss about Beaver's "catching a cold" with those sniffles and to find some indirect way to

make it clear to him that they still love him even if he's not as cute as he used to be. Ward manages to smoothly convey that they've always *loved* Beaver and that, in fact, they now *like* and *respect* him as he's maturing. This does the trick for Beaver, and for the first time in a while he even lets June kiss him.

BEAVER'S LAUNDRY

Richard is on laundromat detail for his family, and Beaver goes along to help. The trip is a disastrous one, as they drop the clothing bundle, have to rescue his father's shorts from a frisky dog, and wind up losing all the money before they get to the machines. Richard asks if they can do the laundry at Beaver's house. Nobody is home, so the two would-be laundrymen stuff the clothes in June's washer and add a whole box of detergent and starch. By the time Wally and Eddie get home, the machine is overflowing suds all over the laundry room. Knowing that he's certain to get blamed for not watching his brother, Wally gives him coins for the laundromat while he gets to work with Eddie mopping up the mess. Ward and June arrive to a spotless laundry room and are suspicious. Then June finds the empty soap and starch boxes and Ward properly connects them to the too-clean floor, but they decide to say nothing to the boys, although Ward is bemused that they usually have to "threaten them with boarding school" to get them to clean up after themselves.

BEAVER'S LONG NIGHT

Ward and June are a little nervous about making good on their promise to Beaver about not having to have a baby-sitter the next time they go out. Wally will be home ony briefly between his basketball game and a masquerade party, so they invite Gilbert to keep Beaver company for the night. The two boys are spooked by the gangster movie they've watched on television, so when they see a gray car pull up outside with two rough-looking characters inside, they believe they're about to get rubbed out. What they don't know is that the goons are Lumpy and Bill Scott, who are in their costumes and masks, waiting to pick up Wally for the party. Beaver, pretending to be his father so he'll be taken seriously, calls the police, and they arrive to arrest the suspicious-looking characters. When Wally returns from the game, he asks if Lumpy has come by yet. The boys realize whom they've had arrested and run up to hide without telling Wally what they've done. An angry late-night phone call from Fred Rutherford demanding to know why a "Mr. Cleaver" has had his lad arrested leads to the boys' being awakened to clear things up. Beaver spends the whole long next day apologizing to everyone involved.

BEAVER'S JACKET

Richard gets a snappy new jacket with leather trim and a pocket that has its own lock, and Beaver wants one, too. Badly. Ward and June feel the $23.76 jacket (tax included) is rather too expensive, but when Beaver looks "so darn sad" and Ward puts himself in his son's place, Beaver gets his wish. Beaver is proud of his new jacket, but Richard is worried about his, which has disappeared in record time. He convinces Beaver to share the remaining jacket between them until his shows up again. Beaver wears it home, then lowers it out the window to Richard, who puts it on and then brings it back in the morning so that Beaver can hoist it through the window, with his parents being none the wiser.

There is a tense moment when Richard spills food on the jacket while he's wearing it, but Beaver is able to avoid spilling the beans. A trickier situation develops when Richard's mother sends the soiled jacket out to be dry-cleaned and Richard arrives at the Cleavers wearing a sweater. They're saved when Richard's jacket shows up in time for them to wear it the next day, but Beaver is caught when Ward notices the jacket being pulled up through the window. Ward and June decide that while the boys were deceptive, no real damage was done.

BEAVER'S FEAR

Wally needs a fifth for a group discount to the Bellport amusement park, and Beaver gets to go by default. He's thrilled to be going with his big brother and his friends, but he gets an attack of queasiness when Whitey and Richard tell him hair-raising stories about the Big Dipper roller coaster, which feels like a parachute drop without a parachute. Before going to the park, Beaver visits Gus, who tells him about being scared before his first jump as a rookie fireman off a high platform into a net. Strengthened by this bit of borrowed courage, Beaver prepares for the Big Dipper. Eddie, who has been particularly obnoxious during the trip, clowns around as the ride starts, while Beaver hugs himself tensely, mumbling, "Gus and the net," over and over. As the coaster hurtles through its twists and turns and plummets, it's Beaver who relaxes and starts to enjoy the thrills, while Eddie screams in sheer terror, grabs Lumpy for security, and winds up practically poured out of his seat. While Lumpy helps a ghostly Eddie back to the car, Beaver and Wally return for another big dip. At home, Beaver receives the supreme accolade from Wally, who tells Ward and June that Beaver was so good he almost forgot Beaver was his kid brother.

EDDIE QUITS SCHOOL

"I'm kissing these ivy halls good-bye," brags Eddie after he has gotten in real trouble for hanging the track coach in effigy in the locker room. He's landed a job at Thompson's Garage for eighty dollars a week and shows up to show off to Wally the new clothes he's bought on time. June suggests Wally talk sense to his friend, but Wally thinks Eddie's doing great. Then he and Lumpy go to the garage to buy a fan belt and watch unseen as Eddie gets a ringing dressing down from his boss. Afterward, Eddie still presents the brassy front to his pals. Soon his old buddies are too wrapped up in their school activities to have time for Eddie, and Wally becomes convinced that lonely Eddie would like to forego the working world and return to academia but would never admit he was wrong to drop out. Wally talks to the principal, Mr. Farmer, who is sympathetic and goes to the garage and tells Eddie they are having a tough time filling Eddie's shoes as manager of the track team. To hear Eddie tell it, there he was with the principal pleading with him to come back and old man Thompson on his knees begging him to stay. Upon Eddie's return, Lumpy jokes, "Now the coach is going to drop out of school."

THREE BOYS AND A BURRO

Beaver, Richard, and Gilbert pool their funds for Pepe, a thirty-dollar burro which they plan to share. Ward agrees only when he is assured it will be boarded at the other houses. The first host is Richard. As soon as Pepe makes lunch out of his mother's flowers, Richard drops the burro off at Gilbert's, where the stay is even shorter once Pepe wreaks havoc with the hanging wash. While the Cleavers are out for the evening, Richard and Gilbert leave Pepe in the backyard, which is where Beaver and Wally discover him in the middle of the night. Pepe proves too noisy a secret to hide from their parents, but they

are forced to keep him tied to a tree for the night. The next morning Pepe breaks free and winds up wearing June's new trellis. Ward lays down the law: the burro must pack up. The boys can't find a buyer, but

Ward manages to sell Pepe for twenty dollars to a nearby farmer. With droopy faces the partners bid farewell to Pepe. Beaver divides the money evenly, with two dollars left over for a new baseball bat the boys will share—that is, until June calls up to Beaver inquiring what he knows about the broken bat someone left on their front lawn.

WALLY'S STAYS AT LUMPY'S

Beaver asks if Gilbert can stay over some night, but June refuses, saying Gilbert can stay some night Wally is away. Separately, Wally asks Ward for permission to spend all of Friday night at Lumpy's to help him throw his first party, and gets told he can stay away only when Beaver has an overnight visitor. Friday night Ward and June are visiting friends and Gilbert is alone with Beaver. Lumpy's party goes well; however, while they're cleaning up, Wally and Lumpy discover a big spot on the Rutherfords' rug, and Lumpy begs Wally to sleep over, since his father will not yell at him so badly in front of company. Wally calls home for permission, and he and Beaver determine that they have met the conditions laid down individually by their parents, so they agree to have Gilbert stay over with Beaver and Wally will stay with Lumpy. The next morning Ward and June are quite surprised to see Gilbert come down for breakfast instead of Wally. When they compare notes, they realize their sons got them on a technicality and they decide that since they frequently force the boys to comply strictly with the rules, they really can't blame them for trying to even the score a little this time.

THE YOUNGER BROTHER

Basketball practice is starting in the park and Ward suggests Beaver try out. The coach, Mr. Doyle, is particularly happy to have another Cleaver on his team, since Wally was a high-scoring star. Eddie tells Beaver that his big athlete brother is the only reason they want him for the team, and Beaver gets so nervous trying to match Wally's reputation that he plays like a complete klutz. In fact, he's so terrible the coach suggests he seek out a more experienced team. Unable to face his family after this humiliation, Beaver continues to stay away from home during practice to keep up the illusion. Ward stops off at the court on the way home from work and is dismayed to learn from the coach that Beaver was cut after the first practice. Wally finds Beaver rubbing dirt on his new sneakers to get them "crummed-up" as if he's been playing hard, and suggests he come clean to his father. Ward tells Beaver that he is not expected to be as good as his brother in everything and that he might very well outperform Wally in some way, which pumps up Beaver's ego, as does his smashing three-straight-game defeat of Wally in checkers.

LUMPY'S CAR TROUBLE

Lumpy's heap is out of commission, so Wally asks permission to have Lumpy drive him and Beaver to a track meet in Ward's car. Ward agrees on the condition that they take no other passengers and stick to the main highway. As soon as he's behind the wheel, Lumpy drives to Eddie's, since he's previously agreed to pick him up. Wally is not happy about this but has no choice. The drive up is safe enough, but on the return trip, over Wally's objections, Lumpy takes the dirt-road shortcut, and tries to show off by speeding through a puddle and winds up stopping the car dead. The boys get out and push the car back onto the highway, and Wally makes them chip in to get a gas-station attendant to repair it. A few days later Ward learns about the boys' adventure from a fellow employee who happened to see them pushing the car. Ward reprimands Wally for breaking his word and points out it was wrong to let Lumpy and Eddie talk him into doing so. Wally and Beaver are unable to figure out how Ward could smoke out their wrongdoing at such a remote location and decide they'd better play it straight in the face of such mysterious power.

BEAVER THE BABY-SITTER

Wally gets Beaver to fill in for him as a baby-sitter for little Chuckie Murdock. Beaver's confidence turns to a sick feeling in his stomach, however, when he learns he's got to care, not for five-year-old Chuckie, but for his "goony" ten-year-old sister, Patricia. In order to placate her, Beaver submits unwillingly to playing house and pretending he and Patricia are the mommy and daddy to six kids. He begins to get into the spirit of the game, but then Wally and Eddie stop by to check up on him and he realizes word of his playing house is bound to get around school. When he gets home he asks permission to stay home sick the next day, which is denied. Patricia follows Beaver all around school, making cow eyes and exhibiting a big crush on him, much to his distress. To help him out, Wally baby-sits for her the next time and she quickly forgets all about Beaver in favor of his older brother. This actually makes Beaver a little sad; he confides to Gilbert that he misses the attentions of the "goony" girl.

BEAVER'S TYPEWRITER

Beaver makes a pitch to Ward for his own typewriter, which he says could help him tremendously with his school assignments. Ward agrees on the condition that Beaver stick with something for a change. He's struggling with an essay on the machine when Eddie comes to borrow money from Wally. Wally turns him down, but when he leaves the room, Eddie makes a deal to type Beaver's essay for a dollar. The essay gets a B-plus, and his teacher, Mr. Bailey, is so delighted by the steps Beaver's taking to "lick that neatness problem" that he writes a note of thanks to his parents. Beaver is uneasy because he knows he got the good notice under false pretenses. He decides to go back to longhand, but Eddie tells him Mr. Bailey will frown on his messy writing again. He gives Beaver a solution by "fixing" the typewriter so he can honestly tell Mr. Bailey his machine is broken. Mr. Bailey mentions the broken typewriter to June at a school meeting and it's a complete surprise to her. Ward decides to leave the disciplining for the deception to Mr. Bailey, but he does urge Beaver not to give up on trying to learn to type. When Wally sees him slowly pecking away at the keys, he's glad to see his brother finally wising up.

BROTHER VERSUS BROTHER

It's a new feeling for Beaver: he's fallen head over heels for a new girl in his class, Mary Tyler. He dresses neatly, douses himself in after-shave, and carries her books home so she won't get a charley horse. When Beaver invites her over to play Monopoly, Mary gets an instant crush on Wally. She insists on following Wally around, which annoys both brothers for differ-

ent reasons. Beaver feels betrayed and Wally views her as a pesky little girl. Beaver stops speaking to Wally and refuses to listen to reason. To straighten things out, Wally tells Mary flat out she's much too young for him to ever be interested in. Angrily she vows she'll never speak to Wally again. She attempts to make up with Beaver, but he passes her a "drop-dead" note in class and makes up with Wally instead. June doesn't know whether to be sad or happy that Beaver's brief romance is over, and Wally says his mother's acting just like a girl.

THE MERCHANT MARINE

Wally is pretty shook-up by Ward's stern talking-to regarding missing dinner and failing to call. He has also had a fight with his girlfriend, Mary Ellen Rogers, so when June finds an envelope of Merchant Marine information with Wally's name on it, she is worried that he might be just upset enough to consider joining up. She and Ward try to show Wally they love him, but get little reaction. Actually, Wally only sent for the material for Lumpy, who sees the Merchant Marine as his passport to freedom from his father, who has angered him. When Wally gets the Merchant Marine application, Lumpy, his duffel bag all packed, thinks that he's as good as in the service and lifts the secrecy vow from Wally, freeing him to tell Ward the full story. As awkward as he feels, Ward is honor-bound to tell Fred. Fred, thinking Ward needs his advice, comes over to the Cleavers', where Wally and Lumpy listen to his long discourse on family harmony, which he delivers without realizing it's *his* son who wants to run away. But listening to his father, Lumpy thinks he's making concessions and decides to go back home with Daddy. The next day Lumpy reclaims his packed duffel bag from Wally, hoping to sneak it home past his father.

THE YARD BIRDS

Ward makes the boys cancel their Saturday plans and clean up the garage and yard while he and June are away. They have to meet an afternoon deadline for the trash hauler. With no concern for the passing time, Beaver and Wally goof around with curve balls, bows and arrows, and such until they've missed the pickup. When Lumpy and Eddie arrive, the boys accept Eddie's offer to use Lumpy's custom heap to haul the trash to the dump—for a modest fee, of course. Ward and June arrive home to a clear yard and are pleased the boys completed their task without parental supervision. Eddie decides it would be silly to drive all the way to

the dump, so he and Lumpy unload the trash on a vacant lot along the way. That afternoon, Mr. Hill, the owner of the lot, carries a magazine with Ward's name on it over to the house, demanding the garbage be removed from his lot. Ward apologizes and marches upstairs to give the boys their orders and a lecture about not trusting someone else to do things they should have done themselves. The following day all four of the boys clean the lot, and for once, neither Eddie nor Lumpy goofs off, because Mr. Hill is there to oversee the workers.

TENNIS, ANYONE?

Instead of Eddie Haskell, Wally winds up playing tennis with a very beautiful—and much older—partner, Carole Martin, who has had a fight with her boyfriend, Don. It's an instant love match for Wally, who isn't aware Carole is just playing with him to spite Don. They play again, and Eddie and Lumpy are very impressed with the girl Wally's now

courting, but somebody else is watching their game: Don. After the match he warns Wally off Carole. Wally seeks out Ward's counsel but doesn't want to follow his father's advice to stay out of the situation. The next day Wally shows up for his tennis date, only to see that Carole and Don have made up and have eyes only for each other. Crushed and disillusioned, Wally now realizes his father was trying to keep him from getting hurt. Wally lets no moss grow on him, though, as he soon heads off to take tennis lessons from a pro who has a niece that he's looking forward to meeting, thereby convincing Beaver that tennis is just a "mushy" game.

SWEATSHIRT MONSTERS

Beaver swoops through the house to get the necessary change from his piggy-bank to join his friends at a special sweatshirt sale. Each of them buys a shirt with a monster's face, one more gruesome than the next. Beaver proudly selects a Martian staring out at the world through three eyeballs. The boys declare they will all wear their new monster shirts to school the next day. Each of them is stopped in this pursuit by their parents at breakfast the next morning, except that Beaver, unlike his pals, merely covers over his Martian with a regulation shirt long enough to get out of the house. When he gets

to school with every eyeball in clear view, he sees that his buddies have not followed suit. Beaver's sent to the principal, who calls June, who in turn sends an angry Ward to deal with it. Back home, Ward lectures Beaver, stressing that if a thing is wrong, no amount of promises to others will make it right. Beaver admits it would be pretty gruesome if everyone wore shirts like his. He is confined to his room for the weekend, but Ward does grant him permission to wear the offending sweatshirt while he does his time.

A NIGHT IN THE WOODS

There's a large mound of camping equipment that's in danger of going unused when Gilbert's father has to cancel the weekend trip he was planning for Gilbert, Beaver, Whitey, and Alan. Beaver resorts to a tried-and-true trick to salvage the overnight by asking—in front of Ward and June—Wally if he would take over as guide. The strategy works, much to Eddie and Lumpy's unhappiness, because they need Wally to be the date of the girl who is providing their dates for Saturday. Eddie decides their best bet is to go to the campgrounds and scare Beaver and his friends so badly they'll beg Wally to take them home. At dusk Lumpy and Eddie approach the campsite armed with a battery-powered phonograph and a record of zoo-animal noises. The sounds don't have the desired effect, but they do manage to awaken Wally, who sets off to scare away the unseen beast. Lumpy and Eddie make a mad dash out of sight and Lumpy soon returns to Wally and the boys to tell them sheepishly that as they fled, Eddie fell over a cliff and is trapped on a ledge. The boys get a ranger to the rescue, who reprimands Eddie for fooling around in the forest.

STOCKS AND BONDS

To teach the boys a practical lesson in economics, Ward gets them to put up twenty-five dollars apiece from their savings, which he matches, to invest in the stock market. Financial wizard Eddie tells them to buy a "swingin' " stock, Jet-Electro, which is involved in "space-age junk." Ward cautions them against speculative stock and they invest in the more stable Mayfield Power and Electric. After a few days though, the big investors discover Jet-Electro has zoomed up to $2.50 per share while theirs has gone up a mere twenty-five cents. They get Ward to switch them to Jet-Electro and are thrilled when it gets to three dollars a share. However, the newspaper reports that Jet-Electro has lost a vital government contract and the stock plummets to seventy-five cents a share. The boys are heartbroken about their loss until Ward informs them that he had advised his broker to sell off Jet-Electro when it went below $2.50 and buy back Mayfield Power and Electric. Everyone is pleased, especially Ward, who says, "When your sons think you're smarter than their friends, you've really got it made."

LONG-DISTANCE CALL

It's phony-phone-call time for Beaver and his friends, and the boys decide to liven things up by calling somebody famous. They have a dollar among them to cover costs, so they place a long-distance call to one of their heroes, Don Drysdale at Dodger Stadium in Los Angeles. The boys decide to hold the phone until the pitcher emerges from the shower. He is nice enough to talk to each of the boys, even though Beaver admits to owning a Warren Spahn glove. The boys are astounded to learn the charges will run to $9.35—plus tax. They make a pact not to mention the call to anyone and advise Beaver not to tell his parents. The secret's short-lived, though, because a schoolmate, Kenny, brags about having a racing driver's picture and Beaver brags back about Drysdale. Three local boys coming into such close contact with a celebrity is too big a story to keep from the media, especially since Kenny's father works for the paper. Ward reads the write-up and angrily confronts Beaver and his friends. He metes out punishment of an hour's worth of yard work after school for a week for the three mad callers.

UNTOGETHERNESS

Ward has made reservations for the family vacation at their usual lakeside cabin. This summer, though, Wally is not thrilled by the news because he is badly smitten with a new girl, Lori Anne, who quotes Tennyson and works at the library. Not wanting to be separated from Lori Anne, Wally tells his parents he wants to stay home, using as his excuse that he can't get away from his job at the drugstore. Since he knows his parents won't want him to stay by himself, he has arranged to stay at the Haskells', even though Eddie

tries to charge him five dollars a week for board until his mother stops him. June is concerned until Ward tells her of his first absence from a family engagement, which turned out to be quite momentous: his first date with June. When Lori Anne reveals to Wally that she is planning to go away with *her* parents, he is shattered but doesn't feel he can go back to his parents and tell them. Instead he sadly watches them pull away with their trunkful of vacation-fun stuff. As they drive away, though, they see Eddie, who tells them about Lori Anne not being around and they immediately drive back to get Wally, who's looking forward to the best family vacation ever.

WALLY'S LICENSE

Since even Eddie has a license, Ward and June can't find any valid reasons to deny Wally's seventeenth-birthday request to begin driving lessons at school. Wally is teamed with know-it-all Shirley for his lessons. She drives smoothly while Wally makes beginner's errors like forgetting to put the key in the ignition or to remove the emergency brake, and driving in reverse. The instructor gives him confidence, telling Wally to keep his mind on driving and off Shirley. Ward takes Wally to his road test and they watch as the examiner flunks Shirley, which makes Wally additionally nervous, but he passes with flying colors, helped no doubt by the "driving prayers" Beaver has said for him back home. The new driver quickly asks Ward for his car for that night. Ward gives him the keys, and the family waits anxiously for Wally's return. Safely back, Wally tells Beaver that he always looked forward to the fun of driving, but sitting alone behind the steering wheel that night, all he could think of was what a big responsibility it was. Flinging a wet towel at Beaver helps relieve some of that new pressure of maturity.

WALLY BUYS A CAR

With $180 saved toward his own car, Wally surprises his parents by telling them he has put down a five-dollar deposit on a "real bomb," a great set of wheels. Once he finds out his likely insurance costs, Wally loses all

hope of ever affording a car, but Ward offers to help him out if Wally's grades don't suffer and if he can check out Wally's bomb. Ward gives the prospective purchase a thorough grilling and rejects it as a sharp-looking but poor-running pile of junk. They visit used-car lots and test-drive a number of cars until they find one which Ward proclaims is "not much for pretty but it gets the job done and it's safe." As they drive up to the house, Wally is very excited and Ward even gets June to show some enthusiasm for Wally's new chariot. Wally very much wants to chauffeur the family out to dinner that night, and so they pile in and Ward and June are good sports, not saying anything about the ragged upholstery, engine noise, and springs poking through at them. After dinner Wally tells Ward his help meant a lot to him because he knows he could have really been taken, and Ward replies, "It means a lot to me to have you say that."

WALLY'S DINNER DATE

June feels that Wally is old enough to take his girlfriend, Julie Foster, on a formal dinner date. Julie suggests the White Fox, which she's heard is simply "the yummiest place on earth." It also happens to be the swankiest restaurant in Mayfield. Wally calls up for a reservation, and— at Eddie's recommendation—to check out the prices for soup and coffee. He's taken aback by the prices, but is shut out of a reservation in any case. Wally knows Julie will be disappointed. Unbeknownst to his son, Ward steps in to place a call to the maître d', whom he knows from his business lunches at the White Fox, and gets him to call Wally back with a sudden availability. Julie is also rather surprised by La Grande Carte prices, and they both order the fish special and have a marvelous dinner. When it comes time to pay the bill, Wally gets a sinking feeling, for he's discovered he's left his wallet home. Luckily June has found it while picking up his room and Ward has made another call to the maître d', arranging credit for Wally, so he is able to just sign the check and look like a real big shot in front of his dinner date.

THE CLOTHING DRIVE

Beaver is determined to amass enough points collecting for the school clothing drive to win the Good Citizen Award and get a certificate signed by the mayor and his picture in the paper. June helps by going through her closets and Ward's. The following morning, a large pile of old clothing awaits Beaver in the hallway. Right next to them, Ward drops three of his suits, with only a note to June stuffed in one of the pockets, asking

her to take them to the cleaners. Beaver easily wins the award with a thousand points—thanks to Ward's suits, which he has mistakenly brought along with his bundle. Ward realizes the error and the next morning has a hard day at school where he sheepishly tries to explain things in the principal's office. Beaver is given twenty-four hours to collect enough clothing to make up for the suits Ward has taken back, and with the whole family's help he does. However, he tells Mr. Bailey, his teacher, that he doesn't want his class to think he's a no-good Good Citizen because he had an extra chance to win. Mr. Bailey tells the class that Beaver has learned an excellent lesson in what a good citizen is. The prize is eventually split between Beaver, his friend Mike, and a "third guy, named Sally Johnson, who gave a lot of good junk."

BEAVER'S AUTOBIOGRAPHY

"I've read some of his compositions," Ward says; "John O'Hara and J. D. Salinger have nothing to worry about"—which is why Beaver turns to some outside help on his autobiography assignment. He hears that Betsy, a new girl in his class, is a good English student, so he asks her to pad out his two messy takes to the required three pages of glistening prose.

Betsy agrees because she thinks Beaver's cute. Then her friend Virginia tells Betsy that Beaver calls her a "goon" to other boys. In a junior fit of pique Betsy sets about coloring Beaver's life with all sorts of extravagant, crazy made-up details. The class rocks with laughter and Beaver cringes when the teacher reads his autobiography, then cringes some more when he gets an F for being a clown. Ward finds out and lectures Beaver about having others do his homework and instructs him to hand in an honest piece, which he does, to receive an honest C. Betsy does tell the teacher about her role in the travesty and Beaver ends up a little more learned about the dangers of slighting a member of the opposite sex.

THE LATE EDITION

Beaver tries out for an open paper route but gets beaten to it by a new boy in the neighborhood. Beaver begins a vigil each evening, keeping track as the paper is repeatedly late and thrown into the bushes, piling up enough evidence to get the new paper boy fired. Ward finally has enough of poor service and asks Beaver to stop the paper boy and ask him to come in to speak to him. The paper boy won't stop so Beaver pulls him off his bike and in the ensuing melee Beaver discovers the paper boy is really a

paper *girl* before she escapes. Beaver is nervous as Wally tells him "getting in a fight with a girl is just about the worst thing that can happen to a guy." Ward now thinks the paper boy is a bully, and Beaver can't find a way to tell him the truth, so Ward is shocked when the paper girl comes collecting that night. He questions her service and the girl starts crying, explaining that she's been filling in for her brother since he came down with the measles so he won't lose his route. Ward, who has placed a call to the paper, asks Beaver what to say when the circulation manager calls back. A thoroughly cowed Beaver tells his father to say they have a fine paper boy.

EDDIE, THE BUSINESSMAN

The teenage job market is tight in town, but Ward is able to get Wally and Eddie work in the shipping department of Mayfield Dairies through the owner, Ted Worden, with whom he plays golf. Eddie, as usual trying to get ahead the easy way, toadies up to the foreman, who asks him to load some ice cream into his car trunk. Unbeknownst to Eddie, the foreman and his assistant have a little racket going of selling the ice cream on their own. When the foreman gives Eddie a bonus of a carton for his extra work, Eddie gives a few packages to Wally. Ward comes home and reports that on the golf course Ted had complained about an irritating series of plant disappearances. He sees the packages from the dairy in the freezer and has a talk with Wally. Without accusing anyone of the thefts, Ward advises Wally to tell Eddie to stop helping the foreman. Eddie thinks his friend is just jealous of his close relationship with the boss and gets caught with another load of pilfered ice cream by Ted. Wally steps in to clear Eddie, who thanks him, admitting he was too busy buttering up people at the plant to see what was going on. Wally doesn't feel much like going out after an exhausting week's work, and he's certain he couldn't face a session in the ice cream parlor.

BEAVER'S FOOTBALL AWARD

At the upcoming Father and Son Awards Night banquet in the school gym Beaver is going to be given his football letter. The team members complain about having to get up in front of everyone and wear jackets and ties, and Terry, the team's star player, announces that he is planning to wear a sweater. Beaver and the others vow that they will also dress casually. The night of the banquet Beaver refuses to get into his good clothes and Ward is ready to let his stubborn son miss the banquet but June insists he cannot miss getting his award, so they let him go in his school sweater. When they enter the gym Beaver gets sick to his stomach when all of the other boys, including Terry, are wearing ties and jackets and their fathers look askance at his attire. He asks Ward if they can go home. Outside in the parking lot Ward produces Beaver's good clothes, which he has had the foresight to pack in the trunk. Beaver asks why his father went to all the trouble after he has been so stupid, instead of clobbering him, and Ward says probably because under the same circumstances his father *would* have clobbered him. Beaver gets his picture in the paper receiving the Most Inspirational Player trophy, agreeing he would have looked awfully silly in his sweater.

DOUBLE DATE

Carolyn Stewart, Wally's new girlfriend, tells him that she can't go to the movies with him on Saturday because she has to watch her younger sister, Susan. Once she meets Beaver, Carolyn suggests Wally talk Beaver into double-dating with Susan. A sure sign he's growing up, Beaver readily agrees and brags to Gilbert about his first date. Beaver's primary concern is that he and Wally share all of the expenses and that his brother not patronize him at the movies. Even Wally admits Beaver looks sharp "for a little squirt," although they have to dilute his overdousing of after-shave. Just before they are ready to pick up their girls, Carolyn calls to say that Susan has chickened out. She suggests Beaver give her sister a call to talk her into changing her mind. Beaver talks to Susan and confides that he is scared himself and the two eighth-graders agree that someday when they get over being scared, they might meet. Beaver heads up to his room to hang up his junior-playboy front for another night.

BEAVER JOINS A RECORD CLUB

An ad for a rock 'n' roll record club offering a record a week for only eighty-seven cents is too good for Beaver to resist, and Ward, in agreeing to let Beaver join, puts him on a fixed allowance and gives him control of his own finances. Beaver turns into a "little cheapskate," watching every penny now that he controls his own cash flow, but what he doesn't watch carefully is the flow of bonus records at additional cost that seem to be a part of each week's mailings. Wally warns him these extra platters will break him if he doesn't send them back, but Beaver ignores him and stuffs

the brochures in a drawer unread. When the threatening bill arrives Beaver knows he's in for it when they refer to him as "Mister," but he's stupefied that he owes $17.60. "I never knew a guy could get in this much trouble just liking music," he says. Ward works out a way for Beaver to pay back the bills on a weekly basis out of his allowance. But when he gets another mailing of bonus records he immediately yells, "Dad, they're after me again."

TELL IT TO ELLA

Beaver's friends Mike and Kevin have tickets to the mid-week jalopy races but Beaver is not allowed to go out on school nights because it might interfere with his grades. Eddie suggests he plead his case through "Tell It to Ella," the teenage advice column in the newspaper. Beaver writes the letter and signs it "Prisoner." Ella answers his letter in the paper but she double-crosses him by agreeing with his parents that he should wait until the weekends to see his friends. Beaver tries to hide the column from his parents, figuring when they see Ella backing them up he'll practically have to "wait until I'm a married man before I get to leave the house on a week night." Ward reads the letter at the barber shop and brings it up at dinner. Before Beaver can confess, Mike and Kevin come over to complain that once their parents saw the letter they were grounded on week nights as well. They tell Beaver they hope "Prisoner gets life." Beaver confesses to Ward and June that he wrote the letter, and they tell him that he should have spoken to them about his distress. He realizes he never should have listened to Eddie, no matter how smart he makes stupid stuff sound.

BACHELOR-AT-LARGE

Eddie has made the big break from his parents, setting himself up in what he describes as a fabulous, swinging bachelor pad. He invites Lumpy and Wally over for dinner to show off his place, but his father has called Ward and asked his cooperation in not having his friends encourage Eddie in this venture. Wally walks over to the apartment with Beaver to tell Eddie he won't be able to make dinner. Eddie is out, but his landlady, Mrs. Evans, shows the boys she is glad he's finally gotten some visitors. She says he's the loneliest boy she ever saw, sitting by himself in his room and eating awful meals. She shows them his humble and messy quarters and the dog Eddie got from the pound for company. The boys run into Eddie on the way home but don't have the heart to tell him what they've learned about him. Wally gives Mrs. Evans the Haskells' phone number and

his parents take him back, though to hear Eddie tell it, his folks came crawling to him and begged him to return.

BEAVER, THE SHEEP DOG

"This is one of our sensitive days," June says about Beaver, and it turns out he is upset because his classmate Shirley has called him a "sheep dog" because of his natural bangs. Beaver tries all sorts of remedies to tame his hair, including hair spray and slicking down his head with hair oil. Ward tries to convince Beaver to take Shirley's comments good-naturedly, but Beaver is miserable over having to face her and his jeering friends. Eddie suggests that instead of trying to do something about his hair, he take care of Shirley by striking back and insulting her personal appearance. The next day Beaver is waiting for her and tells Shirley in front of everyone that she's ugly and has a face like a cuckoo clock. Shirley starts to cry and Beaver wants to go and hide, not because of his hair but because he sees he's really hurt her. He gets in trouble with his teacher, and the two name-callers reach a truce and Beaver can relax his mind—and his hair.

WALLY'S CAR ACCIDENT

Ward's new car is only one week old, yet he lets Wally borrow it for a Friday-night prom while he and June are away for the weekend. At the prom Eddie and Lumpy prod Wally into using his father's "dreamwagon" to give Lumpy's crate a push, and Eddie's careless directions cause Wally to smash a headlight on Ward's car. Eddie warns Wally that when his father sees the damage, "it's back to the coaster wagon for you," so Wally agrees to take the car to a mechanic to get it fixed. The boys pool their funds and pay the eighteen-dollar charge. By the time Ward and June return, the headlight is as good as new and the boys have polished the car to a keen shine, much to Ward's delight. Wally has made up his mind to tell Ward about the accident anyway, but before he gets a chance, Ward answers the phone and listens to Lumpy talk about the headlight until Lumpy realizes it's not Wally on the other end of the line. Ward calls Wally into the den for a session. Afterward, Beaver points out to Wally that he shouldn't be blamed, since the other guys talked him into it, but Wally feels this is no excuse at his age. "Is that what Dad told you?" asks Beaver. "No, that's what I told myself" is Wally's reply.

BEAVER, THE HERO

"Beaver isn't acting much like the Beaver" is Gilbert's analysis of the situation when Beaver gets a swelled head after he scores a winning touchdown at the big game. Suddenly girls who never looked his way are flocking around him, the local paper prints a photo of his feat, and the drugstore even names a sundae after him. Wally tries to put a halt to his arrogance, but Beaver concludes his brother's only jealous of his athletic prowess. Matters take a far worse turn when Eddie gives "Crazy Legs" advice which he guarantees will have Beaver

"endorsing greasy kid stuff" and being courted with scholarships in no time. Beaver decides he's too good and important a star to attend afternoon practice the day before a crucial game. His ego balloon is burst, however, when the coach calls to inform him that inasmuch as he didn't bother to show up for the practice, he need not bother to suit up for the game. Beaver is crushed but learns his lesson. He's reinstated when he regularly shows up for extra practice sessions, and realizes he was going haywire when he saw Eddie Haskell on his side.

THE PARTY SPOILER

Beaver thinks it's such a gyp that Wally has banned him from the party he's throwing at the house that Beaver follows Gilbert's diabolical suggestion that he sabotage the affair with tricks from the magic shop. They plant a fine assortment of plastic ice cubes with bugs in the center, rubber cheese slices, chocolates with soap centers, and a start-stop device in the record-player plug. At Ward and June's behest Wally breaks down just before the party and invites Beaver to attend. It's too late to remove the pranks before the guests arrive, so Beaver watches in miserable silence as Lumpy spits out the soapy candy and Eddie gnaws at an elastic cheese sandwich. Wally's friends are outraged, accusing him of the rankest juvenile behavior, but before the party becomes a fiasco Beaver steps forward to confess his role. Wally is furious and the brothers cease speaking to one another. Eventually they make up. Beaver can't resist one more trick while they're shaking hands as he zaps Wally with an electric buzzer.

THE MUSTACHE

As they watch Wally's girl, Julie Foster, stroll down the school hallway on the arm of another boy, Eddie's assessment of Wally's position is, "You're out, Clyde." Julie's new beau is Wayne Gregory, a transfer student from a swanky Eastern school who affects very sophisticated mannerisms—and a dapper mustache. Wally overhears Julie say he's a nice boy but "so naive and immature," and he's convinced that cultivating a mustache of his own during their school break is the way to lure her back. After a few days and hundreds of close inspections in the mirror, Wally is ready to debut his mustache in school. Beaver is probably the kindest when he tells Wally he's "no Cesar Romero." Every one of his classmates, including

Julie, and even his teacher, laugh in Wally's face. Wally can't shave off his mustache fast enough. Ward points out that the best impression anyone can make is just to be himself. Ward further notes that women are inconsistent, and no man can ever figure out beforehand how they will react. Sure enough, Julie returns to Wally, saying she was very touched that he grew the mustache for her benefit, but does ask him never to do it again.

THE PARKING ATTENDANTS

Wally secures a job parking the cars for a big society-page wedding reception and Eddie agrees to split the job. In their attendants' uniforms the boys look like real pros, even though Eddie thinks the work's "for the birds" and they should just point the drivers to a spot and let them park their cars themselves. He and Wally spend the afternoon running back and forth, and the host is pleased. It gets harder to find nearby spaces, so Eddie parks one of the guests' cars in a restricted private parking lot. The car happens to belong to Fred Rutherford and he raises quite a fuss when Eddie returns with the bad news that his car must have been towed. Indeed, Lumpy calls his father to say the police phoned to say they have his car at the station.

Feeling very guilty, Wally apologizes to the host and refuses to take the fifteen dollars for the day's work, then tells off Eddie in no uncertain terms. Wally tells the whole messy story to Ward, who decides that after working that hard without getting paid and having to cope with Eddie's stupidity to boot, Wally needs no additional punishment or discussions on the subject of responsibility.

MORE BLESSED TO GIVE?

Beaver is infatuated with pretty young Donna Yaeger but hasn't quite worked up the courage to do more than moon around outside her house waiting for her to pass by. He wins a Hoop-A-La prize at the carnival, a twenty-dollar gold locket, and Eddie tells him it's the kind of present you give to "dolls" rather than your mom so that "you don't make your Pop look like a cheapskate." Beaver cuts his picture and Donna's out of the yearbook, puts them in the locket, and hands it over to Donna. She is, of course, delighted. When the Yaegers find out the gift is a rather expensive piece of jewelry and not a trinket, Mr. Yaeger mails it back to Beaver. June finds the locket and assumes Donna sent it to Beaver. Ward also decides the gift is inappropriate, so he brings it over to the Yaegers. When he learns the true turn of events,

Ward comes home, bemoaning that "our sweet little innocent Beaver is a junior Casanova." He commiserates with Beaver over the pangs of puppy love. Beaver shyly gives the locket to June, who accepts it philosophically, knowing that it is a mother's fate to get used to playing second fiddle to her son's girlfriends.

BEAVER'S GOOD DEED

For once Gilbert gives Beaver good advice but he ignores it: Gilbert thinks Beaver's asking for big trouble when he lets a tramp into the house while they're alone. Beaver remembers a recent lecture from Ward about being kinder and more considerate of others, so he offers the tramp, "Mr. Jeff," his full hospitality. This includes food and a "washing up," which turns out to be a luxurious bath in Ward and June's tub. Beaver realizes he's gone a little overboard and enlists Wally's help in asking Mr. Jeff to leave. Leave he does; while the boys are cleaning up the kitchen he walks out with Ward's good gray suit on his back. Wally and Beaver scour the town looking for Mr. Jeff, without success. They return to tell the sad news to Ward and June. Following an admonition not to let any further strangers into the house, Ward assures Beaver that kindness is not usually repaid in this manner. Beaver's spirits are bolstered when a letter arrives from the tramp with a five-dollar bill thanking him and advising him that thanks to the suit he got a job and will pay back five dollars a week until he has paid for the suit.

THE CREDIT CARD

Eddie is the gloating possessor of his own oil-company credit card, but Ward will not let Wally have one because he feels many adults cannot handle such financial responsibility and no teenager could be expected to do so. On a car outing Wally's battery fails and as usual the boys are short of cash, so Eddie proudly whips out his credit card and charges a new fifteen-dollar battery. Wally pays him back out of the money he was saving for seat covers, but instead of putting it aside, Eddie rushes to buy a snazzy vest he's been eyeing for some time, figuring the credit-card bill will be a long time coming. When it arrives, his father is furious that Eddie has disobeyed him by charging something besides oil and gas, and he finds out it was Wally's car that benefited. He calls Ward, but Wally is warned ahead of time by Beaver, so he has time to track down Eddie and threaten him with intense clobbering if Eddie doesn't clear him by coming up with fifteen dollars by that evening. Eddie doesn't learn his lesson, but he does bail out Wally by charging a twenty-five-dollar tire and then selling it for fifteen—and his new vest.

UNCLE BILLY'S VISIT

Ward's Uncle Billy arrives just in time to solve Ward and June's dilemma of who should watch the boys while they're away for a weekend. June is a bit leery of Billy, feeling he's little more than a senior delinquent who frequently bears watching himself, but they head off. Billy and the boys have a ball; he lets them wash the dishes with the garden hose and sleep late and even gives them each money, warning them not to "go spending it foolishly—have a good time." Beaver heads for the movies with his and on the way meets Gilbert, who has already spent his allowance. Gilbert convinces Beaver to sit near the exit and let him in. They're caught, but Beaver is confident his uncle will back him up, but is hurt and surprised when Billy arrives and apologizes for Beaver's behavior. He sends Beaver to his room, saying how disappointed he is that Beaver "took him for some sort of pushover." When Ward and June return, there is no mention of the theater incident and Beaver realizes his Uncle Billy truly is a good guy after all. As Billy says, "The way I look at it, you did it, you got caught, you got punished, and you said you were sorry."

BEAVER ON TV

Beaver's family and friends are all excited about his upcoming appearance as a panelist representing his school on the local TV show *Teenage Forum.* Just before the show is to go on the air, Beaver asks to be excused to get a drink of water and misses the announcement that the show is being taped for airing the following week. June, watching at home, Ward, at the office, and his classmates watching in school are all bewildered about Beaver's not appearing on the show. Even though he displays the transistor radio he was given as a gift from the show, no one in school believes he was on the show. Beaver is so upset he stays away from school for the afternoon. He calls the station and is further confused when he is told he will be "on next week." Beaver fears he has suddenly been transported to the Twilight Zone. By the time Beaver decides to go home, Ward has resolved the spooky situation by calling the station. Beaver is relieved and gets to watch himself on the show with the rest of the class, and they are very proud of his performance.

BOX-OFFICE ATTRACTION

Wally falls for Marlene, an older woman who works in the box office of the local movie theater.

She agrees to a date with him the following Saturday, then leaves, saying she has to meet her aunt. Beaver and Gilbert see her later that afternoon in Hank's beer joint, downing drafts and *smoking cigarettes*. Knowing how flaky Wally is for Marlene, Beaver says nothing about her lie and her bad habits. In order to check out this Marlene, June asks Wally to invite her over for a predate dinner. Marlene is on her best behavior and makes a favorable impression on everyone except June, who thinks her makeup "wasn't what you would call restrained." Once they get settled into Wally's car, Marlene surprises him by lighting up a cigarette and then shocks him by grabbing him for a potent kiss. She takes him to Hank's, his first bar, where Wally gets increasingly nervous as she orders beer and urges him to get into the swing of the "real jumpin' place." When one of Hank's regulars asks Marlene to dance, she tells Wally to run along. Wally comes home, and Ward and June unquestioningly accept his excuse that he and Marlene "just didn't dig each other."

BEAVER, THE CADDY

At Ward's golf club Beaver knows that the man for whom he's caddying, Mr. Langley, is dishonestly juggling his score for each hole. Beaver tries to correct him, but Mr. Langley will hear none of it and is very proud to beat his opponent, Mr. Howard, for the first time ever. Langley tips Beaver a whole five dollars but Beaver feels it's tainted money. He feels even worse when Ward says there was five hundred dollars riding on the match. Unable to stand it any longer, Beaver makes a trip downtown to Langley's office. He tries to give back the money and tells Langley he knows he cheated to win the bet the previous Saturday. Langley tries to explain there were extenuating circumstances but he admits he was wrong and asks Beaver's help in making things right. The following Saturday there's a rematch, and even Langley shoots the greatest game of his golf career, and would have won fair and square, but he fixes his score in Howard's favor, allowing Howard to win back the five hundred dollars. Beaver's conscience scores a hole in one.

LUMPY'S SCHOLARSHIP

Even though Wally and Lumpy both apply for athletic scholarships to State and Wally gets turned down, he offers to throw a party in Lumpy's honor. This is Lumpy's glory time, as most of his life he's been "kind of a pleasant slob," according to Eddie. At the party his classmates cheer the Lump and June even provides a huge cake decorated like a football field. In the middle of the celebration Fred telephones his son and says the university just called him and canceled his scholarship because Lumpy got a D in math. Lumpy feels especially bad about his friends being gathered to celebrate his achievement and he asks his father what he should tell them. Fred calls him a big oaf and tells Lumpy to "tell them you're a big boob." Lumpy decides not to spoil the party for everyone else and manages to put away about fifty yards' worth of cake himself. Lumpy later confesses to Wally and seriously considers leaving town rather than face his friends. On Lumpy's behalf Ward contacts an old friend who is in the university administration and Fred gets a call that the scholarship has been reinstated on the condition that Lumpy pass math in summer school.

THE SILENT TREATMENT

Beaver's all set to goof around with Eddie and Wally, but June stops him by insisting he go to the store for her as he promised. Eddie reminds him there are child labor laws and Beaver is really feeling sorry for himself and decides to give his mom "the big freeze." He plays up to Ward all night and is barely civil to June. Everyone feels awkward about his behavior, but June

doesn't want Ward to intercede. She is confident Beaver will come around on his own. While Beaver helps Ward paint the patio furniture, he is stung by a bee and immediately runs to his mother for aid. As June extracts the sting and eases the pain in his throbbing finger, Beaver realizes how indispensable his mother is and how foolish he has been in trying to "heckle" her. He apologizes, explaining that he was only mad at her because she was annoyed with him. He later confesses that it's harder on the guy who is mad than the person he's mad at— especially when that person is his mother.

EDDIE'S SWEATER

Cindy Andrews is supposed to be Eddie's girl so Ward and June become concerned when Wally keeps going over to her house.

Wally is evasive when questioned about her. He actually is acting as a stand-in for Eddie, but only to model the sweater Cindy is knitting as a surprise for his birthday. At school Lumpy overhears Cindy making a date for Wally to come over to her house that evening and Lumpy convinces Eddie he's being two-timed by his best friend. They go over to spy on Cindy and are convinced she and Wally are smooching when they see two silhouettes on the shade when she's taking neck and waist measurements. The next day at school, goaded by Lumpy, Eddie accuses Wally of being an operator and punches him. Wally will not fight back or spoil the surprise and Eddie is a big shot for the first time in his life. He won't drop Cindy, however, since it's tough enough for him to find a date, but when she hears what he has done to Wally, she gets Eddie over to her house and tells him the truth and gives him the sweater. Wearing his present, Eddie heads straight to Wally's to apologize and hopes that now that there's no secret at stake, Wally won't break his neck.

BEAVER'S PREP SCHOOL

June is thrilled when her Aunt Martha offers to send Beaver to Fallbrook, a prep school that has been a tradition for three generations of her family. When he reads the school catalog and sees the rifle range and ice skating and horseback riding he decides it's the high school for him. Aunt Martha is due for a visit in a few days but just before her arrival Beaver learns that Fallbrook is in New England and then he begins to regret that he will not be able to play on the same high school baseball team as his current friends. On a sentimental tour of his favorite neighborhood places, Beaver begins to get homesick before he's even left. Ward tells him a lot of kids would give their eyeteeth to go to Fallbrook and Beaver tells him he'd rather keep his eyeteeth and go to Mayfield. When Aunt Martha gets to the house she proudly gives Beaver her brother's Fallbrook beanie, which makes Beaver's telling her his revised decision that

much harder. She is very understanding, however, assuring him that it's much more important that he be happy than that his "silly old aunt" follow a family tradition. Beaver asks to keep the cap anyway because "maybe if I have a son he won't be as goofy as I am."

WALLY AND THE FRATERNITY

After Wally and Eddie get into State, Ward's alma mater, Ward recommends his old fraternity, Alpha Kappa, and offers to write a letter on behalf of Wally and one for Eddie. At the malt shop, Wally and Eddie run into an old acquaintance, Chuck, who is now at State. He tells them Alpha Kappa is the worst pig house on the campus. Wally tries to stop his father's letter but it's too late. Eddie tells Wally "the place is full of creeps and squares, the liveliest thing in the house is the termites," and writes to the fraternity renouncing Ward's letter as a mistake. In the school locker room Wally and Eddie run into another former high school friend who is also attending State. Ted tells the boys that Alpha Kappa is one of the best houses on campus and that Chuck is only bitter against it because he was thrown out. Wally is glad to hear this but Eddie is certain that he has ruined his chances for getting into Alpha Kappa. Eddie finally tells

Ward the truth and stops running his mouth long enough to apologize. In turn Ward promises to write another letter trying to clear up Eddie's mess.

THE BOOK REPORT

All weekend pleasures for Beaver are forbidden when his parents find out he's been putting off reading *The Three Musketeers* for a book report that's due the following Monday. Beaver tries to finish the book but finds it slow going. Gilbert tells him it's silly to *read* the book when the movie is going to be on television on Saturday night. With time running out on him, Beaver makes notes from the movie instead, and writes his report. What he doesn't realize is that he's watched the farcical version with Don Ameche and the Ritz Brothers. He reads his paper to the class and they laugh louder and Mrs. Rayburn gets angrier the more he recites about the Three Musketeers singing, plucking chickens, and getting caught up in a windmill. Mrs. Rayburn makes him stay after school and gives him a lecture, saying if he had just told her he hadn't read the book she might have been angry but she would not have been *ashamed* of him as she was now, and she sends a note home to Ward. Wally suggests softening Dad up by getting him to tell stories about goofy things he did as a kid and then springing the note on him. The ploy backfires and gets Beaver another lecture, Mrs. Rayburn assigns him two book reports, and Beaver has learned his lesson— he's going to choose books that haven't even been made into movies.

THE POOR LOSER

He's got only two tickets to what promises to be the season's most exciting baseball game, and Ward can't decide which son to take. Beaver makes it easy for him by declaring he has a date with Gilbert and doesn't care to break it. Gilbert learns he has to make a command appearance at his aunt's house that night and must cancel out on Beaver, but in the process he twists the ticket situation around so that Beaver starts seeing himself as

the younger brother who always gets taken advantage of by the family to the benefit of his more beloved and privileged sibling. At home, Beaver is so surly to Wally about missing the game that Wally offers his ticket to Beaver, hoping to show him that what Beaver has said about his selfishness is not true. To his shock, Beaver accepts the ticket and goes to the game with Ward. But he has a lousy time, because he feels so guilty about Wally during all nine innings. To make up for his childishness, he gives Wally the foul ball he copped, makes his brother's bed, and oils Wally's glove, although he puts so much oil on the mitt that Wally asks him to stop doing him favors and go back to being a creep.

SUMMER IN ALASKA

Lumpy and Wally are envious of Eddie because his uncle has gotten him a great summer job on a fishing boat bound for Alaska. Why, Lumpy says, even the guys on *Route 66* haven't been there. Getting paid for going fishing—Eddie figures he's got it made, and he offers to put in a good word for his buddies. However, their parents won't let them go. The boys suspect Eddie is making up a story so he challenges them to come down to the docks for his interview with the captain. They overhear his conversation, in which the captain shouts a grim picture of Eddie's life at sea, which will be nothing but cleaning fish. "He's a regular Captain Bligh," Lumpy says. "And Eddie's no Marlon Brando," Wally adds. Eddie looks pretty green when he comes out. He later confesses to Wally that he really doesn't want to take the job but is afraid to face his father after raising such a fuss about his right to be a man. Wally pays a visit to Mr. Haskell and suggests he forbid Eddie to make the trip, which will make everyone happy. Beaver tells Wally he'd rather go to sea, but Wally reminds him he gets sick just watching "McHale's Navy" on television.

DON JUAN BEAVER

The entire Cleaver family is surprised when Beaver gets a dinnertime phone call from Peggy MacIntosh, who has asked him to the school graduation dance. Playing it cool, Beaver neither accepts nor rejects her offer, telling her he will let her know his decision the next day. He tells Peggy he'll go with her, but then he meets Melinda Neilson, a new little Southern belle who has moved to Mayfield. She is charmed by Beaver, and vice versa. That evening she invites Beaver to the dance. Beaver would rather go with Melinda because she's prettier, but he doesn't know how to break his obligation to Peggy. Eddie gives

Don Juan the cue by suggesting he make Peggy so angry that she'll call it off herself. Beaver asks his family for ways to make girls angry and uses them all on Peggy the next day, being rude to her, talking about sports, and ignoring her. Peggy tells him she knows the reasons for his actions and she doesn't blame him for preferring Melinda to her. Beaver feels like a cad and that night calls Melinda to tell her he can't go with her, and she gives him a proper Charleston kiss-off, calls him "a cotton-pickin' little creep." By the time Beaver calls Peggy, she has called Whitey and asked him to the dance, and suddenly Beaver is down from two dates to zero. The night of the dance he's left to do the twist by himself in his bedroom.

BEAVER'S GRADUATION

The last few days of classes are messing-around days for Gilbert and Beaver, as they are confident they will not get reprimanded this close to graduation. Beaver comes late to school and accompanies Gilbert on an errand to Mrs. Rayburn's office. They decide to take a look at the class diplomas, which are waiting there, to check if one of the school troublemakers will be allowed to graduate, and in the process, they can't find Beaver's diploma. He's convinced he is being held back and falls into a deep depression, which gets deeper when he hears that his Aunt Martha and Uncle Billy are making special trips to see him graduate. He finally confesses to Ward, who tells him to seek out Mrs. Rayburn. She sets Beaver's mind at ease by telling him she has set aside all of the diplomas of the students who are participating in the graduation ceremony. Beaver is much relieved but fails to share Mrs. Rayburn's amusement over the whole situation.

WALLY'S PRACTICAL JOKE

For a gag Lumpy puts smoke bombs in Eddie's and Wally's car motors. No damage is done but Eddie is bent on revenge. He convinces Wally they should borrow Ward's tow chain and attach one end to Lumpy's rear axle and wrap the other around a tree. To draw Lumpy out of the house, Eddie makes a phone call pretending to be Julie Foster asking for Lumpy to come over and help with her homework. Lumpy comes out of the house in his good suit and tie, and as he starts to drive off, his entire rear axle is jerked back by the chain and the rest of his heap rolls down the driveway. Having misjudged the severity of the gag, the practical jokers run off, but Fred sees Ward's name on the chain and pays a visit to the Cleavers'. Ward tells Wally that he and Eddie will have to repair Lumpy's car as punishment. When Fred finds out Lumpy provoked the attack, he tells him he will have to help the boys fix his car, but Wally convinces Mr. Rutherford the job is tough enough to deal with without having to cope with Lumpy too. After bathing off his grime that evening, Wally advises Beaver that practical jokes are immature. As he lies down on his bed it collapses under him as Beaver laughs knowingly.

THE ALL-NIGHT PARTY

An all-night graduation party is to be given by Wally's class at the country club. The Cleavers and the other parents have laid down strict ground rules, including: No Liquor. Wally invites a new girl, Kathy Gregory, whose parents he has never met, and they refuse her permission to go. She thinks if they meet Wally and see what a fine boy he is, her father will relent, and Wally does win their confidence. The party goes smoothly, with the boys in white dinner jackets and girls in formals, and a lot of food and dancing. At dawn, when Wally and Kathy are leaving, a passing drunk adult accidentally knocks Kathy into a fountain. When Kathy's father sees her in her bedraggled condition and hears that a drunk knocked her into the water, he angrily assumes it was a rowdy partygoer who was drinking and tosses Wally out of his house without listening to any further explanations. When Wally learns from his friends that Kathy will not be permitted to date for a month as punishment, he resolves to tell Kathy's father the facts. Her father's initial appraisal of Wally was correct—he is an upstanding lad after all, and he apologizes to Wally and his daughter for jumping to conclusions.

BEAVER SEES AMERICA

Beaver has been eager to begin a six-week bus trip across the United States but he's infatuated with a new girl and suddenly "Mary Margaret seems a lot more interesting than the Grand Canyon." Especially when Gilbert starts coming around to call on Mary Margaret and mak-

ing plans to entertain her for the summer. She is quite a smooth operator who has both boys wrapped around her finger. Wally tells his parents the reason behind Beaver's flagging enthusiasm for his American tour. Soon Beaver's interest in the trip is revived, and when questioned, he explains to June that Gilbert is now joining him on the bus odyssey. It seems Ward settled the whole problem over lunch with Gilbert's father. After Mr. Bates heard about Mary Margaret, he readily agreed that travel would broaden his son's horizons. As Beaver and Gilbert approach Mary Margaret's house to say good-bye, they see she already has a replacement for them, Whitey, and she's already filling his ears with the same lines she gave each of them. Whitey in turn hopes he doesn't get his hives back this summer, since last year he was scratching the whole month of August.

FAMILY SCRAPBOOK

While cleaning out some cabinets, June comes across a long-forgotten scrapbook of family pictures and calls together Ward and the boys. They go through the book, reminiscing over incidents that are brought to life from the photos they see. Among other golden moments that are celebrated are Beaver discussing his first note from school with Wally while they pretend to take a bath. The night Miss Landers came to dinner, Wally's first attempt at shaving, the time Beaver ran away, a visit from a young Eddie Haskell talking about his first girl, Wally's campaign for class president, Mary Ellen Rogers's doughnut ploy to woo Wally, Andy the drunk, and Beaver and Larry sneaking a peek at his sister's diary. After putting away the scrapbook, both Ward and June realize that Wally and Beaver are no longer little boys but practically grown men. The almost-grown-ups retire to their room to take turns playing with a fiddling clown wind-up toy.

THE ''BEAVER'' I.Q. TEST

1. Ward and June named their son "Theodore" after whom?

2. Who's the first girl whose bedroom Beaver was in?

3. What was Mrs. Mondello's premarital occupation?

4. What does Fred Rutherford have written on his mailbox?

5. Who is the Cleaver family doctor?

6. What role does Beaver perform in the Grant Avenue Grammar School Holiday Festival? In the Fire Prevention Pageant? In the *Flowers and Feathers* school musical?

7. What is the name of Ward's secretary?

8. What does Eddie teach Beaver to say to his Spanish friend? *En español, por favor.*

9. What is Beaver looking for when he gets locked in the principal's office?

10. What is Beaver looking for when he gets his head stuck in the park fence?

11. What is the circulation of Beaver's Maple Drive *News*—including the papers that fell in a puddle?

12. Where does Mrs. Mondello keep her emergency money?

13. Which of Beaver's friends lives in an apartment?

14. What does highfalutin' Judy Hensler's father do for a living?

15. What is Beaver's bike-lock combination?

16. What is the name of Beaver's summer camp?

17. What is Wally's weakest subject in high school?

18. What is Beaver's most solemn oath?

19. What is the address of the soup billboard?

20. What is the vintage of the first car Wally buys?

21. What is Eddie's favorite dessert?

22. What is the Cleaver's phone number at the Pine Street house?

23. What question does Beaver ask Don Drysdale?

24. What is the name of Eddie's mutt?

25. What is a *Beaver Special*?

26. What is Beaver's favorite ice cream combination? Gilbert's?

27. Who is Ward's friend who is even more obnoxious than Fred?

28. When did Ward hit the Beaver?

29. What name baseball glove does Beaver have?

30. Which of Beaver's messes left the two best bathtub rings?

Answers, page 324.

Jerry Mathers, Frank Bank and Barbara Billingsley at a recent get-together.

JERRY MATHERS

When "Beaver" ended in 1963, Gerald Patrick Mathers was not unhappy. The timing was perfect for him to enter a regular high school and leave the studio tutors behind. He was able to try out for the freshman football team and get involved in other normal school activities for a change.

Along with close friend and fellow "Beaver" player Richard Correll, he formed a rock band, Beaver and the Trappers. Jerry played guitar and sang, and Richard manned the drums. They even wrote and recorded a single, "Happiness Is ("Happiness is/Goin' about a hundred and ten/Happiness is/Blowin' your mind and comin', comin' back down again.") that was reportedly a minor hit in, of all places, Alaska and Hawaii.

After serving six years in the Air National Guard, Jerry earned his degree from Berkeley in philosophy, a feat more than a few people have found remarkable for the guy they forever see as the Beav. A resolute pragmatist, he decided to forego being a career philosopher and worked instead in banking and real estate before being bitten by his old acting bug. He was a guest star on a number of television shows including "Batman." During 1979–80, he re-teamed with Tony Dow for a theater tour of the farce, *So Long, Stanley,* written by two TV comedy veterans. He also had a popular weekend radio show in Anaheim, "Jerry Mathers Gathers, Rock 'n' Roll for the Mind, Body and Soul."

Jerry is quite active on the promotional circuit, traveling all over the country to speaking engagements, colleges, autographings and media events—wherever people want to meet the Beav. He makes his home in California's Santa Clara Valley with his second wife, Rhonda, and three children who range in age from 11 years to 1 year. He enjoys camping and reading science fiction and together with Rhonda is responsible for the newsletter of The Loyal Order of the Beaver national fan club which publishes irregularly, Jerry notes, thanks to their seemingly unending chores as—what else?—parents.

TONY DOW

Still in great physical shape and a gifted water athlete, Tony lives about a block away from the Pacific Ocean in Venice, California. He goes swimming, boogey boarding or surfing virtually every day.

Immediately following 1963 he kept busy with TV guest shots including a continuing role on the soap opera, "Never Too Young," until his National Guard duty kept him from being able to make any long-term commitments. After attending journalism school he worked in contracting, construction and sculpting, and even built the house he now lives in with his second wife, Lauren. He has a ten-year-old son from his first marriage.

Tony still gets a lot of fan mail and is amazed at the diligence of some of the viewers. One Beaver-maniac told him he had deciphered Mary Ellen Rogers's phone number by running the videotape of Wally dialing it through a sound analyzer. Another fan insisted he knew Wally's locker combination number which Tony finds particularly amusing since he never learned how to open a combination lock until he recently joined a health club. The crew always made sure to leave the lock open so he could just spin any random numbers on the dial and get into his locker.

Along with his building talents, Tony writes, studies filmmaking and continues to act. In addition to performing on stage with Jerry Mathers, Tony starred with Barbara Billingsley in *Come Blow Your Horn* and during the 1983 season alone played a succession of good supporting roles on "Quincy," "Square Pegs," "Love Boat" and the TV movie, *High School, U.S.A.*, where he made a first-rate modern principal (Mrs. Rayburn would have been proud).

BARBARA BILLINGSLEY

Barbara remains the combination sweetheart and mom to all the "Beaver" players. Mention her name and grown men start to gush about how wonderfully caring she is and what a joy she is to work with.

At the conclusion of the series, Barbara turned down roles in favor of traveling around the world on a freighter with her husband. The mother of two boys "who were both very much like Beaver," she was content to go into semi-retirement in Malibu, devoting her time to her family and to charity work.

With the resurgence of interest in "Beaver," Barbara has once again graced the acting arena, perhaps nowhere more memorably than in her hilarious cameo as the jive-talking passenger in *Airplane* who told two of her black flight-mates, "Just hang loose, blood," and, "Cut me some slack, Jack." She has also appeared as an axe murderess in "Mork and Mindy" and as a judge on "Dance Fever."

HUGH BEAUMONT

Greatly missed by his "Beaver" colleagues, Hugh Beaumont died in 1982 at the age of 72. He was loved and respected not only as a diligent craftsman who brought a very human quality to Ward, but also as a director of a number of "Beaver" episodes and writer of several scripts.

Although from 1964 on he appeared in some series such as "Wagon Train" and "Petticoat Junction," Beaumont spent a lot of his time working with community theaters and church groups. After suffering a stroke in the mid-sixties he divided his time between Los Angeles, South Carolina and a densely forested island in Minnesota.

KEN OSMOND

Ask any ten people what they thought Eddie Haskell would grow up to be and it's doubtful any of them would volunteer "policeman." However, since 1970, Ken Osmond has been a motorcycle traffic officer in the Los Angeles police department.

Ken turned to a law enforcement profession after having problems with a helicopter business he operated with his brother. He takes his police work very seriously. In 1980, he and his partner pursued a stolen cab until it crashed into a parked car on a Los Angeles street. While chasing the gun-toting driver on foot, Ken was knocked to the ground by four bullets and his life was saved by his body armor, his belt buckle, and the fast, brave action of his partner.

Like Jerry Mathers, Ken was the focus of rumors about his post-"Beaver" life. One popular story was that he was really Alice Cooper, the snake-bearing rock star. This grew out of a *Rolling Stone* interview with Cooper who said that as a child he was "Eddie Haskell." An even more bizarre report surfaced that Ken was the porno film celebrity, John Holmes. It seems that there were some porno films in distribution which claimed that Holmes played "Little Eddie Haskel (sic)."

In recent years, Ken has managed to work in a few acting assignments around his police shifts. In addition to "Beaver"

TV reunion appearances Ken played shop teacher Freddie Paskell on an episode of "Happy Days." He lives in a somewhat rural suburb of Los Angeles with his wife and two sons. Oh yes; he thinks Eddie would have grown up to be a used car salesman or a city councilman, "not really corrupt, but kind of shady."

FRANK BANK (*Lumpy*) is a very successful municipal bonds broker in Palm Springs. He's still a figure of considerable size, is a very flashy dresser and sports an impressive beard. He also owns a DeLorean with license plates which read "IM LUMPY."

ROBERT "RUSTY" STEVENS (*Larry*) moved to Philadelphia with his family in 1963. He worked in an advertising agency where he wrote copy and his wife-to-be designed art. They now live in New Jersey and he is an insurance salesman.

STEVEN TALBOT (*Gilbert*) has stayed away from virtually any association with his "Beaver" days. He is a critically acclaimed documentary filmmaker based in San Francisco. He won the distinguished Peabody Award for his 1980 film, *Broken Arrow*, and was highly praised for *The Case of Dashiell Hammett*, which aired on the local PBS station, KQED, where he works.

RICHARD CORRELL (*Richard*) remains a close friend of Jerry Mathers's and was best man at his first wedding. Richard was a cinema major at USC and taught vintage film comedy, even working as the curator of the Harold Lloyd collection. He worked in various production capacities on many TV shows, most recently as associate producer in charge of post-production on "Happy Days." He lives in Los Angeles with his wife and child.

JERI WEIL (*Judy*) has outgrown her pigtails but hair is still an important part of her life as she is a hairdresser in northern California. She recently appeared in the week-long "Beaver" salute on the NBC-TV game show, "The Match Game/Hollywood Squares Hour."

RICHARD DEACON (*Mr. Rutherford*) is perhaps the only actor in TV history to have the distinction of having continuing roles in two classic series simultaneously—"Beaver" and "The Dick Van Dyke Show," where he was Mel Cooley, the frozen faced arch rival of Morey Amsterdam's Buddy. In addition to his continuing acting roles "Deac" is the proud author of a very successful cookbook, *Richard Deacon's Microwave Cookery.*

THE WORLD A.B.
(AFTER ''BEAVER'')

On September 12, 1963, with a rerun of *Wally's Practical Joke* it was all over. "Leave It to Beaver" left prime time network television forever. For the vast majority of series that's the one way ticket to TV Palookaville, but Beaver was soon to prove just how much life was left in the old shows.

Reruns of "Leave It to Beaver" began right away and haven't stopped since. According to MCA Television Limited which manages the syndication of the series to independent television stations around the country, "Beaver" has proven to be one of the most stable and successful series in TV history. Many series are unable to get picked up in as many as 100 markets; the average popular series might be lucky enough to be sold to 125 markets. "Beaver" has been syndicated in nearly 190 markets since 1963 and is currently shown in virtually all of the 50 largest TV cities in addition to being featured on the national super station, WTBS-Atlanta.

With enough episodes to run every weekday for 46 weeks without repeating, and shows that appeal to kids as well as adults, "Beaver" can fit comfortably into any kind of station format at any hour of the day. In fact, more people have now watched the reruns than ever watched the show originally.

While "Leave It to Beaver" has been in perpetual reruns it definitely fell out of favor during the decade between the mid-sixties to mid-seventies. Viewers first favored the corn pone comedies like "The Beverly Hillbillies" and then swung around to more sophisticated character comedies in the tradition of "The Dick Van Dyke Show," with shows like "The Mary Tyler Moore Show" and "M*A*S*H," and to harder-edged, bolder, more realistic family comedies lead by "All in the Family." (One small measure of the "new frankness" in TV comedy was the fact that the producers of "Leave It to Beaver" had to sweat about showing a toilet tank in their first episode in 1957 while "All in the Family" could feature as a running gag the thunderous sound of Archie Bunker flushing his upstairs toilet.)

As the baby-boomers flexed their anger in the student rebellions of the sixties, Beaver Cleaver seemed a lot less relevant than Eldridge Cleaver. Beaver's battles with the grown-up world paled in comparison with the shocks of the Vietnam War. As the singles scene seventies swung into action, the Cleaver boys and their dating rituals seemed positively Victorian. Then the overall popularity of sitcoms began to wane in the eighties. While a comedy program was the top-rated show in each year during the seventies only two of the 1982–83 season's top ten shows were sitcoms.

Still, "Beaver" survived all the trends and mood changes of mercurial TV viewers. In the late seventies and into the eighties, as the nation seemed to have settled into an attitude of numbed perseverance, Beaver, the unflagging optimist who always pulled himself out of the dumpster of life, began to get the shine back on his old image. The baby-boomers remembered him fondly as their ongoing childhood hero and welcomed him back, perhaps wistfully, as a symbol of the warm, wonderful, manageable way the world was supposed to be. A whole new generation of young viewers were watching "Beaver" for the first time and loved his scaled-down approach to life, akin to their own— just trying to get by till tomorrow.

In recent years, Beaver merchandise and memorabilia has been selling all around the country. There is a surprisingly wide variety of Beaver T-shirts and greeting cards with pictures and dialogue from the show; photo buttons of the Beav are displayed right alongside the hottest rock stars, even a checkbook holder with a Cleaver family photo (as if Beaver could ever balance a checkbook!). In 1983, Beaver and Wally were even selected to be featured on packages of Kellogg's Corn Flakes.

The Beaver players have been brought together for all kinds

of reunions within the last year alone, including salutes on "Good Morning, America," "The Match Game/Hollywood Squares Hour" and "Family Feud." Local stations have run Beaver-thons, including two which brought in Jerry Mathers as on-air host, WTXX in Hartford, Connecticut and a 24-hour fest on KXLI in St. Cloud, Minnesota. Radio station WKTI-FM in Milwaukee sponsored one of the more intriguing recent promotions, a concert hosted by Mathers giving fans the opportunity to spend 1984's New Year's Eve with the Beav. Milwaukee is a devoted "Beaver" city—so much so that when the local station bumped the reruns to an early morning slot several years ago, a citywide campaign was started by two disc jockeys who played the TV shows over the radio for their listeners who couldn't get to their sets and also made up their own plaintive ballad, "We've Lost Our Beaver Cleaver," sung to the tune of the Righteous Brothers' "You've Lost That Loving Feeling."

There have been all sorts of oddball tributes as well, such as the intramural softball team at Huron High School in Michigan, which called itself The Almighty Cleavers in honor of their favorite show, adopting a team motto of "We Don't Care." "Second City TV" presented a "Beaver" parody in which Ward stumbles around the house in a drunken stupor, Eddie comes out of the closet and Beaver is unemployed and eventually shoots Eddie through the heart. "Saturday Night" included a "Beaver" send-up in its extended sketch in which guest Ricky Nelson was trapped in the fifties sitcom "Twilight Zone," constantly popping up in the wrong TV kitchen.

Among recent feature films which have saluted "Beaver" are "Fast Times At Ridgemont High" where the "soup" scene is playing in the background during a scene and Blake Edwards's "The Man Who Loved Women," in which Burt Reynolds's character states he "always wanted to live in a Beaver Cleaver house with a white picket fence."

Profiles of the show and its afterlife have appeared within the last two years in *People, USA Today,* hundreds of newspapers, and in *Time,* which referred to Beaver as "a dimpled noble savage" and "the symbol of the melted ice-cream sorrows of an idyllic suburban childhood that never really was." *Time* further observed that the Cleaver household is "the prime time equivalent of John Cheever's sunlit lawns and the immediate ancestor of Steven Spielberg's split-levels."

The key event of the return of "Beaver Fever" was the March 1983 broadcast of *Still the Beaver,* a new, two hour reunion film starring the "Leave It to Beaver" characters twenty years later. Many "Beaver" reunion films had been proposed over the years and several other popular shows like "Father Knows Best" (and who could forget *Return to Gilligan's Island?*) had called back the troops to pick up the pieces but it took the drive and talent of two diehard "Beaver" fanatics, Nick Abdo and Brian Levant to make this one a reality.

Levant recalls watching "Beaver" reruns after school when he grew up in Chicago where "there was nothing else to do on a freezing afternoon except go over to somebody's house whose parents were working and watch the Beav." Both he and Abdo wound up writing and producing for "Happy Days," a natural heir to the Beaver mantle. Their *Still the Beaver* was very carefully and lovingly thought out to try to apply the spirit of the original show to the same characters with 20 hard years of living under their belts. They gathered together as many of the original actors as possible and dug out the old blueprints of the Cleaver home and fixed up the interior sets to be the full-color spitting image of the familiar black-and-white rooms. The hardest obstacle was the prospect of "Beaver" without the late Hugh Beaumont as Ward. Wisely, it was decided to weave in a liberal selection of choice moments from the original series as a counterpoint to the contemporary story. So Ward was very much still part of the family. The show was dedicated to Beaumont.

Life was more messed up than ever for Beaver in 1983. He had moved away from Mayfield, married a girl named Kimberly and had two sons, Oliver and Corey, but as the movie opened Beaver had lost his job, his wife was divorcing him and taking their kids and he even lost his bus ticket back to Mayfield. He moved back home with the widow June and still looked to Wally for help. Wally had his own troubles. Although he married high school sweetheart Mary Ellen Rogers and grew up to be a successful attorney he needed reading glasses, he was going gray—and he was impotent. Now instead of covering for his brother with Dad he was handling the Beaver's divorce proceedings.

June remained the essence of perfect patience and motherly concern. Eddie Haskell, weasly as ever, had his own construction company which was in receivership, thanks in part to his own wife turning him in to the IRS, and was making a complete mess of renovating Wally's house so that Wally, too, had to move back in with Mom. (Ken Osmond's own son, Eric, played Eddie Haskell, Jr., a junior rat in the making.) Many of the old friends were also still hanging on in Mayfield. Richard was now a psychiatrist. Larry was now Avishnu from an Ashram. Whitey (one of the few veteran characters played by a new actor, Ed Begley, Jr., Emmy winner for his "St. Elsewhere" performance) was a corporate headhunter. Miss Canfield took over from Mrs. Rayburn as Grant Avenue Grammar School principal. Fred Rutherford was running things at "the salt mines" where Lumpy was now employed and where Beaver got a new job.

Although the show was hampered by poor direction and by the enforced strictures of wrapping up situations in two hours, there were a lot of funny and even poignant "Beaver" moments, old and new. The adult Beaver walked through the door of 211 Pine and suddenly turned into little nine-year-old black-and-white Beaver shouting to Mom that he was home. In one of the most pointed moments Richard told Beaver, "Didn't you realize a lot of people wanted to be you? Your family did things, you had good things in the icebox and your father was a good role model," to which Beaver, the perplexed adult, replied, "Too bad my kids won't be able to say that." For as a father, Beaver not only had to deal with divorce, he had to deal with two sons who were surly, uncooperative, downright fresh—all the things he and Wally never dreamed of being.

Levant and Abdo managed to fill in and create some interesting Beaver trivia; for instance, that Beaver followed Wally's footsteps to State, that Wally's honeymoon was in Jamaica, that the Rutherfords had Thanksgiving dinner with the Cleavers every year, that Ward worked at "the salt mines" for 35 years and died at age 67 in 1977, and that Mary Ellen's gynecologist was named N. Tokar in tribute to longtime "Beaver" director, Norman Tokar. There were also some jarring notes, like June talking about going to have her legs waxed and serving take-out Chinese food—right out of the containers!—at her dining-room table.

While critical reaction was mixed, *Still the Beaver* was the top-rated program in its time slot and renewed the hopes of rabid fans that perhaps a new series would be spun-off from the movie.

Whether or not new "Beaver" episodes are ever made, fans still get a kick out of the existing 234. And there's always the pilgrimage to the Beaver shrine, 211 Pine Street, now a key site on the Universal Studios tour. As the tourist tram rolls past the water tank with the *Jaws* shark and the flying bikers from *E.T.* it heads for Colonial Street and Circle Drive where the refurbished landmark house stands. (The house also served Marcus Welby, *The Rockford Files*'s Lt. Becker, and the street was recently seen in *Animal House.*)

So there I was on my visit, hopping up and down into the gutter along "Pine Street," like the Beav, turning down the well-beaten path to the front door, past siding that needed painting and a lawn that sported a mushroom or two that would certainly bring a frown to Ward's face. I looked for the key in the mailbox, its old hiding place, found none, reached for the doorknob, turned it and opened the door. To my disappointment, there was just a jerry-built shell of wood beams and platforms behind the exterior, housing nothing more important than the men's and ladies' bathrooms for the street set.

Still, there's something about walking through that door . . . Who could resist yelling, "Hey, Mom, I'm home!" Certainly not I. Just as I think each of us, when we turn on the "Leave It to Beaver" reruns, quietly calls out, "Hey, Mom, I'm home!"

''BEAVER'' SONGS

Perhaps the greatest—and certainly the weirdest—tributes to "Leave It to Beaver" are two songs performed by two of the more colorful acts in contemporary music. The hipper of the two, "Beaver Cleaver Fever" was recorded by the all-girl fifties/punk rock group, Angel and the Reruns, four TV-obsessed alumnae of San Francisco County Jail. The more lugubrious of the Beaver songs, "Somethin's Wrong with the Beaver," was perpetrated by none other than the notorious Kinky Friedman and the Lost Texas Jewboys.

◆

SOMETHIN'S WRONG WITH THE BEAVER
(by Kinky Friedman & Panama Red)

Faithful as a Magnavox
Hung-up on a song
She cried down to the breakfast nook,
"Ward, there's something wrong."

Chorus:
Somethin's wrong with the Beaver
Somethin's wrong with the Beaver
Somethin's wrong with the Beaver
The Beaver I believe-uh is gone

Beaver was a dreamer
Never got it right
Died in livin' color
Lived in black an' white

BEAVER CLEAVER FEVER

(by Hillary Carlip & Miriam Cutler)

I was down in the dumps with no place to go
Listening to nothing on the radio
Turn on the TV receiver
And I see Beaver, Beaver Cleaver
I was never an achiever
Till I got Beaver Cleaver Fever

I got the Beaver Cleaver Fever
I got the Beaver Cleaver Fever
Oh I believe, believe in the Beav

I ain't talking Ward and I ain't talking June
They're not the reasons I'm singing this tune
And you know, by golly
I'm not singing about Wally
Hey man, no need to grieve
I'm singing 'bout the Beav

Beav, have you been back to Mayfield lately?
Three girls got raped on Pine Street
When Miss Landers kept you after school did she have to worry
 about getting stabbed?
No. Well she's dead now, Beav

Where have we gone wrong?
Let's go back to those simple days
When Mom in heels and pearls would have milk and cookies on
 the table
Give me a guy like Theodore J. Cleaver please

Believe in the Beav
Believe in the Beav
Believe in the Beav
Believe in the Beav

A guy gets a girl
And acts like a rascal
He starts being weird like Eddie Haskell
You know who won't deceive her?
Beaver, Beaver Cleaver
And you know who'll never leave her?
Beaver Cleaver

I got the Beaver Cleaver Fever
I got the Beaver Cleaver Fever
Oh I believe, believe in the Beav

I got the Beaver Cleaver Fever
I got the Beaver Cleaver Fever

Beaver in the morning
Beaver Cleaver all through the night

Oh I believe, believe in the Beav
Believe in the Beav
Oh I believe, believe in the Beav
Believe in the Beav
Oh I believe, believe in the Beav
Believe in the Beav
Oh I believe, believe in the Beav
Believe in the Beav

1. June's Uncle Theodore, Aunt Martha's brother; 2. Larry Mondello's sister; 3. Dental nurse; 4. Rancho Rutherford; 5. Dr. Richardson; 6. An angel in the Holiday Festival, Smokey the Bear in the Fire Prevention Pageant, and a mushroom in the *Flowers and Feathers* school musical; 7. Grace; 8. *Usted tiene una cara como puerco*; 9. Mrs. Rayburn's automatic spanking machine; 10. Four leaf clovers; 11. 26 (including 2 papers that fell in the puddle); 12. In her sewing basket; 13. Whitey; 14. Mr. Hensler owns the Circle Garage; 15. 26-4-18; 16. Camp König; 17. History; 18. "Cross my heart and hope to spit!"; 19. Fourth and Oak; 20. 1936 coupe; 21. Chocolate pudding; 22. KL 5-4763; 23. "Do you spit in your glove?"; 24. Wolf; 25. The sundae the drugstore named after Beaver when he scored the winning touchdown; 26. Beaver's favorite combination is carmel tangerine. Gilbert's is watermelon pistachio; 27. Corny Cornelius; 28. According to Beaver, his dad hit him when he spilled ink on the rug; 29. Warren Spahn; 30. When he fell in the new tar road and when he painted the garage;

ANSWERS TO THE BEAVER I.Q. TEST

ABOUT THE AUTHOR

Born nowhere near a mountaintop in Tennessee nor even close to the general vicinity of Mayfield, IRWYN APPLEBAUM grew up in the nonetheless uneventful New York City borough of Queens. No matter what his mother says he was never, on his best day, as cute as the Beaver. He was an honors graduate of the University of Pennsylvania but is prouder of the fact that while there he was the only known disc jockey on the campus radio station to read Robert Benchley essays between Emmylou Harris and Smokey Robinson records, and coedited and wrote numerous features for the arts weekly. After receiving his Master's degree from the Columbia School of Journalism he joined Bantam Books where he has worked for a lucky seven years, holding various administrative positions, most recently Publishing Manager. In addition, he has edited a wide variety of books, including more than a dozen novels by Louis L'Amour, *The Twilight Zone Companion*, and all of Bantam's westerns. In addition to his publishing career, he is the author of several articles on popular culture. He also eats too much Chinese food and pizza, has some of the largest dustballs in captivity in his apartment and spends more time than the law should allow watching television. He claims, "I'd secretly be thrilled to write a situation comedy but I suspect I'm too busy living one." In 1984 he married Lucille Salvino, the loveliest sitcom fanatic he knows.

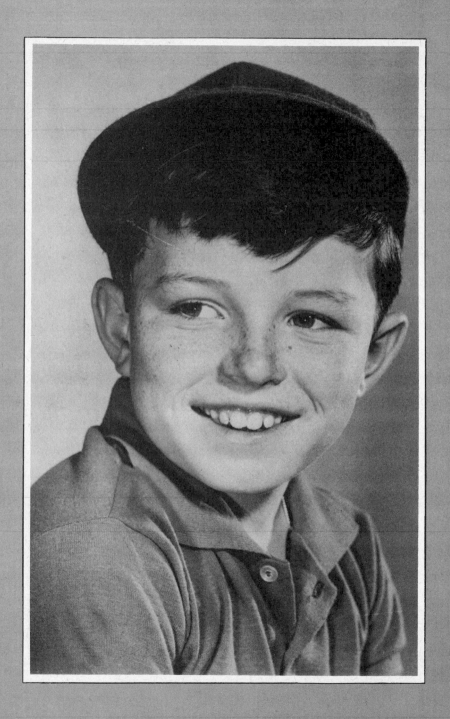